Necessary Trouble

FEB. 12, 1956

DEAR MR. EISENHOWER,

I AM NINE YEARS OLD AND I AM WHITE BUT I HAVE MANY FEELINGS ABOUT SEGREGATION. WHY SHOULD PEOPLE FEEL THAT WAY BECAUSE THE COLOR OF THE SKIN? IF I PAINTED MY FACE BLACK I WOULDN'T BE LET IN ANY PUBLIC SCHOOLS etc. MY FEELINGS HAVEN'T CHANGED, JUST THE COLOR OF MY SKIN.

LONG AGO ON CHRISTMAS DAY JESUS CHRIST WAS BORN. AS YOU REMEMBER HE WAS BORN TO SAVE THE WORLD. NOT ONLY WHITE PEOPLE BUT BLACK YELLOW RED AND BROWN.

COLORED PEOPLE AREN'T GIVEN A CHANCE. "THEY DON'T HAVE A GOOD EDUCATION," SAYS MANY PEOPLE IS IT THEIR FAULT IF THEIR FATHERS ARE SO POOR THEY MUST BE TAKEN OUT AT AN EARLY AGE TO FIND JOBS? ONLY ABOUT 2% of OUR PREP SCHOOLS ARE FOR COLORED PEOPLE. SO WHAT IF THEIR SKIN IS BLACK? THEY STILL HAVE FEELINGS BUT MOST OF ALL ARE GOD'S PEOPLE!

PLEASE MR. EISENHOWER, PLEASE TRY AND HAVE SCHOOLS and other THINGS ACCEPT COLORED PEOPLE.

Sincerly,

CATHERINE DREW GILPIN

Necessary Trouble

GROWING UP AT MIDCENTURY

Drew Gilpin Faust

FARRAR, STRAUS AND GIROUX

New York

Farrar, Straus and Giroux
120 Broadway, New York 10271

Illustration credits can be found on pages 303–304.

Library of Congress Cataloging-in-Publication Data
Names: Faust, Drew Gilpin, author.
Title: Necessary trouble : growing up at midcentury / Drew Gilpin Faust.
Description: First edition. | New York : Farrar, Straus and Giroux, 2023. |
    Includes bibliographical references and index.
Identifiers: LCCN 2023008685 | ISBN 9780374601805 (hardcover)
Subjects: LCSH: Faust, Drew Gilpin—Childhood and youth. | Gilpin family. |
    United States—Race relations—20th century. | Civil rights movements—
    United States—History—20th century. | United States—Social life and
    customs—1945–1970. | Bryn Mawr College—Students—Biography. |
    Concord Academy (Concord, Mass.)—Students—Biography. | Clarke
    County (Va.)—Biography.
Classification: LCC F232.C59 F38 2023 | DDC 975.598092 [B]—
    dc23/eng/20230329
LC record available at https://lccn.loc.gov/2023008685

Our books may be purchased in bulk for promotional, educational, or business
    use. Please contact your local bookseller or the Macmillan Corporate and
Premium Sales Department at 1-800-221-7945, extension 5442, or by email at
    MacmillanSpecialMarkets@macmillan.com.

www.fsgbooks.com
www.twitter.com/fsgbooks • www.facebook.com/fsgbooks

3   5   7   9   10   8   6   4   2

For Jessica

"You want to grow up to be a lady, don't you?"
I said not particularly.

—HARPER LEE, *TO KILL A MOCKINGBIRD*

Thank you for getting into trouble, necessary trouble.

—JOHN LEWIS TO THE AUTHOR, MAY 24, 2018

Contents

Necessary Trouble

PROLOGUE

The past will remain horrible for exactly as long as
we refuse to assess it honestly.

—JAMES BALDWIN[1]

As a historian, I have spent much of my life listening to voices from the past and trying to use them as bridges of understanding to times distant from our own. Here I am seeking to be one of those voices, recounting an era that fewer and fewer living humans can remember. It is time for me not just to listen but to tell. History is about choices and about how individuals make those choices within the structures and circumstances in which they find themselves. I want to illuminate what those choices looked like to one girl trying to become a person during two decades of rapid transformation and powerful reaction in American life. It was a time when new possibilities opened doors and paths my mother and grandmothers could not have imagined; it was a time when ideas and even movements were emerging to challenge assumptions about race, gender, and privilege my parents and grandparents had believed to be immutable; it was a time that inaugurated many of the changes—and divisions—we grapple with still. Yet it was an era that seems like a foreign country to many of those who are still working to carry those advances forward into a more enlightened and just future. The strangeness of that world can perhaps encourage us that at least some things have changed for the better in the course of my life. And at a time when we see many of those advances challenged or even overturned, it can remind us why we don't want to live in such a world again.

The house at Lakeville, the farm in Virginia where I grew up.

A DEATH IN THE FAMILY

Christmas 1966

When grief and shock surpass endurance there occur
phases of exhaustion, of anesthesia in which relatively little
is left and one has the illusion of recognizing,
and understanding, a good deal.

—JAMES AGEE[1]

I still have the bracelet, and I still feel it is somehow not rightfully
mine. Under ordinary circumstances I suppose I might eventually
have inherited it. But my mother never even saw it. When she died on
Christmas Eve, her parents gave what they intended to be her gift to
me instead. I would wear it day and night for months—my own version of a traditional mourning band. We woke up that next day in a
house overflowing both with presents and with stunned, disbelieving
grief. My mother had wrapped most of them, and as we eventually
opened each package, they seemed less objects than posthumous messages, representations of what she thought had mattered to us, a final
gesture of love.

Mounds of newly fallen snow, left by the previous day's blizzard,
surrounded the house, making it difficult to get in or out of the long
driveway and muffling any sound from the farm animals huddled
around the barn or from cars on the highway beyond the woods. We
spoke in whispers as well, astonished by the strange white world that
enveloped us and by the strange new motherless world we inhabited.

My father and mother had set off early the day before as the snow was just beginning to fall. My mother had been ill for several days, with symptoms that puzzled our local doctor, who decided that she should be taken to the University of Virginia hospital in Charlottesville, a hundred miles away. By midday Christmas Eve, as the flakes began to intensify, my father called to say she would be having surgery. He made it clear to me and my brother Donald, at sixteen three years younger than I, that her condition was extremely grave, but we couldn't believe that our mother's life was actually in danger. We decided our ten-year-old brother didn't need to know, so we spent much of the day endeavoring to divert him with snowball fights and cards and board games. When the local minister arrived to pray with us, our ruse was up. Lou insisted he be told what was going on.

The afternoon darkened early as the storm grew stronger, and we played every game we could think of: poker, hearts, Monopoly, Sorry, Clue. Every so often a phone call would break the quiet. Our older brother, Tys, had secured holiday leave from the navy and was making his way to Union Station in Washington to rendezvous with my mother's parents, who had long planned to come from New Jersey to join us for Christmas. Newscasters reported rapid accumulations of snow, and trains and planes ceased to operate as totals mounted. But it was much more than just the storm's upending of travel plans that became a matter for concern. News from Charlottesville was not good. She had survived the surgery but had experienced an interruption of blood flow to her brain. Her prospects for survival were unclear; her prospect for survival with full mental function seemed slim. We waited.

Dice, cards, Monopoly houses and hotels, the lead pipe and the candlestick from Clue were scattered around the den. I moved from sitting cross-legged on the floor to sprawling in the red leather armchair. My brothers arm-wrestled. No one had the energy to light a fire even though the snowy Christmas Eve would have seemed to mandate it. Suddenly I heard a rustle of cloth and quiet footsteps. In swept my father's mother, who lived about three miles down the road. Dressed in a floor-length green satin gown, she had come from a holiday dinner with my uncle and aunt, who followed her into the room. I remember no words, but none were required. Yet I know I needed words and struggled to find them hours later when Tys and my mother's parents at last arrived through the blizzard, still unaware she had died. We had been watching for them for what seemed like hours, and at last the headlights grew larger and larger as their car crept up the driveway through the whirling storm. I can hear the sound of the weather stripping on the back door as it opened and the stomp of their boots on the kitchen linoleum as they tried to shake off the snow. Their eyes darted from me to each of my younger brothers as they eagerly awaited news. Our reluctance to speak was message enough.

I had returned home from college only a few days before, prepared for the confrontation with my mother that I knew was inevitable. We had had a terrible fight about whether I could go visit a friend in Connecticut before I came to Virginia for the rest of the holidays. She insisted she had to have a letter of invitation from his parents before I would be permitted to go. I thought this preposterous, accused her of living in the Middle Ages, and went to Connecticut. I don't think I even told her that my friend was Black and that I had met him as part of a civil rights initiative in Birmingham, Alabama, two summers before. It could only have escalated the battle. But by the time I got home to Virginia, she had no fight in her. She was in bed, and I remember crouching down beside her to talk about plans for Christmas. She barely responded. We never settled the argument.

And we never settled the larger argument that was what we had instead of a relationship. At a reception after her funeral, a neighbor approached me and grabbed a handful of my long straight hair—which had served as grounds for many of our mother-daughter fights. "You killed her, you know," she spat. I smiled politely and turned away as she returned to the bar. But I thought to myself, "At least I didn't kill me." I knew I had had no choice. I had had to fight with my mother in order to survive. And I knew, too, that in some way her failure to fight for her self—for *a* self—had contributed to the tragedy that was her life.

I remember parts of the days after her death as if they just happened; other parts I don't remember at all. In the years since, I have been told by medically sophisticated interlocutors that our family narrative about the cause of my mother's death makes no sense. My Virginia grandmother, my father's mother, whom we called Granny, wrote that it was a "massive embolism of the aorta"; my mother's own mother, Nan, never spoke of a reason or cause at all. I wonder, thinking back, if she might have simply believed that there could not be any good reason for this to have happened to her daughter. My understanding was that colitis had led to a perforated intestine, which resulted in blood clots that required surgery she did not survive.[2]

The reality is that my mother had long been very sick, but we children at least had grown so used to her emaciated frame and her lack of appetite that we had come to take it for granted. She herself never complained or made any overt reference to her health. I look now at photographs of her and wonder what we could have been thinking—and what my father could have been thinking—not to have done more to intervene. As a close friend of Granny's wrote from Richmond upon hearing of her death, my mother had been "so obviously far, <u>far</u>, from well," when she had last seen her two years before. "There was no happy future for her."[3] But what was so plain to a friend at a distance was all but invisible to us. We were a family in which anything difficult or unpleasant was avoided and denied, rather than recognized or addressed. I can remember my alcoholic New Jersey grandfather collapsing in his soup at dinner and simply being quietly removed from the room with no commentary or explanation to the bewildered and frightened grandchildren seated on either side of him at the table.

I wonder now if my mother was an adult anorexic—at the time of her death, she was five feet nine inches tall and weighed no more than ninety pounds—although neither the word nor the concept of anorexia existed in our minds in 1966. She hardly ate, chain-smoked Camels, and consumed what must have been a significant proportion of her caloric intake in whiskey—ritual old-fashioneds before and after dinner. But apart from tobacco and alcohol, she seemed determined to deny herself all pleasures, to make it her purpose to sacrifice herself for children and marriage. She had been a legendary horsewoman—she cut a figure mounted sidesaddle and met my father riding to hounds. There are glorious photographs of them side by side on horseback early in their marriage—she turned out in full riding habit and the two of them almost glistening, just as the horses and even the saddles and bridles shone. But my brothers and I have no memory of ever seeing my mother on a horse. She gave it up—along with tennis and sailing and so many other pursuits she had enjoyed— as she focused increasingly on us.

My mother and father riding to hounds with my father's little sister Bettie in the foreground, late 1940s. My mother, as always, is mounted sidesaddle.

As we entered our teens, we three older children wished avidly that she would find some outlet to replace her all-absorbing interest and interventions in our lives. But for my mother there was no ready alternative. I remember discussing with my older brother, Tys, whether we might persuade her to get a job. But she had never been educated or expected to work, and indeed not one of the other mothers in our social circle was employed outside the home. The conventions that shaped her upbringing and the social constraints on middle- and upper-class women of the 1950s had left her living her life through her children.

My mother, Catharine Ginna Mellick, was born in 1918 in Plainfield, New Jersey. During her earliest months, her father was in the

My mother with her father, Roger Mellick, not long before he was shipped overseas, spring 1918.

army, serving overseas for nearly a year. With the end of World War I, he returned to civilian life and a very remunerative position in the family's odd-lot business on the New York Stock Exchange. In the 1920s, the family moved to the countryside in nearby Far Hills, where my mother enjoyed a childhood of ponies, dogs, excursions to New York City, summers by the sea, and not much education. In 1931, Cath's mother wrote to an old family friend, Mira Hall, founder and headmistress of a school for girls in Pittsfield, Massachusetts, seeking admission for Cath. Their correspondence makes clear that the families were very close, and I remember seeing as a child a photograph of Miss Hall and my great-grandmother each atop a camel in front of the pyramids. My mother's letter of acceptance, dated January 1932, is signed "With much love to you all, I am Affectionately yours," but it also makes clear that admission was contingent upon Cath's passing "our elementary entrance examinations."[4] This would prove no small obstacle.

Miss Hall's was hailed by *Fortune* magazine in 1932 as one of the nation's ten best private girls' schools. But Cath was far from an accomplished student. A tutor delegated to prepare her for the exams noted, "She is reviewing English grammar, as we found that she knew practically nothing about it. She is also reviewing Geography as she failed a very elementary test in it at the start of the year. We started Algebra, Latin and French but had to give up Algebra and Latin as she did not seem to remember anything of Arithmetic." The tutor informed Miss Hall that he was not giving her grades, as they would only discourage her. Although she was fourteen, she was doing "Fourth and Fifth Grade work."[5]

With intensive effort and supervision, Cath at last managed to pass the English exam—although she never did get through spelling. Nevertheless, Miss Hall permitted her to enroll, registered in the general course, not the college preparatory curriculum. In a letter of recommendation, Miss Hall later characterized her as a student of "mediocre ability," "not superior academically" but "rather outstanding in other qualities."[6] Cath completed only three years at the school, departing before graduation and before, it later turned out, accumulating sufficient credits to qualify for further study at Finch Junior College, where she applied and was rejected in 1937.

Perhaps her weak academic record had made further time at Miss Hall's seem pointless, or perhaps it was simply the lure of study abroad that led to her enrollment at Villa Collina Ridente in Florence in the winter of 1936. "I'm out," Cath wrote, "to become a lady." Edith May, a Wellesley graduate who had worked in post–World War I rehabilitation efforts in Europe, had founded the establishment with an eye to providing women college graduates the opportunity to engage with international problems and perspectives. But by the mid-1930s, in the midst of the Great Depression, May seems to have been compelled to shift course, turning to younger girls from prosperous families who needed to be occupied in the years between school and marriage. My mother often referred to her experience as "finishing school"[7]—a distant prospect from what May had originally intended.

Through the winter and spring, Cath and seventeen other young American women were escorted by a phalanx of chaperones—the ratio was five chaperones for eighteen girls—to concerts, museums, and a variety of academic lectures on subjects ranging from the League of Nations to Anatole France to Botticelli. "It is exciting to be right here in Europe where . . . history is being made by the minute," Cath wrote her parents. She was fascinated by Mussolini and kept wishing he would appear at one of the musical or theatrical events the young women attended. "What I wouldn't give to see that gentleman." To fulfill her one major academic assignment, Cath composed a lengthy and unnervingly sympathetic essay on fascism. "I am really beginning to be a loyal Fascist," she wrote her parents, "and don't think he's half as bad as he's made out to be."[8] But the European sojourn and her infatuation with Mussolini were brief. She rendezvoused with her parents in Paris in May and, after a short visit to England, returned to the United States. She would have no more formal education.[9]

It would be six years before she married my father. Her surviving correspondence from that period suggests that she spent her time engaging in one activity after another, searching for something meaningful to do. Parties, friends' engagements and weddings, horses, family, all occupied her attention. But gathering rumors of war and emerging realities of international conflict cast lengthening shadows over what I read as a forced and hollow gaiety of unquestioned privilege among her circle of family and friends. In an increasingly serious world, these young women had never been asked or expected to be serious. A friend from the Villa Collina, an American who in 1938 married an Argentine diplomat, wrote Cath in 1940 from a perspective informed and expanded by her international residence and travel: "Our world is going to change radically, I'm afraid, Cath. Our background, education, cultural interests and refinement are going to stand us of little use . . . The things we subconsciously looked forward to are being swept away."[10]

But among the activities Cath undertook during these years, one did capture her interest and engagement far more deeply. It became a touchstone that she spoke of with nostalgia for the rest of her life, and it always made me think that she longed for something more than the 1950s domesticity to which she would ultimately be consigned. It called on her skills as a horsewoman, directed them toward service to others who lacked the comforts and advantages she had always enjoyed, and placed her in a community of powerful and effective women.

For six weeks in the fall of 1940 and again in 1941, Cath served as a courier in the Frontier Nursing Service in Leslie County, Kentucky. The FNS was founded in 1925 by Mary Breckinridge to provide health care for families, particularly mothers and babies, in the Appalachian hollows of eastern Kentucky. From a prominent Kentucky family, Breckinridge had undertaken nursing and relief work in France at the end of World War I and had struck upon the idea of bringing trained English midwives—like the ones she had encountered in Europe—to deliver care on horseback in the desperately poor and all but inaccessible mountain communities of her home state. She also determined to enlist young American women from privileged families to use their equestrian skills to serve as volunteer couriers, tending to the FNS horses and accompanying and assisting nurse-midwives on their rounds to remote cabins and villages to deliver babies. Frequently—and conveniently for the FNS—the wealthy families of these couriers also became advocates and fundraisers for the enterprise in cities across the nation.[11]

Soon after her arrival, Cath wrote home: "It's the first place I've ever helped in where, as a volunteer worker, you feel you are really needed." Within a week, she was riding alone twenty-four miles through the mountains over two days and a night, from Hyden to Brutus, via Hell for Certain, in order to retrieve a horse from an outlying clinic. "I never thought I would be able to find my way," she wrote, but her experienced mount and the "terribly friendly and pleasant" mountain people enabled her to complete her assignment. Not knowing what she or a midwife might be called on to do next kept her "in a state of excitement every hour of the day and night . . . It is wonderful . . . to see an organization like this not run by the Social Register for want of something better to do, but accomplishing so much . . . It really does make you look forward to tomorrow . . . It is like nothing I've ever seen or done anywhere before. I really do love every bit of it."[12]

By fall 1941, a new name had begun to appear in her letters home. A full-blown romance was well under way and taking on increasing urgency with the approach of war. Tyson Gilpin had grown up in Virginia in a family even more consumed by horses than Cath's. His father bred Thoroughbreds and bought and sold racehorses, in addition to riding and hunting himself. For the Gilpins, horses were a matter of business as well as pleasure. Tyson was enrolled at Princeton, where he was an outstanding student—ranked in the top dozen of his class. He was also stunningly handsome. When *Esquire* sent a staff photographer to Princeton for an article on collegiate fashion for the September 1940 back to school issue, he posed Tyson along the university's legendary Prospect Street and published a shot of him in the "new four-button jacket" with "broad shoulders and flapped chest pockets."[13] Tyson looked as if he had been invented by F. Scott Fitzgerald.

My father
photographed
by *Esquire*
on Prospect Street
in Princeton, fall 1940.

Cath and Tyson had met early in his college career when he came to join her brother Drew foxhunting in Far Hills, an easy drive from the university. Cath's prowess on horseback—her complete mastery over her mount, her fearlessness riding sidesaddle over ditches, walls, and fences—soon made her the focus of Tyson's attention and admiration.

By the time Cath returned from Kentucky in early fall 1941, Tyson was already planning to accelerate his graduation so he could join the army. His draft board in Virginia had called him for a physical in July, and he was eager to volunteer before he was conscripted. By early winter, he was in uniform, and by late the next summer, expectations that he would soon be sent abroad fueled the intensity of their courtship. In early October 1942, the young couple informed their parents that they intended to marry as soon as possible. A whirlwind of hasty preparations ensued—seamstresses summoned to produce a wedding dress, ceremonies and celebrations hurriedly planned, and a photographer already shooting the hunting field deputized to take a picture for the engagement announcement. There would be no equivalent of elegant posing on Prospect Street. The photographer caught her, Cath long complained, just after she had been thrown from her horse, which had then rolled over her. The engagement announcement preceded the wedding by only two days.

On October 23, 1942, Lieutenant Gilpin and Catharine Mellick were married. My father, his father, his uncle, and his new brother-in-law were all in uniform, just as his own father and all his groomsmen had been at his parents' wedding in 1918. For a year and a half after her marriage, my mother shuttled between her parents' home and her husband's various army training camps. Thirteen months after the wedding, my brother Tyson Jr. was born. Often Tys was deposited with a baby nurse at my maternal grandparents' home in New Jersey while Cath followed her husband's army assignments. Soon, however, like their parents before them, Tyson and Cath would be separated by war. In spring 1944, Tyson shipped out to England, and just after D-Day he landed in France with Patton's Third Army. His service in the course of the next year would earn him a Purple Heart and a Croix de Guerre. "The biggest experience of my life was WW2," he reflected on a Princeton 50th Reunion questionnaire.[14] Cath, meanwhile, waited at home with parents and child.

I was born in September 1947, part of a record cohort of 3.8 million American babies who arrived that year.[15] In the vanguard of the postwar baby boom, I represented my parents' commencement of ordinary marriage after five years of wartime disruptions and separations. Now they had to live together and build a life; now we were a family. Soon my mother and father moved away from New Jersey and my mother's parents back to Virginia, where Tyson had grown up. A photograph of my parents holding me at an aunt's wedding in 1948—six years after their own—reveals my mother already getting very thin. Curiously, my father is looking a bit portly, as if weight were being transferred from one to the other. The supposed stability of peace was destabilizing their bodies as well as their lives.

With my parents, May 1948.

My mother was deeply unhappy in 1950s Virginia. It was a place of roles and rules, of revered traditions and rigid expectations not entirely removed from slavery times. An easy day's drive from where she had grown up in New Jersey, this was nevertheless in many ways a world apart. She had come to a community with a sizable Black population, whom she encountered as cooks, cleaners, and menial laborers; a white majority controlled every aspect of the local social and economic order. Segregation was mandated by Virginia law, and the unfamiliar details of racial etiquette and hierarchy were customs she needed to learn. In the suburbs of New York, she had not had to think about being white. But this was the South, and my mother had joined one of the families who regarded themselves as the local gentry, with the privileges and presumptions that entailed.

Being a Gilpin posed its own distinctive challenges as well. The powerful and controlling presence of her mother-in-law, who held the family purse strings, was one factor. My mother was accustomed to having plenty of money to spend, and my father never produced an income stream that adequately provided for what she regarded as the essentials of family and home. They fought regularly about money—and about their dependence on Granny's dispersals—in arguments I heard through my bedroom wall at night even when I was a very small child. And the routines of household and child-rearing underscored my father's sense that the most important episode of his life had likely already occurred—and that no one who hadn't taken part in the liberation of France would ever understand it. As children succeeded horses at the center of my mother's attention, the passion and preoccupation that had originally brought my parents together disappeared.

I cannot imagine my mother ever read *The Feminine Mystique*. It did not even appear until 1963, just three years before her death—when it quickly sold more than a million copies. But much of what Betty Friedan characterized as "the problem that has no name" haunting American women in the postwar era describes my mother and her life: the sense of dissatisfaction and of yearning for something beyond the era's ideals of domestic bliss, the distorting and destructive effects of living one's life through one's children, the dangers of what Friedan called "the forfeited self." Friedan describes "the aggressive energy" a woman "should be using in the world" that "becomes instead the

Me in 1950, age three. With my father and mother and brothers
Tys, age seven, and Donald, seven months. My youngest brother,
Lawrence, known as Lou, was not born until 1956.

terrible anger that she dare not turn against her husband, is ashamed
of turning against her children, and finally turns against herself, until
she feels as if she does not exist."[16] Reading those words now, more
than a half century after my mother's death, I think of my unhappy
and so often angry mother growing thinner and thinner until the day
she indeed did not exist at all.

I am sure she loved her children. But I am less sure she liked or
enjoyed us. Especially me. My birth had been followed in 1950 by the
arrival of my brother Donald and then in 1956 by Lou. I think Lou
was something of a surprise, although national surveys indicated that
since 1940, notions of the ideal number of children had risen from
two to four. But I was the only daughter, and I became the especial
target of my mother's strongly held notions of how things ought to
be. We were on a collision course from as early as I can remember. I
needed to learn to be a lady, with the assumptions of decorousness,

docility, and social position that destiny prescribed. I was not meant to become a woman, for that category carried dangerously sexual and sensual implications. It was a term that seemed almost impolite in its emphasis on the physical aspects of female identity rather than the acquired graces by which a lady was defined. Black people were women; I must be a lady.

The first fights were about clothes. I was only two or three when I declared war against "fancy pants"—frilly panties with lace ruffles she intended for me to wear on top of my regular underwear. They itched and seemed unnecessary, and I would have none of them. Why did so many fabrics for little girls have to itch? What torturer could have invented the organdy of the pale pink dress I was required to wear for a portrait painter when I was four? I can still feel the discomfort of those little bouffant sleeves as I was instructed to sit still for what seemed like hours on end. Why couldn't I just wear a cotton shirt like my brother Donald, who was painted at the same time? The portrait was completed in spite of my attempts at resistance and my incessant wiggling, but I detest pink to this day. It has always seemed to represent a way of controlling and trivializing girls.

Clothes battles became gender battles. What boys could wear, what girls had to wear. What girls couldn't do, what boys could do. "It isn't fair!" became my constant refrain as I challenged what seemed to me so against both logic and justice. "It's a man's world, sweetie," my mother routinely replied, "and the sooner you figure that out, the happier you will be." I should recognize and accept, as she had, the world as it was. She spoke with both resignation and no little anger, which she regularly yet inadvertently signaled with a clenching of the jaw that betrayed to her children more of what she was feeling than she intended to convey.

As I progressed in school, it became clear that I was an excellent student—at the head of my class all through elementary school, a voracious reader, filled with questions and curiosity about how the world worked. For my mother, this was unsettling. It made me not only very unlike her but also unlike what she thought I should be. Years later, the counselor at my high school would capture the essence of our long-standing mother-daughter differences, citing in a college recommendation "Mrs. Gilpin's bewilderment in connection with Drewdie's intellectual gifts." The counselor went on: "Mrs. Gilpin is like a hen that has hatched a duckling and cannot understand having a daughter who is not going to be a 'southern belle.'"[17]

Betty Friedan quoted the psychoanalyst Helene Deutsch to portray the era's prevailing views about bright women. "Women's intellectuality," Deutsch wrote, "is to a large extent paid for by the loss of valuable feminine qualities." And it was not only dangerous for girls to have good minds, it was unnecessary—even wasteful. I once overheard my mother observing to a friend that she wished that my older brother, who struggled a bit with dyslexia, had been the one to inherit my brain. My mother praised me when I collected the class scholarship prize each spring, but she urged me not to attach too much sig-

Walking with my father along the bank of the Shenandoah River at the edge of our farm, early 1950s.

nificance to it, or to act too proud. Other aspects of life, she insisted, mattered far more. In the child-rearing language of the day, she made it clear that it was much more important that I be "well-adjusted."[18] I heard that to mean compliant.

At that I consistently failed. Determined, opinionated, I was far more interested in animals and the outdoors than I was in dolls and clothes. I joined the 4-H club to raise steers with the boys, not to sew and can and bake with the girls. I was convinced I often understood things faster and better than others, and I would argue insistently to defend my ideas. I wasn't much more than two when my grandfather dubbed me "Little Miss Fix-It" after a cartoon character who was always telling others what to do. My mother urged me to lower my voice, not to speak "like a fishwife"; to soften my insistence, not to be so bossy; to defer more to others. I was well aware of my deficiencies in the girl arena. I remember my feeling of relief when I answered the phone in our kitchen in April 1956 to learn that my third sibling had just been born and was a boy. I had dreaded the prospect of a little sister and a lifetime of negative comparisons.

As I grew older, the gap between boys' freedoms and girls' rules became even more stark. Girls were seen to be at risk and needed to be both constrained and protected. Ladies had to be defended from both themselves and others as they became sexual beings. But my mother almost never talked directly about sex. When I first got my period at age eleven, she had not yet mentioned menstruation or addressed the facts of life with me. The morning I told her about the blood on my pajamas, she belatedly and awkwardly began to try to explain, but I had long since educated myself with friends at school. Embarrassed for us both, I dismissed her and turned away.

Our exchanges about sex were always perfunctory and vague, focused exclusively on the prohibitions that surrounded it and the dangers it entailed. But we argued incessantly and angrily about the regime of oversight and control the risks of sex seemed to require. Chaperones had followed her throughout her adolescence and young womanhood, and she expected the same surveillance regime to be in place for me, to ensure both that I didn't behave inappropriately and that others didn't take liberties with me. One ongoing battle of my teenage years involved driving at night once I got my license, which Virginia then permitted at fifteen. My older brother could go wherever and whenever he wished, but if I drove after dark I needed to be accompanied by an adult. I found this double standard absurd and infuriating, unjust and illogical, and I regularly delivered diatribes to make my point.

In retrospect, I can reconstruct my mother's thinking, though she never articulated her reasoning. She saw the world as a dangerous place for women, for their bodies and their reputations. What, I think she worried, might happen to a lone young female if she were stranded on the roadside in our rural county after dark? My mother had grown up in the New Jersey countryside, in a nearly all-white world, yet now she lived in a Virginia county where nearly one in five inhabitants was Black. I am certain this enhanced her fears and her sense of urgency about protecting my white feminine purity. She regarded me as endangered in a way my brothers weren't. And she saw me as far more vulnerable than the boys to my own misjudgments. I had the capacity to "get into trouble" in a way that would be far more devastating for me than it could be for a boy. I did not share her anxieties, resented being cast as weak, and was angered by the lack of trust implicit in this policy. With Tys's complicity, I secretly or not so secretly evaded it whenever I could.

The arguments I had with my mother were structured in a manner that meant they would almost certainly never be resolved. My mother followed often unquestioned instincts; she felt more than she reasoned. I was the opposite—calling on all the intellectual power I could muster to offer what I believed to be irrefutable syllogisms to make my case. She wasn't interested. She would quickly anger and exert her authority: "Because I said so." I would storm off and dissolve in frustrated tears. The outcome of this pattern was that I endeavored from a very young age to protect as much independence from my mother as I could, to preserve the freedom of action I could exercise when she simply did not know what I was up to. It was less about being sneaky or secretive than maintaining distance. In today's world, when college students call or text their parents multiple times a day, this seems unimaginable. But both technology and custom made relationships between parents and children quite different in midcentury America. When I went away to school, I phoned every other week.

As I grew older, it became easier to maintain and even cultivate this distance. I remember discussing with a sympathetic adviser at my boarding school how I could manage to go home as infrequently as possible, and by the time I got to college at Bryn Mawr, I had the institution, with its feminist traditions and its commitment to student self-governance, firmly on my side.

In the winter of my first year at Bryn Mawr, I received a summons to meet with the dean, the indomitable Mary Patterson McPherson, whose six feet two inches of height made her physical presence as impressive as her intellect. I was worried about what I might have done to receive this call to her office, but I could never have imagined what Miss McPherson was about to report. Without telling me, my mother had driven up from Virginia the day before in order to express to the dean her worries about my recently acquired boyfriend and what she feared to be my sex life. She hoped to enlist Miss McPherson on her side of our long-standing battle.

Bryn Mawr permitted us to sign out any night till 2:00 a.m.; chaperones were a long-abandoned relic of the past. Miss McPherson explained to my mother that the college believed in entrusting its students with responsibility for their own lives, and that she would, of course, be informing me of her visit and her concerns. My mother had returned to Virginia without ever confessing she had been there. She never mentioned the trip to me afterward, and I saw no point in bringing it up. I cannot remember what I might have said to the dean in my astonishment, but as I listened to her words I knew the college was on my side—neither in favor of nor opposed to the boyfriend, but in full support of my ability and right to figure it out for myself. I was free. In the long fight with my mother—even though there might be a few further skirmishes—I had won.

Almost exactly two years later, she was dead.

How should I understand my mother's life? She was certainly a child of extraordinary privilege—enjoying foxhunting, boarding school, the sojourn in Florence—all at the same time that so many other Americans had been cast into deprivation and even destitution by the Depression. Domestic workers ensured she never had to cook or clean or take direct responsibility for her own day-to-day needs or those of her children. Yet the 1940s and 1950s proved a time of gradually diminishing wealth for those who since the turn of the century had comprised the financial elite. America's booming prosperity in the years after World War II was a middle-class phenomenon more than an upper-class one. It was accompanied by sharply narrowing inequality that had been inaugurated by the 1929 crash and expanded by the New Deal and the war. My mother's friend from the Villa Collina was right in her perception that many of the expectations nurtured in their circle of young women were being "swept away." In 1930, the top decile of Americans earned 50 percent of national income; by 1940, that figure had fallen to about 45 percent; by 1950, it had dropped to between 30 and 35 percent, where it remained until the 1980s.[19]

My family's particular circumstances reflected an intensified version of this trend, one that—played out on the level of individuals rather than statistical groups—opened seemingly limitless opportunities for blame and resentment. On both my mother's and my father's sides of the family, the generations that came of age with World War I and then World War II did not extend, replenish, or even sustain the financial success enjoyed by my great-grandfathers on both sides of the family at the turn of the twentieth century. By the 1950s, the Gilpins and the Mellicks remained well-off, but less so than they once had been. They were in fact gradually but steadily running out of money, though they remained steeped in the habits of affluence. For my mother, this meant that the resources she had long simply taken for granted were no longer readily and unquestioningly available. She never came to grips with this changed reality, often proceeding—and spending—as she always had, until yet another series of eruptions with my father further undermined their already difficult relationship.

My mother's broader inability to understand or respond to change seems at the heart of the matter. Of a piece with her insistence on rules and expectations for me that I saw as more appropriate to the 1920s—or perhaps the 1820s—than the 1950s or '60s, it was as if she could not see to move beyond the assumptions of a lost and, for her, happier world. She thought it her obligation to teach me to be a lady, complete with the simultaneous privilege and subordination that destiny entailed.

Education has been so important in enabling me to examine my own life and alter its contours and possibilities; I cannot help but think that my mother's lack of education and of capacity for systematic self-reflection did much to imprison her within a set of expectations that she could neither change nor realize. But education for girls was little valued in her era. In 1950, only one in three white women over twenty-five had completed high school, and only one in twenty had completed college.[20] Even if she had been more successful in school, it was unlikely she would have continued on to higher education. From the beginning, her sights were set on Miss Hall's School's general curriculum, not its college preparatory one.

Similarly, young women of her social station rarely took on remunerative work and certainly did not anticipate or pursue careers. Motherhood was the undertaking for which her circumstances designated her. Whatever her advantages of class and wealth, she could not evade the constraints that her era's gender expectations placed upon her. Instead, she embraced much of the ideology of the 1950s with ferocity. Yet the very ferocity with which she defended the strictures of

1950s womanhood was paradoxical. She had no patience for what she called "helpless women" who waited for men to open doors or carry heavy packages. After all, she could bend a thousand-pound horse to her will. Her incessant hard-fought arguments with my father showed her to be anything but docile or deferential. Yet she neither doubted nor challenged the reality that it was a man's world. Few could have done better at achieving what Friedan called "the forfeited self." She would live through her children even as they struggled to escape her control. Her death at age forty-eight was a final act of self-abnegation.

2

A GIRL ISN'T THE SAME

We shall never any of us be . . . as we have been.
—LUCY REBECCA BUCK, FRONT ROYAL, VIRGINIA, 1862[1]

My mother was born when her father was in uniform; she married my father when he was in uniform, and she died while her oldest son was on holiday leave from the navy awaiting orders to ship out to the South China Sea. World War I, World War II, Vietnam. Nearly a half century of conflicts. None of these men was a military professional; all three had enlisted as citizen soldiers. Like so many of their male contemporaries, they were impelled by the inevitability of conscription, but they were motivated more powerfully by deeply held convictions about who they must be as men and about the existential link between manhood and war. As Hector so long ago explained to Andromache in the sixth book of the *Iliad*, it is the men "who must see to the fighting." Men make war, and war makes men.

But war changes more than just those who fight. It turns wives into widows, children into orphans; it makes siblings only children and renders parents childless. It transforms families, distorts marriages, overturns women's choices and assumptions. And it changes societies and even worlds, so that looking back we often define eras by their temporal relationship to military combat.

I grew up in the aftermath of World War II, and the label affixed to my generation identifies us as the direct product of war and its pent-up baby demand. Arriving in unprecedented numbers as our fathers returned from the conflict, we baby boomers entered an era that would itself be conceptualized as the outcome of the conflagration that had preceded it. Instead of peace, we confronted a Cold War, a new kind of conflict generated by the terror of the atom bomb and the polarity of an East and a West divided by an Iron Curtain.

A war to end all wars in the early years of the twentieth century had proved instead to be the opening salvo of seemingly endless conflict, contests without beginnings or conclusions that inspired the invention of a new human capacity to destroy the world. But it was not only the culture and politics of the 1950s that reflected the legacies of three decades of war. My family was in many ways defined by those conflicts, even as it both denied and struggled with their implications. The first half of the twentieth century—the way it shaped my parents and grandparents, the way its wars determined the choices, the experiences, and the relationships of both women and men—would be an inheritance I carried forward into the century's second half.

War transformed Isabella's life. "The wrong one has been left behind," my twenty-four-year-old grandmother wrote from Tennessee to her father in France two days after the 1918 Armistice silenced the guns of the Great War. Scarcely a month before, her older and only brother, Charles McGhee Tyson, an officer in the Naval Flying Corps, had been killed in a seaplane flying a mission over the North Sea. She, not the "much more brilliant" McGhee, should have been the one to die, Isabella protested. Across the English Channel, only a few hundred miles away from the site of the crash, her father, General Lawrence Davis Tyson, commander of the 59th Brigade, 30th Division, was immersed in some of the most desperate fighting of the conflict—"in the midst of a great battlefield with dead on every side," he wrote. And now war's devastation would become personal.[2]

The United States had declared war against Germany in April 1917, but it was the summer of 1918 before American troops arrived in substantial numbers to join the fight on the Western Front. Germany had launched a series of assaults during the preceding spring, hoping to destroy the British and French before Americans could be mobilized, trained, and transported across the Atlantic. The terrible battles of the late summer and fall proved highly costly for the inexperienced American troops. Together with the British Fourth Army, the Americans of the 30th Division had at last broken the Hindenburg Line at St. Quentin Canal at the end of September.

Through October they continued to endure uninterrupted days and nights of heavy shelling, attacking again and again as they sought to push the Germans back and reclaim one occupied village after another—Bellicourt, Montbrehain, Brancourt, Busigny, Ribeauville. The pressure and the losses were unrelenting in what had become a war of attrition. "The Boche is shelling out every town as he retires, blowing out great holes in the roads, mining everything, setting traps that kill people, and doing every dastardly thing possible," General Tyson wrote. "Pompeii is not worse." The 59th Brigade had taken 45 percent casualties. But for its commander, another casualty mattered most—even though he knew he could not let those around him perceive that his son's loss had more significance than any other.[3]

Charles McGhee Tyson fell to his death on Friday, October 11, 1918, at age twenty-nine. Aviation in World War I represented an entirely new form of combat with an irresistible allure for young men imbued with dreams of heroic deeds. Flyers seemed the modern equivalent of knights, mounted on planes rather than horses, ready to do glorious battle. But the primitive nature of aerial technology and the unreliability of almost every World War I airplane brought death instead of glory to thousands of young airmen.[4]

It would take eight days for news of McGhee's death to travel the hundred or so miles from his air base in England to his father in France. Around seven in the evening, after a day of furious fighting, the general's chief of staff delivered a message in the frontline headquarters where Lawrence had been overseeing the battle. "I had been feeling awfully happy to think that I had gained a great victory," he later wrote. After debating whether to give the general the devastating message "at that time," his aides decided they could not hold back the terrible information. "General, I feel I have some pretty bad news," one officer began. "I handed him the message which stated that McGhee Tyson had drowned when his plane fell into the channel." Tyson cried out—"My God"—and fell briefly to his knees. Then turning to his aides, he mumbled, "I think I will lie down a while." Twenty minutes later, he returned to plan for the military movements of the following day. The "Old Man," as his aides affectionately called him, "stood it fine," they reported, "until we were relieved with the tension of the battle over. Then he said, 'Well. We certainly have had a pretty hard time during the last few days.'" From that moment on, General Tyson later wrote, "life seemed without object" and "never the same to me again."[5]

Although she professed to adore her father, Isabella remembered him as "not always a comfortable companion," "often considered stern and superior," "not a generally popular man." His invariably dignified and rather military manner, was, she feared, "frequently misunderstood." But "after his marriage," she explained, "he never had, nor wanted, intimate friends—he and his wife lived in such companionship that it richly sufficed." The contrast between the controlled and controlling man his daughter described and the man revealed in a lifetime of correspondence with his wife is sharp and telling. During their courtship in the 1880s, Lawrence sent Bettie—to whom he gave the pet name Bettina—letters that were passionate, poetic, vulnerable, and numerous: "I fear I should weary you if I wrote oftener." When, after decades of marriage, the Great War separated them, he wrote from France with undimmed devotion. And when their son was killed, Lawrence endured the profound loneliness his unique emotional dependence on her had created, even as he struggled to pay the fearful cost of maintaining a bearing of unperturbable composure.[6]

He was shocked but not surprised by McGhee's death, he admitted to Bettina; the dangers of flight, the unreliability of those "terrible machines" made aviation the most dangerous of all war's assignments. But "a man is not a man if he is not willing to pay the price when it becomes necessary." McGhee died as a soldier; his father felt he must mourn him as one. Yet Lawrence admitted to Bettina, "No one knows what I have suffered the past few days. I have had to keep up an outward appearance for it would never do for me to show too much grief when other men are dying too, but my aspect in life has changed so much—so much . . ." Even as he carried out his command duties till the moment of Armistice on the eleventh hour of the eleventh day of the eleventh month, even as he then quickly departed for England and the site of his son's death, even as he learned that McGhee's body, lost at sea for almost a month, had finally been recovered, Lawrence battled to maintain his self-control. But, he confessed to Bettina, he had been "living in a nightmare of depression . . . going through a terrible ordeal." At last, in a car en route to the British airfield where McGhee had been stationed and where funeral observances were scheduled, he entirely broke down in floods of "bitter tears." Six weeks later, he reported to his wife that his suffering had only intensified: "I try hard to keep down my grief but every time the mail comes in, I break down and have a terrible fit of weeping. Instead of getting better I am not controlling myself as well as I did a month ago." The force of his sorrow challenged his dedication to the self-discipline and mastery so central to his identity; it challenged his sense of manhood and of himself.[7]

Four thousand miles away in Knoxville, Tennessee, Bettie and Isabella had received the news more promptly, just three days after McGhee's death. The women had taken over Lawrence's managerial duties at the Knoxville Spinning Mill and had been busily distracting themselves from worry about the war with concerns about gear valves and labor's escalating wartime demands. A friend wrote Bettie in amazement at the responsibilities the Tyson women had assumed in the family businesses. "To think of you and Isabella undertaking the work carried on by the men of the family! . . . These are indeed strange times!"[8]

And Bettie and Isabella had reason to worry about their own health and safety. The worldwide influenza epidemic had appeared in their small southern city. Although they both had only mild cases, Bettie reported that the local death toll had risen so high that caskets had become almost unavailable. Schools, churches, and theaters were closed, and eighty University of Tennessee students were in the infirmary. The disease was surging through the mills as well, and the manager reported that so many were stricken that the finishing room was "cleaned out" of workers.[9]

But the personal impact of the war was to become more direct and searing. As they readied themselves for bed around eleven one evening, they were startled by the doorbell and then by a messenger baldly announcing "Death Telegram." As the reality set in over the days that followed, the women—joined by McGhee's wife of just four months, similarly named Betty—strived to contain their grief. As a dear friend wrote, "Soldiers wives and mothers have to be soldiers too."[10]

For McGhee's mother, Bettie, this was her worst fear come true. She had visited her son during his flight training in Pensacola and was so alarmed by the unreliability of the new flying machines that she wrote to Josephus Daniels, the secretary of the navy, "with an appeal for greater care in examining airplanes before our boys are allowed to use them." Daniels dismissed her concerns: "I assure you that we are exercising every care possible to protect our aviators from accidents and injuries." For McGhee, it would not be care enough.[11]

The war would be won within days, but Isabella understood how hollow a victory this was for her father. "All your plans and building for the future and for the [family] name are defeated," she wrote to him. The male line of Tysons had been extinguished. "I know a girl isn't the same papa." Decades later, toward the end of a long life, with children and grandchildren of her own, Isabella would write that McGhee's death had been "the end of everything."[12]

Everything had begun for Isabella in 1894,[13] when she was born to a prominent Knoxville, Tennessee, family. Her grandparents on both sides had been slaveholders. But her father, Lawrence, born in

Isabella Tyson, age four,
Knoxville, Tennessee.

1861, saw his best chance for personal advancement in the Civil War's chaotic aftermath to lie in the U.S. military. Securing a nomination to West Point from a local congressman, Lawrence headed north and graduated from the academy in 1883. After a decade of service, he left the army to become, first, a professor of military science at the University of Tennessee and, then, a lawyer, a politician, and a textile manufacturer. Isabella's mother, Bettie, was the daughter of a Knoxville railroad magnate who had been shrewd enough to exchange his landholdings for railroad stock at the end of the Civil War.

Isabella and her older brother, McGhee, born in 1889, grew up in a world of privilege, performing the rituals of the local gentry: learning to shoot, playing golf and tennis—and Isabella excelled at all these—attending the annual weeklong appearance of the Metropolitan Opera in Atlanta, traveling to Europe and across the United States. In 1898, Lawrence returned briefly to military service in command of a regiment in the Spanish-American War, and the whole family joined

Lawrence Davis Tyson,
West Point graduation
photo, 1883.

him for several months in Puerto Rico at the end of the conflict when
he was assigned as administrator of the Arecibo area in the northern
half of the island. Rooted in Tennessee, they nevertheless sought to
be part of a cosmopolitan national elite.

Isabella and McGhee were both sent north to be educated. Mc-
Ghee graduated from St. Paul's School in New Hampshire and then,
like many elite southerners, enrolled at Princeton. Isabella, four years
behind him, arrived at Miss Spence's School in New York City as
a boarding student at age fifteen. Its aim, the school brochure declared, was "the cultivation of a perfect gentlewoman, intellectually
firm and having poise, simplicity and graciousness." It was no place
for "delicate or idle girls," and students were expected to "dress simply
and work faithfully." The school proclaimed itself to be "nonsectarian,
but pupils attend either the Episcopal or Presbyterian Church."[14] No
room even for a Methodist.

Isabella sent flurries of letters to her parents describing the performances and exhibitions around the city to which Miss Spence introduced her—concerts, Shakespeare, dancer Isadora Duncan at Carnegie Hall—the "essence of grace." And she proved to be an outstanding student. Her first-year science teacher was eager to have her go to college; they could prepare her in two years, Isabella reported to her parents. "But," she added, underlining the words in thick black ink, "I don't want to go to college." Late in her life, she proudly recorded that she had been at the very top of her class, but she nevertheless had internalized the limited educational ambitions of young women of her station. In the 1910s, only 3 percent of American women graduated from college, and Isabella had learned to look down on those unconventional "bluestockings." In dark, bold strokes, she dismissed the possibility of higher education.[15]

Yet at the very same moment, while Isabella was impressing her teachers and classmates, her brother, McGhee, was at Princeton, charming everyone he met, while busily failing his courses, drinking and partying, overspending his allowance, and writing home regularly for additional funds to buy such necessities as a raccoon coat. But there would be no college education for Isabella. Instead, her university experience would be the social whirl of "Harvard Class Day with Hasty Pudding," "Princeton Prom," and University of Virginia "Easter Week." On a European tour, she later remembered, she had attended "dozens of parties" and "danced a million miles" with "lovely young men most of whom were killed in the war the next year." She once proudly reported to her daughter that she had received forty marriage proposals. Testimonials to her beauty abound—from a comment by the bishop of the Episcopal Diocese of Tennessee that the loveliness of her person was exceeded only by that of her soul, to a relative describing how everyone in the Copley Plaza dining room in Boston stopped eating when she entered, to descriptions of what a "sensation" she caused at one appearance or another. She was, more than one admirer declared, "a queen."[16]

During a visit to the University of Virginia in the spring of 1913,

Isabella Tyson Gilpin,
1920s.

Isabella had danced with Kenneth Gilpin, a recent graduate who had returned to attend a party with his friends. Kenneth was smitten from the time of their first encounter. Isabella was friendly but distant as Kenneth continued in hot pursuit with repeated proposals and showers of orchids. Son of a wealthy family from the northern end of the Shenandoah Valley, Kenneth was interested in politics and horses, and not long after his college graduation he was elected to the Virginia House of Delegates as its youngest member.

His romantic persistence would pay off. "Finally found out that I was in love with Kenneth Gilpin 4 years after his first proposal," Isabella later wrote. In 1917, she informed her suitor offhandedly, toward the close of a long and newsy letter, "Also, I am beginning to think I'd like to marry you."[17] Kenneth was overjoyed at his good fortune, but Isabella would retain the whip hand. In this time of national crisis, she insisted, "every able-bodied man should have on a uniform."[18] That included her husband-to-be.

By the fall of 1917, the United States was already at war with Germany, and Isabella's brother and her fifty-six-year-old father had both promptly volunteered. Her father had been appointed to command a brigade in an army division created out of the National Guard in Tennessee and the Carolinas. The general would come to think of the "Old Hickory," the 30th Division, as the best in the U.S. Army because it was the "purest." Not just segregated, as was every U.S. military unit in World War I, it was "Anglo Saxon," composed "completely of native born American citizens." These white southern boys, Tyson was sure, knew how to fight in a manner far superior to the mixed ethnic stock from New York that made up the bulk of the 27th Division, their companion in service with the British Fourth Army.[19]

Kenneth had anticipated the entry of the United States into the raging global conflict. As part of the pro-intervention American Preparedness Movement, he had spent much of the summer of 1916 in upstate New York at the Plattsburg Training Camp for citizen soldiers—the "Business Men's Regiment"—where sons of the East Coast elite paid their own expenses for a month of drill, war games, and military science.[20] Isabella had even visited him there. But his participation had only raised her expectations that he would be eager to join up now that the real war had begun. In her eyes, Kenneth seemed intolerably slow to act. "If I were a man," Isabella wrote her intended, "I should enlist to-night!" Kenneth dutifully began to explore his options and told Isabella he was "determined to do something." Should it be the Quartermaster Corps as a purchaser of horses for the army? Or the Naval Flying Corps in the footsteps of his beloved's brother? Isabella continued to push, making it clear that marriage and military service had to go hand in hand. "I must tell you that when I mentioned to McGhee the fact that I was 'considering you seriously' he only said 'Get him into uniform.'" At first, Isabella expressed disdain for the Quartermaster Corps, which she declared to be the "Dept. of Fat Old Men." She seemed little more impressed with Ordnance or the Signal Corps. "I do like you better every time I see you," she tantalized him. "But I am afraid I am very strong for the uniform." The excitement of aviation had yielded an oversupply of applicants for the Naval Flying Corps, so Kenneth was stymied. Isabella relented on the Quartermaster opportunity and announced herself "thrilled" when she thought "your uniform is in sight." The engagement announcement was prepared, and Bettie began to examine samples of invitations for her daughter's wedding. When Kenneth was stricken with appendicitis, Isabella wrote her fiancé, "I find I care more than I knew."[21]

Unexpectedly, a place in the flying corps became available, but it required Kenneth to wait till midsummer for his orders. Isabella would have none of it: "Well—Kenneth—dear—then that means to me <u>no wedding until after the war. Definitely.</u>" She insisted that he must "get into active service <u>to-morrow—today</u>!!" Kenneth got the message. Somehow he found a way to enter active duty as a naval flyer

Kenneth N. Gilpin.

My grandfather Kenneth Newcomer Gilpin, 1918, in the World War I uniform my grandmother was so insistent upon.

almost immediately, and Isabella had her way. The wedding would take place in late March 1918. Declaring himself "mighty mighty happy," Kenneth reported to Isabella that he was off to get "my wedding gown in the shape of a uniform." A cousin wrote Kenneth to congratulate him on his engagement, noting, "You have been very persevering." It seems an understatement. As Kenneth himself confessed to Isabella, he would "always wonder and be thankful that I got you."[22]

Isabella got not just one uniform but a party full of them for her wedding—her father and brother both on furlough for the occasion, the groomsmen who were able to procure leave to attend, and her new husband. It would be the last family occasion where the Tysons would be all together. Lawrence would be on his way to France in a little

McGhee Tyson sails off to war aboard the USS *Leviathan*, August 1918.

more than a month; McGhee would embark in midsummer; and after aviation training at MIT, Pensacola, and Miami, Kenneth would
follow them in the fall to join the Northern Bombing Group a short
distance from Paris.

Isabella's romantic notions of war would prove a poisoned chalice.
Before the year was out, McGhee was dead, and so was his Princeton roommate. Kenneth's brother Donald had been gassed, two of
his University of Virginia roommates had been killed, and a third
was "down with nervous prostration"[23]—what we might call PTSD.
Kenneth himself had been torpedoed en route to France and, after
taking up his post in the bomber squadron, had narrowly escaped
capture when a faulty engine brought his plane down in no-man's-
land. "Sherman was right was he not," Kenneth wrote home.[24] War
was indeed hell—for men and women alike.

And for families. McGhee's young widow, Betty, remarried only
after two decades had passed. Isabella's mother, in mourning for her
son, wore black the rest of her life. Lawrence attained the pinnacle
of his career when he was elected to the U.S. Senate in 1924, yet he
never escaped his sense of depression and futility. "I shall never have
the same interest in life again," he confided to his wife, "and the heart
has been taken out of me to . . . struggle for place and power." He
devoted his congressional service to veterans' affairs and could not
understand why his colleagues did not share his commitment to an
international order that would sustain world peace. When support
for the Permanent Court of International Justice, also known as the
World Court, came to the floor of the Senate early in his term, Lawrence broke with the protocol that mandated respectful silence from
new members:

> As one of those who went out and fought in the World War,
> and who appreciates as fully as any man can the value and ne-
> cessity of maintaining peace in the world and as one who has
> seen the devastation and the horrible effects of war upon the

nations which were involved in the last great war, as one who has suffered in spirit and mind and has sacrificed as much as anyone can sacrifice by reason of the destructive effects of war . . . I am keenly interested in preserving peace, and in the hope of doing something, at least, during the remainder of my life to prevent the sons of men and women from being sacrificed in any wars which may come in the future.

He begged his colleagues to "keep faith" with the dead and wounded by "seeing that America adheres to the Permanent Court of International Justice."[25] The United States never joined.

Lawrence Davis Tyson died of a stroke, which he suffered in the midst of delivering a speech in Johnson City, Tennessee, on July 4, 1929, his sixty-eighth birthday.

Isabella, who had worried that McGhee's death would leave her without any blood relatives, quickly began her own family upon Kenneth's return from Europe in January 1919. The baby born not quite a year after McGhee's death was given his name: McGhee Tyson Gilpin, my father. And Isabella settled into the role she had trained herself to perform: the belle who grew into a grande dame; the steel magnolia skilled at managing and suppressing her emotions and her needs; the devoted wife, mother, and grandmother. But something ended for her, too, in 1918 when she was the one "left behind." Little more than two decades later, she confronted with "terror" the outbreak of World War II, fearing that McGhee's fate might be duplicated by his namesake or her younger son, Kay. Her husband, Kenneth, returned to uniform, too, serving as a major in the Army Air Forces, training young pilots for this new war. All three survived, but the consolations of peace proved to be short-lived, for Kenneth, plagued with a series of health conditions through most of his adult life, died of a heart attack in 1947, leaving her a widow at age fifty-three.[26]

When Isabella wrote late in her life of "dancing a million miles," her words carried a special poignancy, for by then she was no longer

General Lawrence Davis Tyson (second from right) sails home from the war aboard the USS *Mercury*, wearing his mourning armband, March 1919.

General Lawrence Davis Tyson in his Senate office, 1925.

My grandmother
Isabella Tyson Gilpin
and my father,
McGhee Tyson Gilpin,
1919.

able to walk. Stricken by painful arthritis in her fifties, she spent her last three decades on crutches and then in a wheelchair—and in persistent physical pain. Episodes of hospitalization for bleeding ulcers compounded her suffering. Yet she silently endured, and she continued to exert over her children and grandchildren—and most of those who came in contact with her—the sway she had wielded over Kenneth as she hastened him into uniform. But her power and her performance made her in essential ways inaccessible, and simultaneously generated and concealed a deep loneliness. She maintained a formality and distance not unlike that she ascribed to her father, even as she presided over endless social occasions and surrounded herself with people.

I remember a family party she hosted one summer evening—it might even have been for her own birthday—when I was eleven or

twelve. After we all had departed, she went upstairs and took an overdose of pills. I only overheard whispers about it, but there had been
an earlier attempt as well. Such matters were, of course, never openly
discussed, and her children had been instructed by her local physician
not to mention it. She later told her daughter she had tried again because no one had even appeared to notice. But a second effort seemed
to require a response. For a time she disappeared—hurried off by my
father and uncle to Connecticut's Hartford Retreat, where prominent
figures from socialites to movie stars were sequestered during episodes of emotional crisis. And then she returned to Virginia, and life
continued. She soldiered on as she had learned to do so well from her
father the general and from the crucible of war.[27]

She lived into her late eighties, the brains and the power in the
family until the very last years of her life. But even as her mental
capacities began to fail, her performance as belle, as queen, as grande
dame persisted. The gracious phrase and gesture remained ready at
hand even when her children's and grandchildren's names eluded her.
So strong were the lessons and expectations and prescriptions that defined her, they outlasted rational thought or self-conscious intention.
They remained when the self beneath them had departed.

3

SHOOTING THE DOG

The greatest way to live with honor in this world
is to be what we pretend to be.

—SOCRATES[1]

I had long since grown up and left home. But the call from my brother
wrenched me back into a time and place that still held the power
to confound and dismay. At first, I didn't think I had heard right.
Maybe the phone connection was bad. Daddy had shot the dog? His
dog? Teddy? His constant companion? It wasn't an accident? No, it
was the middle of the night and Teddy was in agony from his cancer
and so Dad shot him. Right in the head. Right in the kitchen. Then
he rolled the big Rottweiler up in a rug. The next day he had someone
take him to be cremated.

A terrible thought flashed through my mind. If my stepmother
were suffering, would he shoot her? She was about the same size as
the dog. Had he shot people in such circumstances when he was in
the army? I had read accounts of that happening in wars—comrades
obliging when soldiers begged to be saved from pain and anguish.
Maybe Dad somehow knew Teddy didn't want to live. Certainly he
believed he was using the gun as an instrument of mercy. But that
mercy must have come at an awful cost. How do you come to kill
something you love? You must believe it is a valiant and generous act,
that it is necessary, that it is your duty and responsibility. A gun was
an emblem and a vehicle of that honorableness, of the privilege and
the burden of being a man.

I can remember another time he shot a pet. This he did in a combination of sorrow and rage. We had a duck that arrived as a baby one
Easter morning. As it grew, waddling in and out of the house, I think
it had an identity crisis. It didn't know if it was a dog or a person,
and it had no role model for how to be a duck. But this confusion
made it a wonderful, enchanted creature. Dad was devoted to horses
and to dogs—we had a pack of five assorted dogs through most of
my childhood. But he didn't usually pay much attention to what I
would call our minor pets—the many cats, chicks, lambs, goats, ca-
naries, parakeets, hamsters, lizards, goldfish, and turtles with which
we cohabited. This duck was an exception. It had at least dog status in his animal pantheon. He had a little pen built for it in a large
shed near the back door, and he went out to greet it every morning.
One day as he opened the shed, the duck's quack was not a welcome
but a call of distress. There the animal stood, half-destroyed, its beak
chewed off by a predator. Dad returned to the house to fetch a rifle,
and first he shot the duck. But this circumstance required more than
mercy. There must be revenge. Saying not a word, he headed out on
the farm determined to punish the murderous possum for its crime.
When we saw our father next, the deed was done. It was not a hunt
but an execution. The gun served as his instrument of justice.

The guns in our house were kept in the den—although Dad also
had a pistol in the drawer next to his bed. Rifles and shotguns hung
on racks on the wall; handguns rested on a shelf below. I was always
fascinated by the Luger my father had captured from a German prisoner and brought home after the war. My brothers sometimes picked
it up to show it off to friends, but I didn't want to touch or go near
it. I had a toy Davy Crockett rifle and insisted on being given a BB
gun when I was eight or nine so that I could be adequately armed for
our endless reenactments of Civil War battles in the fields and woods
around our house. But I don't think I ever so much as shot at a squir-
rel with it.

I was scared of guns, scared of the responsibility they demanded,

The den at Lakeville with the arsenal visible in the background.

scared of the power they bestowed, a power of life and death I did not believe it was my part to claim. And I knew the stories of neighbors whose household guns had yielded tragedy—the suicide of a close friend of the family; the woman who accidentally shot her husband one night, allegedly mistaking him for an intruder. With my brothers it was a different matter. Less a choice than an expectation, a necessity, a foundation and signal of manhood. My brother Donald remembers receiving a .22 rifle and then a 410 shotgun for his eleventh and twelfth birthdays; it was a bit like graduating from short pants.

My grandmother Isabella was said to have been a crack shot as a young woman. She might have excelled at target practice or with clay pigeons, but the serious work of guns was reserved for men. That work began with learning to handle the weapon, but it included learning the customs of hunting as well—the choreography of how to stand and move in relation to others in the field, the hierarchy of who shot when, so that participants did not endanger one another. My brother Tys has no recollection of "any female shooting or bird hunting." Nor does he remember ever seeing a Black man with a gun. African American men hunted for food and for pleasure, but did so beyond white men's eyes. Long-standing legacies of race and power had made guns a white man's privilege. From the time of slavery, white Virginians had preserved their mastery by endeavoring to monopolize the instruments of violence. Before the Civil War, it was officially against the law for a Black man to have a gun, and after the war, whites continued to seek to control Black access to guns and hunting rights. It was not accidental that in the mid-twentieth-century South learning to shoot was a rite of passage for young white men.[2]

I did not envy my brothers this privilege. I had no desire to kill animals, and I was, I confess, relieved not to bear the burden of being expected to protect or even, as in the case of my father and the duck, avenge others. The nineteenth-century Virginian George Fitzhugh, who regarded his influential defenses of slavery as a broader "sociology" for antebellum southern society, had a century earlier explained the fundamental premise of white southern ladyhood. "Woman has one right," he wrote, the "right to protection."[3]

Slavery may have given way to Jim Crow, but, like assumptions about race, ideas about white southern womanhood lingered tenaciously. In one sense, this female right to protection was empowering; it represented a prerogative and a demand that women could make of men. But it was inextricably tied to concessions of frailty and incapacity. The reassurance that one would be taken care of could be all too alluring: chivalry, with its implicit acknowledgment of dependence, came at considerable cost to those it claimed to defend. But I was proud that my father was so comfortable with this power and that, as the Luger reminded me, he had used it for genuinely admirable purposes. Framed photographs of my father, grandfather, and uncles in their World War II uniforms rested on every side table in our living room as a testament to how they had saved me—not to mention the nation and the world—from Hitler and the apocalypse of Nazism.

Like the photographs themselves, the war was a lingering presence in our lives. We children all knew that our father had been away for a long time fighting our enemies. We had seen his formal portraits in uniform, as well as a much more thrilling faded sepia snapshot buried in a desk drawer of Dad aiming a pistol at a German prisoner. But he never talked about any of it apart from an occasional brief and hagiographic mention of General Patton.

When, in 1995, my thirteen-year-old daughter sent her grandfather a postcard from Paris, he replied, "I spent a year and a half in France during World War II and enjoyed a lot of it; we marched down the Champs Élysées on Victory Day in May 1945. I'll never forget the whole thing."[4] This was more than I had ever heard before. But what were those experiences—the enjoyable and the less so? What were his memories, and how did they affect us all as we grew up in a strange, foggy aftermath of war that no one explained or ever overtly discussed?

My father in Paris on V-E Day, May 8, 1945.

In 1941, the summer after his junior year at Princeton, the Clarke County, Virginia, draft board called McGhee Tyson Gilpin for a physical. Negotiations among his father, the local board, and Princeton deans yielded a compromise about his draft status. He could return to college in the fall so long as he could complete his academic work and be available for military service by March 1. Under the provisions of a special program approved by the Princeton faculty for students of "high scholastic standing," Tyson could be excused from second-semester senior courses yet still graduate in June if he completed his thesis, a study of Anthony Trollope, and passed a comprehensive examination in his major, English literature. Although ultimately more than four-fifths of the Princeton Class of 1942 would serve in the war, only 17 of its 683 members accelerated their degrees in this manner. After taking the required examinations in late February, Tyson joined an antiaircraft training battalion at Fort Eustis, Virginia. Basic was, Tyson wrote his parents, "unsympathetic to the general spirit." Serving as "latrine admiral" was a far cry from the college routine that had occupied him such a short time before, but soon he proclaimed himself "well & happy," with hopes to be sent to officer training school.[5]

By the fall of 1943, Tyson was a lieutenant, stationed at Maryland's Camp Ritchie, a Military Intelligence Service training center perhaps best known for producing the Ritchie Boys—primarily German-speaking Jewish immigrants who had fled the Nazis and were readying themselves for U.S. operations in Europe.[6] Camp Ritchie in fact trained intelligence officers in a dozen languages, including French, which was Tyson's specialty. After eight weeks of classes such as Terrain and Signal Intelligence, Aerial Photo Interpretation, Foreign Maps, and Combat and Operations, Tyson stayed on into the spring as an instructor. But as rumors of a cross-channel invasion of Europe multiplied, it became increasingly likely that he would be deployed overseas.

In the meantime, however, he seemed to spend only part of his life as a soldier. In October 1942, he had married, and Camp Ritchie was close enough to his family home in Virginia to enable him to spend Christmas in 1943 with Cath, his parents, and his baby son, Tyson Jr., born in mid-November. Cath returned to Ritchie with him, leaving the baby at her in-laws' with a nurse, and Tyson managed as well to get frequent time off to foxhunt during the winter. Wherever the army took him, however close or far from battle, he seemed to find a horse. One of the million and a half American soldiers who poured into Britain after January 1944, Tyson wrote home about attending a local horse show and tried in June to maneuver his way to the legendary English Derby, the apogee of what he often referred to as "the

Christmas in uniform, Virginia 1943. Top to bottom, left to right: Lewis Allen (my great-uncle); my father holding my brother Tys; Dorothy Gilpin Allen (my great-aunt); my mother; Isabella Tyson Gilpin (my grandmother); Kenneth Newcomer Gilpin (my grandfather); Douglas Allen (Dorothy and Lewis's son); Bettie Gilpin (my aunt); Kay Gilpin (my uncle).

sport of kings." Later that year, in post-invasion France with Patton, Bradley, and Montgomery speeding toward Germany, he managed to attend the races at Auteuil in the Bois de Boulogne. Until I read my father's letters home, it had never occurred to me that horse racing would continue as usual while the Allied and German armies struggled for dominance across the French landscape.

Tyson had arrived in France in mid-July 1944, part of the wave of troops that crossed the English Channel in the weeks after D-Day. He landed amid wrecked and sunken ships on Utah Beach with the 6th Armored Division, part of what soon became Patton's Third Army. Government files documenting the service of some eighteen million men, including these troops, burned in a tragic fire in a National Archives building in St. Louis in 1973, so the official record is even more silent about Tyson's experiences than he was himself. But his surviving letters to his family and general histories of the war make it possible to piece together his year and a half in France.

Once in Normandy, Patton's army headed south from the Channel coast and west toward Brittany, setting its sights on the city of Brest, designated a likely harbor for importing necessary supplies for Allied troops moving through France. Tyson was assigned command of Military Intelligence Interpreter Team #437, six soldiers who worked as a unit, interviewing prisoners and locals who could provide information useful to the advancing troops—enemy numbers and movements, the character of the terrain, the loyalties of its residents. A bit like a newspaper reporter, he explained in an effort to reassure his family. Many of those he interacted with were French Forces of the Interior, the Resistance, and he was charged with locating and reaching out to them. One memorable contact was a poet and painter who claimed to have been a friend of Marcel Proust and welcomed Tyson with both information and a glass of Breton cider.[7]

The division slogged its way across Brittany, devising a special hedgerow cutter—known as the "hedge-spade"—for the front of its tanks so they could make their way through the almost impassable

barrier posed by the bocage, the traditional raised embankments sur-
mounted with trees and shrubs that enclosed every field throughout
the countryside. On August 6, as American troops cleared enemy
forces from Plouvien, eighteen kilometers north of Brest, Tyson was
wounded sufficiently seriously to merit a Purple Heart, but not badly
enough to keep him long out of action. Military censorship limited
what he could communicate to those at home, but his own reluctance
seems to have played a larger role.

"What with . . . just unpleasantness about some aspects and general inability to describe what went on without taking time to do a
careful job it is awfully hard to write a good combat letter," he explained to his aunt and uncle. "Somehow I am not in the mood these
days." He might tell people more when he got home, he allowed, but
he warned about relying on the news: "It's on too large a scale & without any Ernie Pyle style description."[8]

The fighting in Brittany was intense, but Tyson relished it. "Some
of the farmers & welcoming villagers make . . . parts of the war well
worth fighting," he told his parents. At the end of the campaign, he
jokingly declared himself "the unofficial, or perhaps even authorized
savior & liberator of Brittany." He had "crashed through," he wrote, to
a promotion to captain.[9]

With Brittany under Allied control, Patton moved east, eager to
race toward Berlin and strike the final blow against Germany, but
shortages of fuel slowed his army through the end of the summer.
The Germans took advantage of the American delay to build up their
forces in Lorraine so that the campaign to take Nancy and Metz and
advance across the German border proved more difficult than the
Third Army anticipated. Patton disliked Lorraine—calling it a "nasty
country where it rains every day and where the whole wealth of the
people consists in assorted manure piles."[10] Tyson seemed to agree,
similarly citing the manure piles and complaining about the "ger-
manophile" character of that part of France. Lorraine "in the winter-
time," he wrote, "should give any place east of hell a good run for its

money."[11] The opposition seemed "tougher with more arty. [artillery] fire & so forth" here as well, but, he added, "I can't complain as I was always lucky." Tyson was fighting the Germans just a few miles from where his grandfather had struggled to break the Hindenburg Line only a quarter century before. The cold and rainy fall weather and the seas of mud had not changed.[12]

Patton and the 6th Armored Division were by late December engaged in the grim warfare of Bastogne and the Battle of the Bulge, Germany's last desperate and all-out effort to stave off defeat. But Tyson seems not to have been there—he was perhaps on furlough or perhaps reassigned. Although he was glad "to be in one piece and not exposed to dangers," he wrote to his mother, "the days were still an awful anticlimax."[13] It was an anticlimax that Isabella, who understood war all too well, must have welcomed.

V-E Day on May 8, 1945, found Tyson marching down the Champs Élysées. By summer, he was writing home from occupied Germany, consulting with French friends he had made in Nancy about business opportunities after the war, and returning to his old unit to visit his former G-2—intelligence—officer, Lieutenant Colonel Ernest Mitchell, and to find the "nucleus of my best friends . . . still there, scattered all over the various battalions." A brief five-day trip to Brittany in September enabled him to say goodbye to his old associates from the Resistance and an "intelligence chief of the local FF" and to tour what had been the German submarine base at Lorient. Its size and quality were a "little awing—almost frightening," reminding him how formidable a foe the Germans had been. But the Allies had attained victory. The war in Europe was now over, and he would be headed home. A half century later, he remembered the war as "something real, with a chance to do something significant, with a wonderful (and genuine) group around you." There would be, he wrote, "NOTHING like it" again.[14]

Tyson admired the journalist Ernie Pyle's columns, widely circulated among the troops through the GI newspaper, *Stars and Stripes.*

But his own communications about the war were strikingly different. It was not just that Pyle was a gifted storyteller who used a wealth of on-the-ground detail to convey war's human face, men's suffering and their heroism. Pyle felt a combination of awed admiration and compassionate sympathy for the ordinary soldier, and this emotional engagement with his subjects came at a considerable price. Overwhelmed and exhausted, Pyle left France in the fall of 1944 to recover from what he described as incipient "war neurosis." Later, reluctantly returning to the front to cover the war with Japan, Pyle was killed in April 1945 at Okinawa.

The very different tone and style of Tyson's letters can be only partially explained by the censorship to which he knew his words would be subjected. Tyson consistently emphasized the aspects of his experience most like life at home—going to the races, doing work like that of a newspaper reporter, casting a war ballot. "The way I spend my time is traveling and talking to Frenchmen," he told his parents. Perhaps he hoped they would forget there was a war on. Or perhaps by not speaking of it, he could for a moment forget it himself. Always cheerful, always controlled and contained, he wrote of the war only in generalities. And at the same time, he seemed curiously disengaged from what was happening at home. When after a visit to her grandson, his mother reported that Tyson Jr. was a very attractive child, Tyson responded with almost indifferent detachment from his baby son: "It'd be fun to see how he does look myself. This far away, it all tends to seem sort of farther and more unreal than the routine of our every day life."[15]

The daily routine established and cherished in defiance of the uncertainty and chaos of war absorbed him in a way that the abstraction of an unfamiliar baby could not. Tyson's letters reveal a man with his emotions in check keeping a measured distance from his family an ocean away. I can't help but wonder if he kept his emotions similarly inaccessible to himself.

In August 1944, Pyle wrote from a "lovely green orchard" in

France, anticipating Germany's inevitable defeat and the approaching end of the war: "It will seem odd when, at some given hour, the shooting stops and everything suddenly changes again . . . odd to have your spirit released from the perpetual weight that is compounded of fear and death and dirt and noise and anguish." Pyle had a message for those at home:

> Thousands of our men will soon be returning to you. They have been gone a long time and they have seen and done and felt things you cannot know. They will be changed. They will have to learn how to adjust themselves to peace. Last night we had a violent electrical storm around our countryside. The storm was half over before we realized that the flashes and the crashings around us were not artillery but plain old-fashioned thunder and lightning. It will be odd to hear only thunder again. You must remember that such little things as that are in our souls, and will take time.[16]

Tyson came home with his Purple Heart and a Croix de Guerre and those countless "little things" in his soul. Like his father and grandfather, he had tested himself in war. He had been "too green," he later reflected, to take full advantage of Princeton; it was in the army that he had "hit stride."[17] But Uncle Sam had been in control of the last four years of his life. Now he needed to figure out what to do with the rest of it.

I have always been puzzled by what came next. He could have done anything. He had an outstanding record as an honors graduate of Princeton; he had been decorated in the war; he was extraordinarily handsome—"unusually attractive," one of his college recommendations put it[18]—photographed as a male model by *Esquire*, voted the best dressed in his Princeton class. He had means, talent, and connections. But he seemed directionless. He dabbled with the idea of a business that turned seaweed into pharmaceuticals, but the only enduring upshot of that venture was names for two dogs, Moss and Kelp, Irish setters who lived on well into my childhood.

In June 1947, Tyson's father, Kenneth, died. Although he was only fifty-seven, Kenneth had been hospitalized much of the preceding year with congestive heart failure. But no one had expected his death, and his business interests were far from settled. He was running a considerable Thoroughbred horse breeding operation in Virginia, and together with a partner, he had recently bought the venerable horse auction company Fasig-Tipton, which had been founded in 1898 and since the time of World War I had run the storied annual Saratoga yearling sales. Man o' War, widely considered the greatest horse of the twentieth century, had been sold at Saratoga in 1918 and was but one of Fasig-Tipton's claims to distinction. In our household, the horse's name was synonymous with unrivaled excellence; when any one of us did something outstanding—a prize, a bull's-eye, a home run—Dad would tell us we had "come on like Man o' War."

With his father's death, Tyson could no longer be directionless. He took over as president of Fasig-Tipton, commuting to its offices on East Forty-Eighth Street in New York City from the New Jersey town where Cath had grown up, and managing the Virginia farm long distance. I was born three months after my grandfather died. I have no memories of those early years in New Jersey. By the time I was two and a half, we had joined my father's family in Virginia. He had felt trapped in the city, hated the routines of business and commuting, and missed the farm and the horses. He worked to syndicate Fasig-Tipton to permit his exit as president and became instead—in the designation he always instructed us to use on forms in the blank for "Father's Occupation"—just "Horseman." "I'd rather lose money in the horse business," he explained, "than make it by working 9 to 5 doing anything else."[19]

I wonder if my parents understood all the ramifications of the return to Virginia. It was terrible for my mother. If she did not know that right away, it would soon become evident as she was cast into the unrelenting struggle to resist her mother-in-law's imperiousness and control. The move was as comfortable for my father as it was uncomfortable for my mother. He was home, living near his mother and brother and an array of friends—and even aging horses—he had grown up with. His father had given him a farm; his mother would pay to renovate the old farmhouse where we would live. Perhaps it is unfair for me to think my father should have wanted something more, should have taken greater advantage of his considerable talents. Ambition is not an unalloyed virtue. Perhaps what would prove to be a fantastical ambition to breed a Kentucky Derby winner could have sufficed. Perhaps he just wanted life to be easy and happy. But it would be neither.

Money—or its insufficiency—would prove the evil that gnawed at my parents' marriage—and indeed all our family ties. Whether as a result of skill or luck, the breeding operation performed only moderately well. My grandfather Kenneth had hit the jackpot when in 1931 he imported a French horse named Teddy (the original namesake for the ill-fated dog) to stand at stud on the Virginia farm. Teddy sired more than sixty-five stakes winners, and his line produced some of the most significant horses in twentieth-century racing. In contrast, the stallions my father acquired two decades later—Beau Gem, Kingsway, Double Eclipse—proved less successful than their pedigrees and racing records had promised; the broodmares produced foals that underperformed my father's expectations. The horse business would not prove to be a winning bet, at least in the way my father had hoped. In the course of the 1950s, Dad scaled back breeding operations and in 1960 founded the Stallion Service Bureau, a business in which he would not run a racing or breeding operation but would instead act as an agent for others in matching dams and sires, syndicating stallions, and purchasing and selling horses for novices eager to enter the racing field. His own pedigree and experience served as the currency for the business, replacing the infusion of monetary capital that would have been necessary to reinvigorate a breeding farm.

While we were growing up, he usually also had a horse or two in training, often at the track in nearby Charles Town, just over the border in West Virginia. They were an ill-assorted bunch, often washed-up or broken-down racehorses, well past whatever prime they might have enjoyed, thrown in as afterthoughts in various deals. "Sell the best and race the rest," my father often proclaimed. But we loved it when he took us to see them run. Their names were entrancing: Picture Window, Serendipity, Bright Gem, Example, Twice Shy, Perfectly Clear. A Thoroughbred's name, Dad explained, ideally should combine the names of its sire and dam in some new and clever manner. I pored over the listings of pedigrees in the racing program, renaming horses in my head or assessing how well owners had done with this word game. We would proudly accompany Dad to the paddock to see his horse saddled and sometimes even more proudly proceed to be photographed with the victor in the winner's circle. But this was pretty small-time racing: Charles Town was what was known as a "half-miler"—not a Saratoga or a Churchill Downs—and almost all the races were "claimers," not stakes, in which both the horses and the purses were better. Tyson Gilpin lived his life as a highly respected member of the racing establishment, elected president of the Virginia Thoroughbred Association and inducted into the Virginia Racing Hall of Fame. There is even an annual stakes race named after him at Colonial Downs, near Richmond. But he never attained the financial rewards he sought and never got to cheer his own Triple Crown or even Derby champion across the finish line.

And he never generated the resources to support the life his family led. Within months of Tyson's marriage, his parents were corresponding about his seeming obliviousness to costs and budgets. Perhaps, Kenneth mused, Tyson and Cath might get stationed somewhere near other fellow officers and their wives "where they could learn all of the various economies practiced by young people in the smaller brackets." Isabella thought Cath was responsible for their extravagance, but Kenneth was "not at all sure that Cath thinking it bottomless isn't the result of Tyson thinking it bottomless also." Kenneth worried that Tyson took too much for granted. He wrote to Isabella, "Heard him arguing with Cath on the subject . . . Of course I will say nothing but I just don't like the set up for years to come."[20]

Kenneth was prescient. By the early 1950s, Tyson's financial challenges had begun to come into clearer focus. His choice to move back to Virginia and endeavor to live his father's life would constrain his own opportunities to make money, and in the years after the New Deal and World War II the existing resources of the very wealthy were being taxed and curtailed. In the 1950s, the marginal tax rate on an income of $100,000 was nearly 70 percent. Tyson could not take for granted the circumstances in which his father had lived. At the same time, the demands upon him were steadily growing. With the birth of a third child, my brother Donald, in 1950, Tyson was now responsible for a sizable family and a wife with deep-seated—and expensive—assumptions about the material requirements for raising children and running a household.

My most prominent memories of my father as we were growing up were of his endless efforts, as he often put it, to "make a buck." It meant that every family meal was interrupted by phone calls because the big deal might be on the other end of the line. It meant he was engaged in an endless search for moneymaking ventures that might substitute for the elusive Derby winner. He got involved in founding a company to import Thai silk in partnership with an old family friend who almost certainly was a spy and ultimately disappeared mysteriously and permanently in Malaysia. Dad created a trampoline park in a town near where we lived, but it quickly shut down because of liability claims from injured patrons. A restaurant venture failed nearly as rapidly. A bowling alley that he, my grandmother, and my uncle launched in the mid-1950s lives on.

It was all a distant cry from his studies of Trollope—or from his days as "savior" and "liberator" of Brittany. At one point, he announced a plan to plant acres of paulownia trees on our farm, assured

by their purveyor that Asian demand for paulownia wood was certain
to yield a rich return. Quickly persuaded, Dad set about—with much
hype—to purchase dozens of seedlings and create a paulownia forest.
One or two of the trees did eventually grow to maturity, but there was
no harvesting of wood and no financial windfall. My father's suscep-
tibility to such hustles seemed to surprise even himself, for he always
cultivated—and displayed—a rational, controlled, imperturbable, and
coolly competent manner. The war hero; the dog's merciful savior; the
duck's avenger. The closest approach to self-awareness often came in
the guise of humor and irony. I remember once, years after leaving
home, when I was complaining to him about the ill-conceived nature
of some venture my brother Tys had embarked on. Dad looked at me,
arched his eyebrows, and whispered, "Son of Paulownia."

For me, the apogee of this scramble against downward mobility
came many years later, when I was well into my adulthood. I was
visiting a plumbing store on Cape Cod with an eye to replacing a

My grandmother's
front hall as the setting
for a plumbing
advertisement,
1986.

boiler in my house there. As I waited to speak to a salesperson, I sat down and picked up a glossy plumbing brochure from a showroom table. To my astonishment, I saw—under the title "The Lexington Suite in a Virginia Hunt Country Estate"—photographs of the elegant front hall and stairway of my grandmother's Virginia mansion serving as background for an American Standard toilet, bidet, lavatory, and soaking tub artfully posed for display. My father and uncle had moved my grandmother out of the enormous and costly dwelling into a small and more economical house, but, unable to sell the white elephant, they had found another way for it to pay the bills.[21]

Dad's entrepreneurial spirit was accompanied by all-but-futile attempts to contain expenses. For many years, he drove an ancient and dilapidated brown Ford with a trunk that didn't open but emitted a suspicious smell. We all speculated about what might have died inside. He was a fervent advocate of "basic transportation": there was no reason to have a fancy—or even, it seemed, respectable car. Bargains—which always turned out not to be—exerted an irresistible lure. One Christmas my mother hoped for what was then called a console—a record player disguised as a fashionable piece of living room furniture. Dad went off on Christmas Eve to find one. Baited and switched, he returned with an ugly and unwieldly boxlike apparatus that emitted an electric shock every time it was turned on. Its brand name was Phonola. The name lived on in infamy in our family, representing my father's perverse and ill-fated infatuation with the bargain.

Charles Dickens explained it well: "Annual income twenty pounds, annual expenditure nineteen nineteen six, result happiness. Annual income twenty pounds, annual expenditure twenty pounds ought and six, result misery."[22] The gap put my father perpetually in thrall to his mother—who would be entreated to make up shortfalls or assume basic costs like children's tuitions or orthodonture—as well as, as he might have phrased it, "in the doghouse" with my mother, who felt he was not providing adequately for the only kind of household and family life she could imagine. This tension was the backdrop for our childhood—overheard as loud quarrels after my parents had gone up to bed at night, though more customarily unspoken but understood.

My father seemed inevitably pleasant. Unlike my mother, who was quick to anger, he rarely reacted, maintaining a certain distance from most child-rearing decisions and challenges. It was my mother who battled with me about continuing piano lessons for years against my will. I could not get my father to intervene on my behalf. It was my mother who was insistent about my clothes and hair. My father didn't seem to notice. It was my mother who warned me endlessly about the dangers of premarital sex; Dad looked bemused and said nothing. But Dad excelled at the rituals of fatherhood: showing up at official parents' events, kissing us when we came bathed and pajamaed to the den in the evening, when he would wish us a Shakespearean good night: "May flights of angels sing thee to thy rest."[23] Or sometimes he would choose a more vernacular verse that ended with our being "whisked up the chimney"—lifted high in the air in his arms before we were sent upstairs.

We were proud of him and his polished performances—when he would give funny toasts at family gatherings, claiming the floor, glass aloft, as "the oldest living male Gilpin," or when he sang in the church choir—even featured in an annual Christmas solo as one of the Three Kings. I remember how excited I was when at age eight or nine I learned that he would be serving as a substitute teacher in my Sunday school class. We were reading the story of Samson and Delilah. He listened to us all prattle on for a while, then closed the Bible study book with a snap and ended the discussion with a declaration of the story's moral: "Never trust a woman." The class and I were both dismissed.

Dad loved aphorisms. I think, in retrospect, they served as handy ways for him not to have to work out or express what he actually thought. "Horses don't bet on people," he'd say, meaning, I think, that horses had better judgment, and people were too unpredictable.[24] "Any one you walk away from is a good one," he'd declare as we beat our retreat from fraught family holiday gatherings where the opportunity for overt conflict among my mother, grandmother, aunt, and other relatives abounded. I was startled to discover, just a few years ago, that this saying originated among early pilots and applied to their frequent crashes. A choice of words that for the son and nephew of World War I pilots, including one who had died in an air accident, perhaps revealed more about his attitudes toward family life than he ever knew or intended.

But in my mind the most memorable of Dad's maxims is "There is no excuse for being lousy." It illuminates in him both a great weakness and a great strength. You should be respectful to everyone, treat everyone well. Always act like a gentleman. But you need to bury your true feelings, show no weakness, be unflappable and, on some fundamental level, disengaged, distant. That is how he always was with us children. I don't think we ever knew him. He certainly didn't know us. I am not sure he wanted to.

4

MANY FEELINGS ABOUT SEGREGATION

Children, not yet aware that it is dangerous to look
too deeply at anything, look at everything, look at each other,
and draw their own conclusions.

—JAMES BALDWIN[1]

The farm where I grew up was located on the western bank of the Shenandoah River at the foot of the Blue Ridge Mountains. The front gate was just an opening in the fence off a road officially known as the Lee-Jackson Highway, commemorating the route across the river and through nearby Ashby's Gap that had served as a critical military corridor for Stonewall Jackson's troops at Manassas and in his 1862 Shenandoah Valley campaign. An old oxbow of the Shenandoah, long cut off by our bottom pasture, formed a lake that gave the five-hundred-acre farm its name and provided us with somewhere to canoe and fish in the summer and skate in the winter—if we were lucky and had enough cold days in a row. Lakeville was an odd name for the property, though, for there was no hint of city or town. The driveway stretched a quarter mile or so from the main road to our house, crossing two fields, variously occupied by a few cows, a small herd of sheep, and, often, one or two elderly or broken-down racehorses. For many years, my brothers and I quarreled daily over who would have to get out of the car and open the gate that separated the two pastures as we were driven to and from school.

Our house had been built in the first decades of the nineteenth century as what is known as a traditional "I-house," a common vernacular

The Blue Ridge Mountains from the backyard at Lakeville.

form in the Shenandoah Valley popular among aspiring planters and farmers during the early decades of the new nation. But the original classic two-story, four-room frame structure had been altered over the years by additions to the side and rear that included a kitchen (built just before we moved in) and a tiny bedroom appendage, suspended on stilts, that was constructed after my youngest brother later arrived to surprise us all.

No more than a hundred yards from the house stood the barn, painted a fading green, with stalls on the ground floor and hayloft above, next to the tractor shed, the sheep pen, the pigsty, and the chicken coop. Beyond the muddy barnyard pond was the house occupied by the tenant farmer, Mr. Walter Johnson, who took care of crops and animals. It was a beautiful setting, with the sweep of rolling fields surrounding our house, the pastoral scene of grazing animals and the picturesque barn, and the changing colors of the softly undulating ridges of the mountains on the horizon, often foggy or hazy blue, as befitted their name. But as a child, I took the landscape for granted and only began truly to see its beauty when I grew older and heard others—often friends from afar—remark upon it.

Walter Johnson, the tenant farmer at Lakeville,
who taught me how to raise my steers.

The farm had another dwelling, out of sight of our house, in the woods perhaps a half mile from our door. For much of my childhood, it was empty and increasingly dilapidated, but at some point a man, white and of indeterminate age, took up residence with his legions of cats. His real name was Ernest Taylor, but he was universally known as Tootsie. He was just about the only white adult I can remember calling by a first name. He wasn't exactly a squatter, though he paid no rent, and he wasn't exactly a homeless person, because he lived in that house until he accidentally burned it down and moved into his car, permanently parked next to the charred remains. He had served in the military, had worked at some point as a plumber, and survived by doing odd jobs, including dubious plumbing work at my father's behest. Dad felt somehow responsible for him, and Tootsie often appeared at our back door in hopes of receiving a bottle of vodka or some cash or to sneak what he called "girlie magazines" to my brothers.

Our farm was about a mile and a half from the town of Millwood, home in the 1950s to some two hundred persons, most of them Black and occupying dwellings without running water. My childhood friends—all white—lived on surrounding farms like ours. These properties almost invariably had names, and many had stood since the time of the American Revolution. Saratoga had been built by Daniel Morgan in the 1780s to commemorate his 1777 battlefield victory. Carter Hall, Pagebrook, and Long Branch were all erected after the Revolution by younger sons of the Tidewater gentry, who had moved to the western part of the state in search of fresh land and opportunities. Burwells, Byrds, Randolphs, and Carters—the FFVs, the First Families of Virginia—had brought their enslaved workers with them, and the descendants of the white owners and Black laborers remained, joined by newer families like mine, which had come to the valley at the turn of the twentieth century.

The Lakeville barn in snow as seen from my bedroom window.

In 1950, the population of my county, Clarke, was 17 percent Black. Every adult Black person I knew worked for whites as either a laborer or a domestic. The established practices of Jim Crow had changed little for more than a half century. Nevertheless, this was not the Deep South. There were no signs designating water fountains or waiting rooms COLORED or WHITE. In my small rural Virginia community, people just knew. Or learned. This, too, was part of a landscape that I came to take for granted but did not really see. Even my own house was segregated. The African Americans who cooked and cleaned ate in the kitchen and used the back door. We ate in the dining room, except for Sunday supper, when the workers had the evening off and my mother, who could scarcely cook at all, contrived to produce a meal, while we all longed for Monday and the cook's return. Behind the kitchen was a separate servants' bathroom. When I used it once, my mother reprimanded me for invading their privacy.

I never witnessed physical cruelty toward Black people; I never heard the N-word. Prejudice was hidden beneath a surface of politeness and civility that scarcely masked the assumption of superiority, of greater intelligence, of entitlement. Amused condescension, mockery cast as patronizing affection, often inflected white attitudes toward "the colored people." Yet as I think back, there was a nervousness about the laughter, a need for mutual reassurance as the adults around me recounted tales of people so close at hand yet so mysteriously and ominously different from themselves.

Racial custom was carefully yet obliquely taught. It encompassed all the contradictions that had confronted white Virginians for centuries. Home of Washington, Jefferson, and Madison, the architects of American freedom and nationhood, Virginia was also the place where, beginning in 1619, American slavery first took root. Nearly two and a half centuries later, it became the site of the capital of a new Confederate nation dedicated to the proposition that Black men and women were decidedly not created equal but destined for perpetual bondage. When emancipation brought slavery officially to an end, unfreedom simply took on new forms—convict lease, Jim Crow, seg-regation. By the middle of the twentieth century, there had been little visible change in the patterns of racial separation and white domi-nance. I grew up in the constant company of Black people, human beings central to my life, yet I somehow came to understand that an unspoken hierarchy required our distance—both physical and emotional—from them. We had—and came to assume we deserved—better houses, better education, a better future.

The women who cooked for us, first Victoria Wilson, then Cor-nelia Anderson—addressed by their first names though they were a generation if not two older than I—were magicians in the kitchen. As a child, I ate cakes and pies and breads and roasts always made from scratch; I was not subjected to the repellent 1950s cuisine of the instant, the frozen, the artificial, the canned. But I was never allowed behind the scenes into the kitchen, and I grew up as incompetent a cook as my mother.

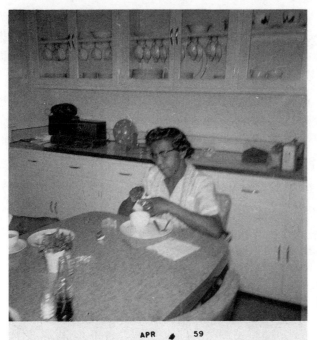

Victoria Wilson in our kitchen, 1959.

An African American man who worked for my family for decades did everything from shining shoes, to mowing the lawn, to driving us around the county—to school, to piano lessons, to scout meetings. Raphael Johnson (who pronounced his name "Rayfield") was as present in my childhood as my brothers and my parents. He quizzed us on state capitals and the order of the presidents, made sure we remembered our lunch boxes and homework, and told us jokes and riddles. He always spoke not of "driving" us here or there but of "carrying" us, a usage that to my child's ears communicated a kind of concerned protectiveness. But I scarcely knew anything about his own life. He had a daughter not far from my age, but I rarely saw her because she, of course, went to the segregated Black school. I never even knew where it was.

I am certain that part of why my mother hated Virginia was that she was never comfortable around Black people. She did not know that some of her New England and New Jersey ancestors had enslaved Black workers in the eighteenth century, and the countryside of her childhood was entirely white. Although she was certainly accustomed to servants, those she had encountered were likely to have been Irish immigrants. They were set apart by their accents and their Catholicism, but not by their skin color or the prejudices it generated. My father, by contrast, had grown up in close and constant contact with Black domestic and farm workers. He never would have doubted that he held—and deserved—a more elevated position economically, socially, and intellectually than they, but he interacted with the many Black people in his life regularly and familiarly, adopting the posture of benevolent paternalistic concern with which whites had endeavored to cloak the injustices of southern race relations for generations.

Alone among the families in her Virginia circle, my mother relied not on Black workers, but on a white woman, for childcare. We had a nanny, who came to our family from England a month before I was born, and, unlike Mary Poppins, never left. But, like Mary Poppins, she seemed enchanted in her intuitive understanding of children's innermost workings and entrancing in the stories she recounted as she brushed our hair, supervised our baths, or listened to us recite our prayers. She told us how her father, a bobby, arrested Christabel Pankhurst as she protested for women's suffrage; she described her own work in a munitions factory during the First World War and reported her experiences in London during the Blitz in the Second, before she and the little girl she was caring for were evacuated to New York. And she indoctrinated us with an endless stream of moral tales about children she had known—good ones who were kind and obedient, and bad ones who were spiteful and who grizzled. She believed in us unreservedly. To borrow a Poppins-ism: we were in her eyes "practically perfect in every way." She instilled in me a desire to prove I could be just as perfect as she envisioned. She gave me a faith in myself that pushed back against my perception that my parents found me both inadequate and vexing. On the extremely rare occasions that she took a vacation and left us directly in our mother's care, we mourned until she returned.

My mother wielded her authority over the Black workers in our household uncertainly and as a result often ineffectively, creating tensions and further contributing to her dissatisfaction with her Virginia life. These conflicts appeared most clearly in her interactions with Raphael, who, in addition to "carrying" us children around, did whatever house or yard work needed attention. He and my mother were at constant odds as he devised his own style and timing for his assigned duties. It was rarely the schedule my mother would have preferred. He mowed the lawn, for example, in phases, usually several days apart, so the grass always looked striped, often with the mower temporarily abandoned in the middle of the lawn awaiting the next segment. My mother was persuaded of the truth of a whispered rumor that Raphael had started a secret local chapter of the National Association for the Advancement of Colored People.

My father's relationship with Raphael was entirely different. Raphael always seemed eager to please him, shining his shoes until the

Raphael Johnson,
early 1950s.

leather was soft and glowing, and seeking out assignments he might undertake, especially if they involved anything related to horses or the track. When my mother died, Raphael assumed it his duty to take care of my father—cooking his breakfast, making his bed, taking his suits to be cleaned. On a visit home a few years after my mother's death, I realized that in this relationship, my father was dependent not just on Raphael but also on Raphael's opinion. Dad had begun to keep company with the woman who later became my stepmother. She lived about an hour's drive away, and Dad would often stay over. But he always came home early enough to disarrange his bed to be sure Raphael would not know. I am certain Raphael did know, and surely my father knew that he knew. But everyone had to keep up appearances.

When Raphael died, his family asked my father to deliver a eulogy at his funeral. A few years before, Dad had attended his baptismal ceremony, when Raphael was immersed in nearby Spout Run. Now he would play a role in Raphael's last rites. Although the all-Black

Guilford Baptist Church was just down the road from the all-white Episcopal Church where my father served on the vestry, it represented a different universe of liturgy and ritual. At an Episcopal funeral, one suppressed tears, music was subdued and mournful, and speaking was reserved for those standing behind the pulpit. At Guilford, my father's every phrase was partially repeated back to him or greeted with Hallelujahs and Amens. He joined the rhythm of the call-and-response with his audience as he praised and bid farewell to the man he hailed as "Brother Raphael." Two decades later, when Dad died, members of the Guilford choir came to sing at his funeral. It was the first time I had seen Black people in our church.[2]

The world of the racetrack—where large numbers of grooms, walkers, stable boys, and even trainers were African American—represented another setting in which my father interacted closely with Black people. African Americans had been central to the culture of Thoroughbred breeding and racing since the era of slavery. The sport had its American origins among the southern elite in the eighteenth century and depended, like every other aspect of plantation life, on the labor and skill of enslaved workers. African Americans continued to play a major role in racing after emancipation. In the first Kentucky Derby, run in 1875, thirteen of the fifteen riders were Black. The imposition of Jim Crow at the turn of the century, however, led to the elimination of Black men as jockeys and relegated them to more backstage roles caring for and preparing the horses that others rode to glory. Between 1911 and 2000, no Black jockeys competed in the Kentucky Derby. African Americans continued, however, to work as trainers, especially at smaller tracks with less prominent horses. They bore responsibility for the animals' conditioning and readiness, strategizing with owners about where and when and how a horse should compete. My father had deep respect for accomplished trainers' professionalism, skills, and acumen. When I was growing up, trainer was the most prestigious position I saw occupied by a Black person.[3]

For several years beginning in the early 1960s, my father employed

Sylvia Bishop, the first Black woman licensed to train racehorses in the United States. My father knew she was gifted and gave her his complete trust in managing a number of runners at tracks where she worked in nearby West Virginia and Maryland. A collection of winner's circle photographs depicts my father and Sylvia Bishop posing triumphantly together with a parade of successful horses: Bright Gem, Twice Shy, Odd Lot, Wounded Knee, In Hock. A recent biography of the pathbreaking trainer describes them as the "Gilpin/Sylvia" team.[4] To me, she was Mrs. Bishop, the only Black woman in my childhood whom I did not call by a first name.

The winner's circle, 1962. A muddy triumph. Left to right: my brothers Tys and Donald, my father's sister Bettie, the legendary jockey Eddie Arcaro presenting the trophy to the trainer Sylvia Bishop, the jockey Carl Gambardella, my father.

Manifestations of the past in our lives did not just involve the unquestioned persistence of patterns of racial separation and white supremacy. I knew I lived in history. Nearly a century after Appomattox, Virginia was still breathing the air of war and defeat. It was in the names of places all around us, on the ubiquitous Confederate-gray historical markers memorializing battles like Cedar Creek, Belle Grove, or Bethel, or skirmishes along the Opequon and Shenandoah. Seven marble slabs noted the presence of unnamed Confederate dead just behind our family plot in the nearby Episcopal cemetery. Our games in the woods and fields around our house most often involved the refighting of Civil War battles, when my older brother forced me to be Grant so he could be Lee. Years went by before I learned that Grant had actually won the war. Inside we played with my brothers' metal soldiers, uniforms carefully painted blue or gray, generals portrayed in lifelike renditions astride their famous mounts. Lee on Traveller was always my favorite but rarely my lot. My grandmother spoke of "The War" as if it had happened in her own lifetime. "Sherman. Such an unattractive man," she declared as she sought to inspire and instruct us with choruses of "I'm a good old rebel / That's just what I am / For this fair land of freedom / I do not give a damn." This entirely uncharacteristic use of profanity succeeded in impressing us with the depth of her passion.

If Sherman and Grant were the enemy, Robert E. Lee was the unquestioned hero—the gallant knight whose honor, sacrifice, and martial prowess represented the best of our Virginia past. He embodied the same values of manliness and chivalry that led my father to fight to protect us from the Nazis—or any of the myriad other dangers that might threaten our family and fireside. At one point, Dad even acquired a hood ornament, a miniature statue of Lee mounted on Traveller, to adorn his car.

This thorough embrace of the Lost Cause was taken for granted among the white people in my community; it was passed along to us children as an explanation of our origins and a truth in our lives. From our perspective in the twenty-first century, we can see so clearly the pernicious overturning of the war's emancipationist purposes that is at the heart of this rendering of the past. We can recognize the assumptions of white supremacy inherent in a celebration of those who built a nation to perpetuate human unfreedom. But to a young white child growing up in Virginia in the 1950s, the relationship between Confederate legends and past and persisting racial inequality was obscured and all but erased. When we children played Civil War, we were not thinking of the shameful history of slavery and injustice. Imagining ourselves surrounded by the ghosts of Mosby's rangers or Stonewall's legions who had not so very long ago galloped through these very fields and woods, we were unaware that in refighting their fight we were in some fundamental way affirming the racial order in which we lived. Yet we were, however unwittingly, enacting rituals that were preparing us to take our privileged places in the adult world that the legacies of race and slavery had made.

Of course, the veneration of the Confederacy was all but inseparable from a romanticized view of the South and its racial arrangements both during and after slavery, and these myths took on a powerful presence in my own time. Celebration of the Lost Cause and nostalgia for the era of "moonlight and magnolias" went hand in hand. And at the heart of both was an understanding of southern slavery sharply at odds with the realities of the regional past. In white history and memory, slavery was not a system of cruelty and exploitation that stole millions of Black lives over nearly three centuries. Instead, white southerners reminisced about gracious plantations peopled with benevolent masters and docile, devoted, and grateful slaves. This widespread view even drew academic validation well into the 1950s and '60s from the much-acclaimed historical research and writing of scholars like Ulrich B. Phillips, a Georgia native and Yale professor who characterized southern slavery as essentially a school that had protected an inferior race and had uplifted Black people from the barbarism of Africa by bringing them to civilization and Christianity.

This sanguine view of slavery's oppressions slid easily into a justification of the persistence of white supremacy. The white people I grew up with had convinced themselves that Black people both accepted and deserved their assigned, separate, and subordinated place.

Mid-twentieth-century Virginia congratulated itself on having devised the "Virginia Way," a distinctive form of Jim Crow in which Blacks and whites lived peaceably together in lives of "separation by consent," in the words of Douglas Southall Freeman, a Richmond newspaper editor and renowned Robert E. Lee biographer. Freeman acknowledged that this was a social order designed to perpetuate "the continued and unchallengeable dominance of Southern whites," who, he told his readers, would work to provide the assurance of safety and security to Black Virginians in return for their acquiescence in the status quo. "Southern Negroes," he explained, "have far more to gain by conforming than by rebellion . . . by deserving rather than demanding more." Elite white Virginians, he posited, had inherited a legacy of gentility accompanied by the imperatives of noblesse oblige; Virginia's Black people, in turn, were "inherently of a higher type than those of any other state." Nowhere else, Freeman insisted, "are the Negroes more encouraged through the influence of friendship for and confidence in them, on the part of whites, to be law abiding and industrious." But never to claim equality.[5]

This was the image of white Virginia with which I grew up. Yet even in Freeman's seemingly blithe confidence one can see an emerging crack in the "unchallengeable dominance" he sought to claim. His words represented more an effort of persuasion than actual description of an unwavering status quo, for Freeman's very language anticipated the possibility of challenge: of Black demands for change and even the threat of Black rebellion against the structures of injustice he sought to establish as the timeless and immutable contours of Virginia life.

But life is not timeless. History happens, and it was happening to the American South. World War II had accelerated the pace of change in many dimensions of American society, and race was central among them. The war with Germany had been waged against an enemy whose despicable racist ideology had challenged Americans to examine their own commitments to equality and human dignity. Like

all American soldiers, my father had fought in a segregated unit, as the
military imposed the practices of Jim Crow on citizens of both North
and South. Often Black troops were relegated to demeaning physical labor rather than full military participation. But the distinguished
contributions and sacrifices of Black soldiers who did serve in combat
cast the injustice of their segregation into full view and led President
Harry S. Truman officially to integrate the armed forces by executive
order in 1948. Black Americans had fought for what they called a
"Double V" victory—triumph over the Axis powers abroad and over
discrimination at home. Long-accepted hierarchies of race were under siege in the postwar world, and the civil rights movement, often
seen to begin with the Montgomery bus boycott in 1955, might better
be understood as the almost immediate outcome of the war. Even
in Clarke County, Virginia, the possibility of change, the emerging
challenge to long-held racial assumptions and arrangements, could
not be entirely silenced or denied.

In 1957, my grandmother Isabella arranged for a plaque to be
installed in the form of a grave marker near the back of the Old
Chapel Cemetery, where my parents, uncles, aunts, grandparents, and
great-grandparents are buried in a family plot just a dozen steps away.[6]
The historic stone chapel at the cemetery's front corner was built in
the 1790s, and the earliest gravestones memorialize such Virginia
worthies as Edmund Randolph, the nation's first attorney general and
a secretary of state, Virginia governor, and member of the Constitutional Convention. My grandmother's act of commemoration was
also about history, but it addressed a dimension of the Virginia past
previously unrepresented and unspoken within the cemetery's rough
stone walls:

TO THE GLORY OF GOD

AND IN REMEMBRANCE OF THE MANY PERSONAL

SERVANTS BURIED HERE BEFORE 1865.

FAITHFUL AND DEVOTED IN LIFE, THEIR FRIENDS

AND MASTERS LAID THEM NEAR THEM IN DEATH

WITH AFFECTION AND GRATITUDE

THEIR MEMORY REMAINS, THOUGH THEIR WOODEN MARKERS,

LIKE THE WAY OF LIFE OF THAT DAY,

ARE GONE FOREVER

I.T.G. 1957

There is a monument to the Confederate dead in this cemetery; there are graves for many who fought in the Confederate cause. But these had been erected decades before. What is to be made of this invocation of slavery offered during my own lifetime? Of this tangible link between who we are now and who we were more than a century and a half ago? Between attitudes and practices taught to me as a child and the person I could or would become? Between the Virginia of 1857 and that of 1957? What had my grandmother been thinking?

I turned ten years old in September of the year she erected the plaque, but I have no memory of any family conversation about it or any ceremony of dedication or celebration. The language and tone of the memorial are right out of white mythology of the Old South—the romanticization of plantation culture, the erasure of slavery and its brutalities. On the plaque we have not "enslaved people" but "servants," "faithful and devoted" rather than "subjugated against their will." The words describe affectionate and appreciative masters—a benign domination, not the cruel system of physical brutality, stolen lives, and human beings bought and sold that we know slavery to have been. The marker proclaims a nostalgia for an era, a "way of life" that is "gone forever." Gone, we might say, with the wind. Margaret Mitchell's book, published in 1936, and the movie that followed in 1939 were still exerting their influence, romanticizing the Old South and its slave institution, as they have well into our own time.

But this wasn't 1857 or even 1936. It was 1957. Why did my grandmother go to the trouble—and expense—of erecting the plaque at this particular time? It was more than just an expression of views that had persisted since the idealization of the Old South had solidified in the years after Appomattox, views that she had been indoctrinated to embrace from the time of her birth in Tennessee in 1894.

The year 1957 was a crucial time in Virginia and in the South generally. Three years earlier, the Supreme Court had struck down school segregation in *Brown v. Board of Education*, and the implications of the decision were beginning to become clear. Now integration was to become the law of the land; schools, and then all of southern society, were to be transformed with "all deliberate speed." In September 1957, nine African American students entering the previously all-white Central High School in Little Rock, Arkansas, were greeted by a segregationist mob supported, per order of the governor, by the state's National Guard. President Dwight Eisenhower was compelled to mobilize the 101st Airborne Division to enforce integration and uphold the law. Close to home, U.S. senator Harry Byrd—who lived just a few miles from the Old Chapel graveyard—had called for "Massive Resistance" to the Supreme Court ruling. Engineering a plan to close rather than desegregate schools, Byrd and his aroused followers were transforming the 1957 Virginia governor's election into a referendum on race and, in a broader sense, on the morality and legitimacy of the white South's discriminatory assumptions and practices. In the face of such controversy and opprobrium, the plaque invoked a redemptive narrative of the southern past, one designed to reassure a society under siege that it was not just right but righteous. It proclaimed a virtuousness fashioned out of a fantastical history, a virtuousness to be reinforced by the generous act of noticing and remembering that the plaque was meant to be.

But why did my grandmother choose this graveyard and this statement to subdue her unease about the challenges to her taken-for-granted world—her unease, I imagine (and hope) about that very world itself? Why a plaque? It wasn't filling a gaping need. In both its language and its very existence, it protests too much.

Local circumstances had generated an additional motivation. The far end of the cemetery—the land beyond the plaque—had housed graves of enslaved people, though their locations and markers had all but disappeared. As a child, I remember hearing discussions among the adults in my family about how a growing demand for graveyard plots had led to a consideration of extending the white cemetery into the area the slave cemetery had occupied. This was not understood as sharing—and certainly not as integrating the space. Instead, the older graves would essentially be erased from the landscape and from the minds and memories of the white church and its members.

But not from my grandmother's. The puzzling plaque represented her discomfort with (though not, significantly, any overt objection to) a plan to callously disrespect the dead. She intended to remember them with a permanent stone marker that would not rot and disappear. But as a white southern woman imbued with a conventional understanding of the past and its racial practices, she was memorializing a world and a history that had never been. Her gesture of reconciliation was undoubtedly prompted in part by the winds of change that penetrated even into her world of racial silence and denial; it was intended as an expression of benevolence. Yet she had no language or understanding that could take her beyond the assumptions of white dominance and Black subservience that had shaped her life. Her earnest and well-meaning intervention was perpetuating a narrative about race that has continued to poison Virginia and the nation more than a century and a half after slavery's end.

Though still in elementary school, I, too, was hearing the winds of change and the disruptions to the fixed silences about race. For many white southerners of my generation, a life-defining question has been how long it took us to notice the contradictions between the democratic and Christian ideals intoned in church and school and the patterns of injustice in which our lives were imbedded.[7] When did the contradictions become troubling? When did they become unbearable? What was the moment of epiphany, the circumstance that made the inconsistencies undeniable? When did it become imperative to confront the legacies of slavery and segregation, to be honest with ourselves and one another and purge the untruths that, like malignancies, had permeated our society and our lives? "It's that obliviousness, the unexamined assumption, that so pains me now," the photographer Sally Mann has written about her own 1950s Virginia upbringing. "How could I not have wondered, not have asked." For her, going north to school and encountering the writings of William Faulkner "threw wide the door of my ignorant childhood, and the future, the heartbroken future filled with hitherto unasked questions, strolled easefully in. It wounded me, then and there, with the great sadness and tragedy of our American life, with the truth of all that I had not seen, had not known, and had not asked."[8]

For many, the civil rights movement and the racist pushback it provoked served as a wake-up call, forcing an end to silences, exposing the violence on which Jim Crow rested, and removing the veneer of timeless inevitability that whites had strived to create. And a growing assertiveness by Black Virginians made it ever more difficult to maintain the fiction of separation and subjugation "by consent."

My epiphany occurred the same year as my grandmother's plaque, when news reports about "Massive Resistance" and battles over segregation made me suddenly realize that it was not a matter of accident that my school was all white. I was nine years old, in fifth grade, and in the car with Raphael being driven home from school when I heard something on the radio that startled me: Black children were, by Virginia law, not permitted to go to school with white children. It had never occurred to me. I asked Raphael if what I had understood was true, whether I would be excluded from my school if I was a different color, if I painted my face black. I remember that Raphael never answered my question. My probings about rules of racial interaction made him acutely uncomfortable. He was evasive, but for me his evasion was answer enough. No one talked openly about race in my family. It would have been considered rude, not unlike talking about sex, another prohibited topic. Yet somehow I knew that, as with sex, talking about race was not just impolite but dangerous. When I asked Raphael about my school, I crossed the lines of both propriety and safety. To even acknowledge race was a first step toward change. Raphael knew far better than I the perils involved in any questioning of his place. But even at nine I knew enough to recognize my questions as a transgression. We rode the rest of the way home in silence.

But I remember being upset. Upset at what seemed so completely unfair. And upset that I had not known, that no one had told me that this was how the world worked. I was not supposed to know or see, and yet now I did. I felt compelled to do something with this new information. I had to speak. Not to my parents, who had known about this all along and never told me, much less objected to such patent unfairness. I wanted to express myself to someone who might do something about it.

What I did was write to the president. Why did I think of this? My guess is that some edition of *My Weekly Reader*, a newspaper for children regularly distributed in our school and around the country, had featured an article about writing to elected officials. The publication was filled with stories intended to nurture good citizenship and civic consciousness. And President Eisenhower seemed somehow approachable. He had been, of course, the general in charge of Patton and thus of my father in the legendary events of the war. My parents, like a majority of Virginians, had voted for him in 1952 and 1956. The preceding fall, as part of the campaign season, I had been taken to an Eisenhower rally in a nearby town. The candidate himself appeared, and although I remember nothing of what he said, the man's benevolent appearance and generous smile made me glad to wear my "I Like Ike" button. I had seen the president; the White House had a human face. I could certainly write to him. I addressed my letter to "Mr.," not "President," Eisenhower.[9]

I composed my letter on February 12, 1957. (It is clear, both from my own declaration of my age in the text and from the reply that came back from the White House, that I made a mistake when I gave the year as 1956 at the top of the page.) It now rests among twenty-three million pages of manuscripts in the Eisenhower Library in Abilene, Kansas. It is officially the property of the National Archives and Records Administration of the U.S. government. I have always remembered and often told the story of writing it, not telling my parents until they were alerted by the arrival of a formulaic acknowledgment from the White House. But I had little memory of the details of what I had written until nearly a half century later, when I decided to look for the letter. I had recently completed a book based in considerable part on letters Confederate women had penned to their president, Jefferson Davis, and it dawned on me that what I had written to my president would likely have been preserved as well. "I have located a letter," the archivist Herbert Pankratz responded to my inquiry, "in the White House Central Files. In the letter Miss Gilpin expresses her feelings about how Black Americans are treated and urges the president to make schools more open to minorities." In 1957, I would, of course, not have written about "Black Americans"; that was a usage introduced in the mid-1960s. I had probably, I thought ruefully, as I awaited the envelope from Abilene, written about "colored people."

"Dear Mr. Eisenhower," the letter began. "I am nine years old and I am white, but I have many feelings about segregation." The letter is written on lined, three-holed notebook paper, which I must have taken out of my school binder. I printed in block letters, perhaps worried that my handwriting would otherwise be illegible. I wrote the letter, fittingly, though I doubt I was aware of this, on Lincoln's birthday. I wanted the president to know in my first sentence that even if I was very young, even if I was not among those feeling the force of discrimination, I felt strongly about segregation. "If I painted my face black, I wouldn't be let in any public schools, etc." I wanted to share the outrage I had felt in my exchange with Raphael. "Why should people feel that way because [of] the color of the skin?"

This was not Christian, I reminded the president, invoking the strongest force I could imagine in defense of my position. I had God on my side. "Long ago on Christmas Day Jesus Christ was born. As you remember," I continued, lest the president miss my point, "he was born to save the world. Not only white people but black yellow red and brown." I have never thought of my childhood or my family as particularly religious. Ours was the detached faith of Episcopalianism, not the enthusiastic piety of the evangelical South. Talk about God was confined to Sunday-morning church, Sunday school, and a daily rendition of the Lord's Prayer recited so fast at bedtime as to be almost one long word: "whoartinheavenhallowedbethyname." Any other invocation of religion was almost as indecorous as discussing sex or race. We did not even say grace at meals. Yet I had imbibed some sort of egalitarian message, some sort of human empathy from the church nonetheless; here I was demanding justice in God's name. "So what if their skin is black? They still have feelings but most of all are God's people!" In the red leather-bound prayer book and hymnal that I was given as a child, hymn number 263 reads:

> In Christ there is no East or West
> In Him no South or North;
> But one great fellowship of love
> Throughout the whole wide earth . . .
> Join hands, then, brothers of the faith
> What e'er your race may be;
> Who serves my Father as a son
> Is surely kin to me.

The words are attributed to "John Oxenham, 1908"; the notes appear above the stanzas on two treble staves marked simply "Negro Melody."[10]

Christianity in the mid-twentieth-century South, as in many other times and places, contained powerful ambiguities, so often serving, as Martin Luther King, Jr., charged in his 1963 *Letter from Birmingham City Jail,* as "the arch supporter of the status quo." Yet at the same time, in the hands of King and others, Christianity came to serve as the weapon of the oppressed, the ideology for the mass civil rights activism that would make the transformation of southern race relations possible by invoking "the light of human conscience."[11] King would effectively appeal to thousands of Americans like me who had begun to recognize the contradictions between their fundamental religious and moral commitments and their participation in the South's system of racial cruelty.

Segregation, I insisted to the president, was not only unchristian. It was not fair. "Colored people aren't given a chance. 'They don't have a good education,' says many people. Is it their fault if their fathers are so poor they must be taken out at an early age to find jobs?" As a child, I was close to obsessed with what was and wasn't fair. I think many

In my bedroom at Lakeville, February 1957, the same month I wrote my letter to the president.

children regularly protest receiving what seems clearly a smaller piece of cake or being given the second rather than the first turn or being punished for a fight they didn't start. But for me, the battle was about what girls couldn't do that boys could. I grew up in a man's world and a white world. Did I see a connection between the two? Did my finely honed sense of personal injustice translate into an empathy for injustices done to others? The urgent tone of my letter suggests a deep personal investment in my plea. "Please Mr. Eisenhower," I closed, "please try and have schools and other things accept colored people."

I ended the letter in a manner that is both curious and revealing. My signature is out of alignment on the page. It looks as if I wrote "Drew Gilpin," which was indeed what I was called, for I had been named to honor my mother's brother Drew. And then I decided I should include my official first name, one my father had insisted on adding when I was christened to ensure an unbroken four-generation line of Catharines. It is a name I never used except to identify myself as female. So "Catharine" is attached in front—looking quite out of place. I wanted to be known not just as white and nine but also as a girl. I am sure that had I not added the "Catharine," the response from the White House would have come to Mr. Gilpin; the description of the letter in the Eisenhower Library catalog would now note that "Mr. Gilpin expresses his feelings." I had begun, even by the age of nine, to learn the realities of having been given a boy's name. I knew I had to act to claim my femaleness and my own identity. I wanted to speak to Eisenhower as the person I was, and an important part of that was being a girl.

There is a clarity about how children see the world that the complexities of adult life often muddy. And there is a fervor children feel when they believe adults have misled them or disguised or hidden the truth. My epiphany in the car with Raphael represented a shock of recognition. A combination of silence and denial was obscuring the realities of my world. I was being taught one set of values and being told to live another. I refused to be quiet about this or any hypocrisy or injustice I was given to endure or embrace, whether it meant arguing with my mother or petitioning the president. "Why be difficult," my father would come to ask me regularly, "when you can be impossible?" I did not relish being difficult; I had no aspiration to be impossible. But I could see how the lives of so many around me had been deformed and diminished by the constraints of custom and conformity, as well as by the unjust social hierarchies that structured our world. I wanted to understand that world, to see it fully without distortion or illusion.

The civil rights leader John Lewis often referred to what he called "necessary trouble." I did not have the privilege of getting to know Congressman Lewis until very much later in my life, but I have often thought that his words captured something of the essence of my childhood rebelliousness. It was urgent and imperative; I did not feel that I had a choice. Partly it was that youthful clarity and determination about doing the right thing. But perhaps even more fundamentally, it was necessary for *me*—necessary to enable me to survive amid the stifling silences that threatened to define my life. I had to make my own kind of necessary trouble. Penetrating the blindness and the taken-for-grantedness of the present and coming to terms with the real meaning of the misrepresented past would become for me work for a lifetime.

5

LIFE IN THE FIFTIES

A nation up to its ears in domestic tranquility.
—EDITORIAL, *LIFE*, JULY 4, 1955

I have often wondered how I came to know about the world beyond my own isolated existence on a farm miles away from town or neighbors, hours away from any city. Where did I hear enough about the emerging battles over integration to feel myself implicated in the conflict? How did I come to be afraid of Russia and communism? Where did I learn of the terrors of radioactive fallout and nuclear war?

We didn't receive a regular daily newspaper. My mother, clinging to the world she had been forced to leave in the move to Virginia, subscribed to the *New York Herald Tribune*, but it arrived by mail several days after publication. I don't remember ever looking at it. *The Morning Telegraph*—the bible of Thoroughbred racing—appeared every day at the breakfast table. I was proud when my father taught me to decipher the complicated past performance charts printed for every horse running that day, detailing previous outings, weight carried, split times, race outcomes: win, place, show, or also ran. The *Telegraph* contained all the news one could want about the world of the track, but next to nothing about the world of public affairs. The radio was always on in the car as we were driven around to our various activities, so I must have heard at least snippets of news in between the Hit Parade and baseball games. My parents resisted bringing a TV into the house until well after almost every other family we knew, but it was

The Lone Ranger, Superman, The Mickey Mouse Club, and later *American Bandstand,* not news shows, that absorbed my attention.

We had subscriptions to many magazines. My father bought *Playboy* as a one-off, concealing it in corners of bookcases around the house where we children inevitably found it. I remember poring over its contents, always astounded by the centerfold, who looked like no woman I had ever encountered, clothed or otherwise. Most magazines, however, were placed in a wooden rack in the den, next to a comfortable overstuffed chair tucked under the stairs. It was an inviting place to read, with an inviting library of publications—*Sports Illustrated, The Saturday Evening Post,* and *The Chronicle of the Horse* were regulars, as was *The New Yorker,* which lured me with its cartoons. More often than not, however, I didn't understand them and had to ask my parents to explain why one or another was funny. And I read *Life.* In its heyday in the 1950s, an estimated half of all Americans looked at the magazine.[1]

As I return to *Life* now, more than six decades later, I am struck by how the world of the 1950s it portrayed seems both so familiar and so strange. Davy Crockett coonskin hats, hula hoops, pogo sticks, Elvis: *Life* chronicled crazes that reached even to rural Virginia. I recognize nearly every product pitched in the dozens of pages of advertising that filled the magazine, even though many have not existed for years. The back cover of most issues displayed a full-page cigarette ad: "Luckies—Cleaner, Fresher, Smoother"; or Camels: "It is a psychological fact: Pleasure helps your disposition. That's why everyday pleasures—like smoking for instance—mean so much." One news story *Life* published about childbirth even depicted a woman smoking during labor.[2]

This startles me now, but then I took for granted a home that must have been filled with clouds of smoke from my mother's daily pack of Camels and my father's cigars. Multipage spreads in the magazine presented the newest models of enormous cars, designed like our family station wagon to transport large families of baby boomer children. These illustrations featured vehicles that were lavishly finned and often stylishly two-tone, though by the end of the decade smaller models like the Nash Rambler, the Ford Falcon, and even the VW bug had begun to mount their challenge.

The food that appeared in *Life* now seems perhaps the most unimaginable. A soda ad urged customers to fill half of babies' bottles with 7-Up in order to coax them to drink their milk. Another advertisement proclaimed National-Use-Up-Your-Leftovers-in-a-Jell-O-Salad Week. In an elaborate southwest barbecue, "everything, even the meat, comes from cans." In the mid-1950s, the average American family ate 850 cans of food annually. A special issue on food in January 1955 extolled "the servants who come built into the frozen, canned, dehydrated and precooked foods which lend busy women a thousand extra hands in preparing daily meals."[3] These busy women were perpetually in a hurry and would welcome such innovations as instant oatmeal, instant coffee, and Swanson's TV dinners. In my household, the hard work and virtuosity of Black cooks—Victoria, then Cornelia—rescued us from such misfortune.

Life chronicled the emergence of aspects of contemporary existence that I tend to think of as present since the beginning of time: this was the decade that credit cards entered American life; the Interstate Highway System was launched in 1956; jet passenger travel began in 1958. In the first part of the decade, *Life* reported plane crashes with disturbing regularity, perhaps because, astoundingly, air traffic control existed only near airports, and pilots were themselves charged to spot other planes when they weren't taking off or landing. When two pilots failed at this assignment over the Grand Canyon in 1956 and 128 people died, the Federal Aviation Administration at last took over responsibility nationwide. It is not surprising that my mother hated to fly and did her best for years to have her children avoid air travel.

If I had read *Life* in search of models for my adult self, I would have been hard-pressed to find much that was encouraging about what lay ahead. Every third or fourth *Life* cover featured a glamour shot of a woman—almost always an established or emerging movie star: Shelley Winters in a tub of bubbles, "Lovely Liz Taylor," Joan Collins on a swing, Sophia Loren, Audrey Hepburn, Kim Novak. Such lives were clearly unattainable—and to my mind, of little interest. Stories about women were scarce and overwhelmingly reflected an unease about who American women were becoming. In 1955, "The 80-Hour Week" described housewives as the nation's "largest, hardest-working, least-paid occupational group." In interviews for the piece, women— exclusively white—did not overtly complain about their burdens, but their words conveyed a kind of stunned desperation. "There are times when I just wish I was away on a long trip," one remarked.[4]

In December 1956, *Life* published a special double issue titled "The American Woman: Her Achievements and Troubles." Once again, the focus was exclusively on middle-class white women, with an opening story about American "beauties" that hailed their derivation from "many racial stocks"—which, *Life* proudly noted, extended beyond English and Irish to include German and Scandinavian. The new freedoms women enjoyed in postwar America, one contributor concluded, had created a "backwash of . . . emotional and psychological problems." As the issue's editorial observed, the "American woman is often discussed . . . as a problem to herself and others." *Life* seems to have been anticipating Betty Friedan by nearly a decade. I hope I skipped over these stories as I paged my way through the magazine. They could only have filled me with dread. Perhaps, though, I stopped to look at one article with a more inspiring message that would prove to have direct relevance to my later life: "Tough Training Ground for Women's Minds: Bryn Mawr Sets High Goals for Its Girls," offering "some of the most intensive intellectual training available in any college in the U.S."[5] Nearly a decade later, Bryn Mawr would provide me with a lifeline.

It was in many ways highly forward-looking of *Life* to offer such recognition to women and, more especially, to their discontent. One disgruntled reader assailed the editors for even taking up the sub-ject. "Bah! With the world situation being as it is . . . you clutter up 172 pages of *Life* with women."[6] *Life* in fact regularly cluttered up dozens of its pages with women—promoting cars, appliances, beauty products, and fashion in the advertisements that filled the magazine. These women were not dissatisfied housewives, however, but exuber-ant consumers. Such a portrait sat more easily with the magazine's readers than any effort to look beneath the surface of the myths about gender that rested at the heart of 1950s self-satisfaction.

Throughout the decade, countless advertisements in *Life* displayed women encased in girdles—such as Playtex's aptly named "Magic Controller"—and featured elaborately engineered bras as well as a dia-bolical apparatus first introduced in 1952 called a "Merry Widow." It extended from breasts to girdle top, ensuring no flesh could escape appropriately corseted discipline. The doctrine of "containment" that made its appearance in foreign policy seems to have had its counter-part in feminine fashion. Men's bodies were not subjected to such restraint, but their "unruly" hair required attention. Vitalis hair tonic promised to restore order, casting its oil upon waves of curls or wind-blown locks.[7]

Pale pink, proclaimed "fashion's favorite color" in 1955, was ev-erywhere: cars, stoves, typewriters, washing machines, refrigerators, toilets, and bathtubs. Mamie Eisenhower was pink's greatest cham-pion, introducing it into the White House—"First Lady Pink" was the particular hue—as well as in plumbing fixtures in her own Get-tysburg house.[8] Yet for me, pink was the color that marked girls—and women—as frail and sweet and irrelevant. Not unlike a girdle or a Merry Widow, pink seemed intended to contain and constrain. A color for a First Lady but not for a president.

Life's pages of advertisements were an advertisement for America, its abundance and its complacency, a mood reflected in much of the magazine's news content as well. Americans of the 1950s, the maga-zine editorialized, were "mightily pleased with themselves."[9] But who were these Americans *Life* addressed and portrayed? With the exception of a butler serving a drink on a silver tray, every individual pictured in the hundreds of sheets of advertisements *Life* published in the 1950s was white, as were the middle-class aspirations and achievements *Life* celebrated.

The magazine's news stories exhibited more variety. *Life* wrote regularly about Black athletes and entertainers. Marian Anderson, Sidney Poitier, Harry Belafonte, W. C. Handy, Floyd Patterson, Bill Russell, Sugar Ray Robinson, Althea Gibson, and Willie Mays occupied categories in which midcentury America had come to acknowledge Black achievement. In the course of the decade, the magazine increasingly covered other Black Americans as well, but these stories were neither appreciations nor celebrations. Instead, they were focused on what was often called the "Negro Problem"—how Black people constituted a crisis in American life and a challenge to the idealized images of American democracy and prosperity the magazine consistently foregrounded.

From the *Brown v. Board* decision in 1954 onward, *Life* demonstrated steady support for the emerging civil rights movement, even as it sought to present both sides of the escalating national debate about race. Voices of white southerners who opposed integration or thought it should not be mandated by federal courts were given respectful attention. *Life* even enlisted William Faulkner to warn the nation: "Go slow now. Stop for a time, a moment." The white southerner, the Nobel Prize–winning writer observed, "faces an obsolescence in his own land which only he can cure." But *Life*'s gestures at what it prized as objectivity and evenhandedness appeared alongside a clear commitment to Black progress and equality, evident in both editorial and news content. Between 1954 and 1956, *Life* published 46 articles about civil rights, filling 160 pages of the magazine. Overwhelmingly, these chronicled the stories of Black efforts to advance integration and the ensuing white backlash of cruelty and violence—from racist schoolyard taunts and threats to bombings, beatings, and lynchings.[10]

As challenges to Jim Crow intensified, *Life* told the cruel history of slavery and segregation.

In 1956, the magazine published a five-part series on segregation, introduced with a dramatic and disturbing cover illustration depicting an antebellum Charleston slave auction. *Life*'s rendering of the nation's past was remarkably critical in the context of both its time and its middlebrow identity; the magazine eschewed any romanticized or sanitized version of America's racial history. Disturbing portraits of the nation's past included illustrations of Confederates shooting wounded Black prisoners during the Civil War, whites slaughtering Blacks seeking political rights in Louisiana's 1873 Colfax massacre, and a horrifying photograph from the early twentieth century of a Black man being burned alive by a crowd of jeering white men.[11]

These were not stories regularly told in the era's history books. They are indeed the kinds of stories that a number of governors and state legislatures are today trying to exclude from school curricula.

But they were images that would have riveted my attention, because the world they portrayed differed so markedly from the narrative of benevolent white paternalism and genteel racial harmony that I had absorbed since my earliest childhood. And they contrasted sharply as well with *Life*'s own prevailing assumptions about 1950s America as a nation "up to its ears in domestic tranquility." Contradictions like these and the denial on which they fed pushed me to question the assumptions of the world around me and the lessons I had been taught. I resented what I began to perceive as the blindness or even bad faith of those who had misled me. This was the source of the tone of indignation and surprise in my letter to Eisenhower. How could I have not known why my school was all white? How could I have been taught about ideals of American democracy and Christian love when such terrible injustices did not just exist but were so vigorously defended, often by the very same people mouthing those civic and religious pieties?

And *Life* was not just recounting a distant past. In nearly every issue during the mid-1950s, the magazine confronted readers—in shocking photographs as well as words—with a new set of outrages. Stories depicted the murder of Emmett Till in 1955, the lynching of Mack Charles Parker in 1959, and the assaults on Black students seeking to integrate schools from Little Rock to Charlotte to Greenville—and even in a Virginia county adjacent to our own. In *Life*'s pages, I would have encountered boys and girls close to my own age, including a number seeking to attend schools not far from my home. I could see children, sometimes even younger than I, bravely facing angry mobs as they seized a right I could simply take for granted.

Almost as soon as I learned to read, I devoured a series of biographies describing the noble—and I now know mostly invented—childhood deeds of famous Americans. I can still see those books in my mind's eye, uniformly bound in orange, enthralling me with what young Americans had accomplished even before they became their famous adult selves: *Abraham Lincoln: Frontier Boy*, *Tom Edison: Boy*

Inventor; *George Washington: Boy Leader*; *Robert E. Lee: Boy of Old Virginia*; and perhaps most notably *Susan Anthony: Girl Who Dared*. And now children of my generation were creating their own heroic stories. It was not the Montgomery bus boycott or the Mack Charles Parker lynching or the 1957 Prayer Pilgrimage for Freedom—all of which were fully reported in *Life*—that had moved me to write to Eisenhower. It was school integration. I identified and empathized with these girls and boys. In many ways, the civil rights movement of the 1950s and '60s originated as a children's crusade, a designation later explicitly used by civil rights leaders when children—some even as young as six or seven—filled the streets and jails of Birmingham in the summer of 1963.[12] But half a decade earlier, the courage of such young people seeking justice both inspired me and filled me with a sobering sense of responsibility.

And it was not just American children who were fighting for freedom. In October 1956, Hungary erupted in the first threat to Soviet control in Eastern Europe since the end of World War II. The uprising caught the imagination of an American public steeped in the evils of communism and wholly convinced of the existential threat posed by Russian aggressions around the world. *Life* hailed this "magnificent revolution" and the "incredible bravery" of the Hungarian people whose "ancient love of liberty" had led them to risk all to end a twelve-year reign of "Communist terror." The revolt began as a student protest, and Hungarian youth remained at the center of the conflict—and of its portrayal in the Western press. *Life* published photographs of teenagers—male and female—armed with rifles and even submachine guns, as well as a distressing picture of a young girl killed on the street in Budapest. "They shot our children," one fighter exclaimed. Young boys and girls battled on, but it was only a matter of days before Soviet might brought a swift end to the insurrection. "Russia Crushes Hungary," declared the headline in *My Weekly Reader*.[13]

But Hungary did not disappear from American consciousness.

Tens of thousands of refugees fled the country to escape the Russian crackdown, and Help Hungary meetings were organized across the United States to offer assistance and asylum. On his popular Sunday-night variety show, Ed Sullivan urged viewers to contribute to refugee aid, but an appeal on the same show a few weeks later from his guest Elvis Presley stimulated an even greater outpouring of generosity. *Time* named "the Hungarian Freedom Fighter" the Man of the Year. *Life*'s first cover of 1957 pictured Richard Nixon with his arms around two refugee Hungarian girls. Ultimately more than thirty thousand Hungarians would resettle in the United States.

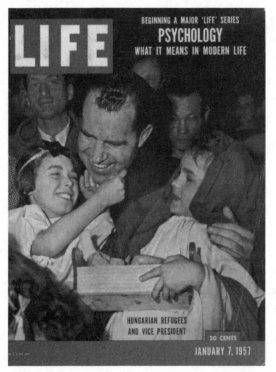

Vice President Nixon welcomed young refugees from the Hungarian Revolution.

I was much affected by this narrative of courage and idealism in which, once again, individuals not far from my own age were playing such a central and daring role. The Hungarian Revolution appeared to me as another episode in the ongoing battle of good versus evil, not unlike the forces I identified at play in the school integration battles, and of a piece with the war my father had so nobly fought before I was even born. Reflecting on her own childhood in the aftermath of World War II, the writer Annie Dillard has observed, "You couldn't view much about the war without figuring out that the world was a moral arena that required your strength."[14] That was my inheritance as well. Growing up white and female in conservative, segregated Virginia, in a nation fighting a Cold War it regarded as essential to the future of global freedom, I found almost limitless possibilities for the moral combat that World War II's legacy seemed to require. The Hungarian Revolution fit perfectly with my Manichaean child's-eye view of the world and inspired me with a vision of what humans, even very young ones, might summon the strength to dare.

I was moved by the appeal from Ed Sullivan, who was a Sunday-night regular in our house, and glad when the collection plate at church one week was designated to support refugees. I wanted to do more, but not knowing what that might be, I decided to write a play to dramatize Hungary's plight. No trace of it survives, which, given my memories, is probably a good thing. It depicted a family trying to escape from Hungary after the father was killed in the uprising, and it was no doubt maudlin in the extreme. At least it was likely to have been very brief. My fifth-grade class performed it, and I was gratified to be communicating what I felt to those who did not share my absorption with events taking place five thousand miles away.

If World War II appeared in my mind as a morality play, its Cold War aftermath only intensified such an understanding of my country's place in a wider world. We were the defenders of freedom and justice in the face of the advancing and godless Red Menace. The fear of communism within our borders and the threat of communism beyond them served as constant messages in mid-1950s American life, ones that did not exempt even the youngest children from their reach. Growing anxiety about nuclear war and a slowly emerging recognition of the devastating effects of radioactive fallout were not just matters for adult concern. Many schools instituted duck-and-cover maneuvers in which students dived under desks to protect themselves in the event of nuclear attack. I don't remember any such drills in my school, but I do recall many conversations about fallout shelters and whether we should build one. In 1955, the national administrator of civil defense advised all families to create shelters in which they could protect themselves for days or weeks from the radioactivity that would follow the detonation of a nuclear bomb. *Life* and many other magazines and newspapers offered examples and even blueprints of units in which a family might manage to survive, readied with supplies of canned water and food as well as "safety suits" to wear when they emerged.

I regarded the dangers of nuclear war as all too real. Politicians and pundits discussed nuclear options as entirely plausible. *Life*, in an editorial titled "Nuclear Wars Can Be Small," claimed that such conflicts might have real benefits: "A limited war doesn't have to be an old-fashioned war." In March 1958, on a routine training mission, a B-47 from the Strategic Air Command accidentally dropped a 7,600-pound atomic bomb on Mars Bluff, South Carolina. Its triggering mechanism was being carried separately, so the nuclear warhead was not set off, but the conventional explosives designed to ignite the bomb destroyed a house and left a crater seventy feet wide and thirty feet deep. The *Life* headline read, "A Scare Felt Around the World," a sobering reminder of the knife's edge on which we lived.[15]

In the face of such threats, fallout shelters seemed to me more imperative than far-fetched, but my parents had no interest, telling me a shelter probably wouldn't work and wondering who would want to survive a nuclear conflagration anyway. There was also the challenging problem, warranting extensive speculation and discussion, about who would be allowed into our shelter if we built it. Would we turn neighbors and relatives away if we did not have enough room—not to mention water and food and safety suits—to provide for them? Images of slamming the door in the face of cousins or my best friends troubled me. And what about Victoria and Raphael? Would the fallout shelter be segregated? And what about the dogs? And the cats? (I assumed there was no hope for the horses or other beloved pets.) I decided my parents were right: it was better not to have a shelter at all than to be confronted with such impossible decisions.

On October 4, 1957, the Soviet Union successfully launched Sputnik, the world's first artificial satellite. The size of a beach ball, it weighed 184 pounds and circled the globe every ninety-six minutes, chirping regularly in the key of A-flat. The news of this Russian triumph gripped the United States with fear, as well as with a crisis of confidence about what Americans had comfortably assumed was their technological dominance. It was, in the words of Senator Henry "Scoop" Jackson, "a devastating blow to U.S. prestige." Americans feared that the Russians would be able not just to build satellites but also to launch intercontinental ballistic missiles and directly threaten the United States. As Senator Mike Mansfield put it, "What is at stake is nothing less than our survival."[16] Sputnik was flying over the United States, violating our skies, multiple times every day, no doubt spying on us and our deepest security secrets. In the early morning and evening, I could even see it with the naked eye, and I imagined it watching me as it passed overhead.

I was stunned and scared by this news. Might Sputnik or some other Russian spacecraft drop a bomb on me as it flew by? After all, we lived only sixty miles from the White House. Poor aim might make us the unintended target. And what did this mean about America's vaunted invincibility? Was this yet another set of untruths adults had imposed on me? Another instance of bad faith? I decided that henceforth I would sleep on my back so that at least I would see the bombs before they struck.

It is difficult more than a half century later to grasp how devastating the Sputnik launch seemed in American eyes. Recriminations abounded within the military establishment; Congress formed new committees to address issues of U.S. preparedness; commentators demanded an overhaul of the American education system to place more emphasis on science and homework, and less on "life adjustment"; cultural critics welcomed the challenge Sputnik posed to American self-satisfaction and complacency. I am sure I understood little of this, but the aura of fear and betrayal that surrounded it was communicated clearly, even to a ten-year-old.

And I was far from the only ten-year-old for whom this was a defining event. The writer Stephen King, who was born just three days after I was, regards the launch of Sputnik as life-changing, and he postulates this was true for a great many of us born in the years just after the war:

> For me, the terror—the real terror . . . began on an afternoon in October 1957 . . . I am guessing that a great many kids—the war babies, we were called—remember the event as well as I do . . .
>
> We were told that we were the greatest nation on earth and that any Iron Curtain outlaw who tried to draw down on us in that great saloon of international politics would discover who the fastest gun in the West was . . .
>
> We were and always had been, in that pungent American phrase, fastest and bestest with the mostest . . .
>
> This was the cradle of elementary political theory . . . in which I and a great many other war babies were rocked until that day in October, when the cradle was rudely upended and all of us fell out. For me, it was the end of the sweet dream . . . and the beginning of the nightmare.[17]

From Sputnik to horror fiction.

I made no such passage, though perhaps a career writing about slavery and war could be seen as in some ways equivalent. But I, too, felt my cradle upended. America was not what I had been told it was. It was not all-powerful, and it could not protect me. I had discovered that its racial injustices belied the ideals of democracy and equality that I had been taught defined it. Nor did the United States exert the unrivaled power to enforce these ideals in the wider world. Or even to protect its citizens from fallout and rockets and bombs.

Fissures had begun to appear in the celebratory postwar myths of American virtue and omnipotence. The year 1957 brought not just Sputnik but a recession; beloved President Eisenhower's heart attack, which had hospitalized him for seven weeks in 1955, was followed by a stroke; the 101st Airborne had to be dispatched to Little Rock to safeguard Black students seeking to enter Central High, pitting the American military against American citizens; and the Russian leader Nikita Khrushchev was threatening to "bury" us. The complacency and self-satisfaction emblematic of the 1950s were eroding well before the decade came to an end.

I understood very little of all this, but enough trickled down to instill fear and doubt in my mind. Fear of the dangerous world of missiles and satellites and international confrontations in which I now found myself; doubt nurtured by the overturning of so many of my fundamental assumptions about the society in which I lived. Fear and doubt might be mitigated or assuaged, but something even more profound was at risk. And that was trust. If so many things were not as they had seemed, who had misled me? Who and what could I believe? What could be taken for granted? I began to see that I would have to discover and define the world for myself.

I was not alone. A generation of children began, like me and like Stephen King, to see through the comforting illusions at the heart of postwar American culture, to ask the questions that by the time of our adolescence would transform American society. The Sixties began with Little Rock and with Sputnik and with the seeds of doubt and disappointment they sowed. As my generation approached adolescence, other seeds of the future began to take root as well. The hypocrisy and denial evident in public life also had their personal dimensions. As we grew up and our bodies began to change, we found that here, too, things were not exactly as we had been told.

As the children of the 1950s became the teenagers of the 1960s, our parents' repressive attitudes about sex began to seem at odds with our emerging understanding of human nature—and, often, with our knowledge of their own behavior. For girls, these conflicts were especially acute. Growing up meant repressing emergent sexuality as dangerous and forbidden. Developing a woman's body meant being contained and controlled by girdles and bras. To menstruate was to have "the curse." To acknowledge sexual feelings was the first step on the slippery slope to "getting in trouble."

My own mother's approach was to ignore the fact that I was entering puberty—first by staying silent about it and acting as if I were still a little girl, then by refusing to supply what friends had convinced me were essential accoutrements. Perhaps she thought that if she didn't acknowledge I was growing up, I wouldn't. I would remain a child, and the messy issues of sexuality and the disappointments of womanhood could be avoided altogether. My best friend urged me to insist to my mother that I be provided with a bra, and I remember a set of seemingly endless battles about whether I would be allowed to have a garter belt and stockings or would humiliate myself by continuing to appear at dress-up occasions in short white socks. If I confronted her with questions about sex, I received platitudes and generalities: it was part of a loving marriage, something you did for your husband, something men cared about more than women. Never did she describe what "it" was—perhaps in the hope that if I didn't understand "it," I wouldn't be able to do it. But of course, I managed to learn all those details elsewhere: from classmates and from books about sex—ranging from marriage manuals to *Lady Chatterley's Lover*—that I found hidden in a dark alcove of my parents' bedroom.

But perhaps the most direct path toward recognition and expression of sexual feelings and longings came through the new music emerging all around me. While I was a fan of singers like Pat Boone and Frankie Avalon, who crooned in the romantic traditions of my parents' era, I was increasingly captivated by the rhythms of rock and roll, which seemed to invite me to forget rules and inhibitions, forget the lofty romantic dreams invoked by ballads accompanied by whole orchestras of strings. Let the music touch your body, not your mind. Don't think, just move. Dance.

The combination of this new music's intensity and its lyrics ("leerics," one worried journalist called them) opened doors into interior worlds and feelings that middle-class white American culture had strived to keep firmly closed. Elvis's pelvic gyrations on *The Ed Sullivan Show* in September 1956 invited us to imagine and move our bodies in new ways, freed from containment or control. Girls had been indoctrinated to believe love was all about waiting, but Elvis insisted otherwise. "It's now or never," he warned. "My love won't wait." Chuck Berry introduced us to the irresistible beat of rhythm and blues as he implored Maybellene to be true; Little Richard's hypnotic and unrestrained performances enthralled us, as did the words he sang, suggestive even in their expurgated form. "Will you still love me tomorrow?" asked the Shirelles—one of the earliest girl groups bringing female voices and perspectives into what would ultimately prove to be both a musical and a social revolution.[18] Their first hit spoke to exactly what we "nice girls" were repeatedly warned about: a boy may want you tonight, but if you let him go too far, he won't respect you in the morning. When Chubby Checker invited us to do the twist in 1960, we delighted in our ability to join in the dance's full-body exuberance, which most of our parents regarded alternatively as impossible to master or outright threatening. As we twisted, we girls moved independently with no need to follow a male partner's lead; everyone had an equal opportunity to invent and improvise. (My father had long bewailed my inadequacies at traditional ballroom dancing: I had never, he complained, learned to *follow*; I always wanted to lead.)

Even though much of the pop music of the era—Elvis, the girl groups, Motown—has been criticized as a commercialized dilution and even expropriation of Black artists and traditions, we understood none of these complexities. Even in altered or distorted form, this music enticed and enchanted. Rock and roll's foundations in Black music offered a degree of liberation from the constraints at the heart of white 1950s culture, and we greeted it as the vehicle of a kind of authenticity absent from the lives our parents had intended for us.

I grew up in a world in which Blacks and whites were in one sense impossibly distant, separated by the hierarchies of racism and the legal strictures of segregation. Yet we were at once paradoxically together and apart. I encountered and interacted with Black people every day within an environment that demanded I think of them as different and other. That required me constantly to ask who I was as well as who they were. I was exposed to glimpses of another reality that provided a perspective and often an implicit critique of my own. Whatever I could discern about Blackness cast my whiteness into sharper relief and, as I grew older and more aware, repeatedly challenged the assumptions of white superiority with which I had been inculcated. Black music contained attractions and mysteries that made it both admirable and desirable—and even just plain better than the anemic popular canon that our parents had embraced.

I was only about thirteen, so I think I was trading on my older brother's status when I became the organizer of a series of dances over the course of two years—at the local fire hall during Christmas vacation and during summer holidays at what passed for a country club in Millwood, Virginia. It was a one-room building with a wide wraparound porch and a tiny kitchen, but it served our purposes. My job was to raise money for a band and refreshments from my friends and my brother's friends—a few dozen boys and girls ranging from my age up to seventeen or eighteen. The bulk of the funds would go to signing up the Solid Senders. In the collective opinion of Millwood's white teenage inhabitants, the Solid Senders were thrilling—at once familiar and a little dangerous. All Black, performing R and B and rock and roll, they had taken their name, an old jive phrase, from a successful 1940s blues band. We felt that their live performances had a power unmatched by even the best existing recordings of the very best contemporary music stars available to us on our record players. Their music transported me to some other realm and transformed me into a person I had not previously known.

Their signature song was a cover of the Ray Charles hit released in the summer of 1959, "What'd I Say." When the Solid Senders broke into this number, this crowd of white Virginia children, dressed in khaki pants and bow ties, dresses and crinolines, erupted, first responding to the demand they "shake that thing," then engaging in full-throated embrace of the call-and-response chorus—"Uuunh / uuunh, Ahhh / Ahhh, uunh / ahhh / uunh / aahh"—shouting and dancing faster and faster until the band returned to its opening words, "Tell me what'd I say. Tell me what'd I say." We would urge the Solid Senders to repeat the sequence again and again. I don't remember how much, if anything, we knew about the controversy the song and its runaway popularity had ignited with its sexual suggestiveness. *Rolling Stone* later remarked that "What'd I Say" was "the closest you could get to the sound of orgasm on Top Forty radio during the Eisenhower Era." This we on some unspoken level understood. We had come a long distance from dancing school and the foxtrot.[19]

By the end of the 1950s, I was suffused with skepticism and even dismay about the path my life was expected to take. The white Virginia society in which I lived was seriously at odds with its own professed values; my country was in a crisis about its position and its role in the world. And my own future—growing to be a woman in a man's world—seemed increasingly unappealing as its various dimensions and requirements became clear. I responded to my mother's new demand that I wear a skirt to dinner by retreating to the barn and the company of my 4-H club steer and refusing to come to the table at all. I chafed at my mother's activated insistence that I be chaperoned and surveilled whenever I was with boys. I sneaked off with my older brother to escape the rules and strictures that applied to me alone. To borrow some words from Scout in *To Kill a Mockingbird*, "I felt the starched walls of a pink cotton penitentiary closing in on me."[20] Idealistic notions of justice, equality, and patriotism combined with a more self-interested concern about my own freedoms to put me on a collision course with my parents. The most serious breaks and confrontations did not occur till the 1960s, supported and fueled by the broader youth movements of that era. But it was the 1950s that opened this generational gulf. We recoiled at what we regarded as the dishonesty and denial at the core of our parents' existence. We were determined to find a way to live otherwise.

6

GIRLS WHO DARE: NANCY, ANNE, AND SCOUT

Without books we wouldn't know who we were.

—JASON EPSTEIN[1]

In June 1954, my parents received the school report card summarizing my year in second grade. I received a 99 in spelling, a 98 in English, and a 93 in arithmetic. Even my messy handwriting had improved to "Very Good." My teacher, Mrs. McNally, offered congratulations: "Another excellent year's work. Drew continues to lead her class." The headmaster took a somewhat different perspective in remarks he added at the bottom of the page. Mr. Bradley had been uneasy when I had arrived in first grade a year younger than the rest of my class and already a proficient reader. He firmly believed children should not be taught reading until they were at least six years old. By the end of my first-grade year, however, he acknowledged all had seemed to go well. But he continued to express his view—and his hope—that "this remarkable record will not keep up indefinitely . . . perfection can be an awful axe over one's head." I had completed another strong year, and he felt compelled not just to indicate his ambivalence about this bright little girl but also to offer quite explicit advice: "I suggest she have a summer of fun and not try to break her reading record of last summer: enough is enough."[2]

From the time I began amassing a collection of Little Golden Books, from *The Poky Little Puppy* to *The Saggy Baggy Elephant*, I found few things more fun than reading. I read not to break records but for pleasure, for company, and for escape. As I grew older, I read to look beyond my contained Virginia world and to be able to see it through different eyes. Books enabled me to explore other lives and to imagine myself into them, lives that went beyond the limited choices available to my mother and the women of her circle. I read because I loved words and loved seeing what could be created with them. And I read because I wanted access to a realm where only imagination could set its limits, and where a strong record in first and second grades would not be proclaimed to be "enough."

Discussions of women's changing lives in the second half of the twentieth century often invoke the notion of "role models" who have attained positions of power and influence and can thus help young girls envision themselves in similar circumstances. To see the accomplishments of someone who looks like themselves is to recognize possibilities that might not have been conceivable without that example and inspiration. As a young child, I encountered no such living models. No female politicians, writers, artists, scientists. Nothing beyond the occasional elementary school teacher. None of my friends' mothers worked outside the home; ladies became wives and parents unless financial hardship required otherwise, a circumstance to be pitied, not admired. My role models had to come from the world of books.

I cannot remember when I did not know how to read. I must have been read to as a small child, and as we grew older my parents from time to time still dutifully gathered us in the living room to listen to some worthy volume that was inevitably unsuited to one or more of us, given our different ages. Perhaps the most ill-conceived of these—and thus immortal in family legend—was Charles Lindbergh's *The Spirit of St. Louis*, an account of his 1927 solo flight across the Atlantic, which we found as boring and interminable as any actual thirty-three-and-a-half-hour journey would seem to children ranging from five to eleven. But for me the issue wasn't just Lindbergh. I hated being read to. I did not want another person between me and the power of the book; I wanted the rest of the world to disappear when I was reading. I wanted to read at my pace and on my terms. I wanted to be in control.

Summer reading fun in my elementary school years was closely associated with what I viewed as the miracle of the public library. Our Virginia county had no such facility, but when we made long visits to vacation with my mother's parents at Marion, a picture-book village on the Massachusetts coast, a new world opened for me. First was the freedom of being in a New England town instead of isolated on a farm a quarter mile from the road. I could ride my bike, a shiny green Schwinn, to the general store, to my tennis lessons, or to what seemed an infinite world of books. I can still smell the odor of mildewing pages that greeted me when I opened the door to the cool, dark Victorian mansion repurposed to house the town library. Room after room of shelves crowded with books greeted me, and I could have any of them. It was as if I could now ride my bicycle to any corner of the world. I took as many books as I could fit in my bike basket and returned for more almost every day. Enough was never enough.

In Marion, Massachusetts, in the mid-1950s. Off to the library?

From as early as I can remember, one of my favorites was Nancy Drew. Thirty-six books appeared in the series before the end of the 1950s, so there was always a long shelf of matching blue bindings from which to choose. Although I was only six or seven and Nancy was sixteen when we met, she was an inspiration.[3] It turns out that Nancy Pelosi, Hillary Clinton, Sonia Sotomayor, Gayle King, Ruth Bader Ginsburg, Sandra Day O'Connor, Oprah Winfrey, Beverly Sills, and Diane Sawyer all felt the same.[4]

Nancy, as she herself put it, had a "talent for unearthing mysteries,"[5] and in each volume she confronted a different one—the puzzle of a hidden staircase or a hidden window, of secret passwords or a clue found in a locket or perhaps in an old trunk, an old album, or an old clock. Menaced, threatened, even kidnapped, Nancy fearlessly persevered. Extravagant coincidences abounded; long-lost twins were reunited; missing maps and fortunes were found. But the mystery was always solved. The most satisfying aspect of the books was that justice was always done; truth was revealed; the world was righted. And it was all because of Nancy. The Little Miss Fix-It in me found this deeply satisfying. But the attributes that enabled Nancy to achieve these feats were equally alluring. She was accomplished at everything: she could pick locks, pilot a speedboat, sew, paint, execute necessary chemical analyses, change tires, repair cars, analyze handwriting. The blue roadster she drove with the skill of a professional was the agent and emblem of her freedom—a more grown-up version of my summer bicycle. "Left motherless at an early age," Nancy had no one to show her how to occupy a woman's place. In an era when females were taught it was their foremost duty to look out for others, Nancy had "an ability to look out for herself." Her adoring father was in Nancy's eyes "a peach." She congratulated him, "You let me do anything I like and never make fun of my wild ideas." Her boyfriend, Ned, appeared only occasionally, usually to take direction from Nancy about how he could help with some aspect of the mystery at hand. He seemed a handy accessory but less central to her life and purpose than her blue roadster.[6]

Nancy was free, independent, resourceful, and brave. Carolyn Heilbrun, the late feminist literary critic and a mystery author in her own right, saw Nancy Drew representing "a moment in the history of fem-

Nancy Drew's daring exploits. Endpapers from *The Haunted Bridge* by Carolyn Keene, illustrated by Russell H. Tandy, 1937.

inism" and serving as a "model for early second wave feminists," those of my generation who would launch the Women's Movement of the late 1960s and '70s. Nancy's readers were empowered to imagine a different kind of womanhood before them, one in which they could be beautiful and admired while they dazzled the world with their accomplishments. Perhaps it was Nancy Drew who persuaded us we could Have It All.

We live our lives in accordance with the stories we tell ourselves about what those lives ought to be. Feminism, Heilbrun has written, required women to find new narratives, new directions for the plot, new notions of what made for a happy ending. Men have traditionally been offered "quest" plots, stories tracing life trajectories toward action, power, and accomplishment. Women's lives, by contrast, have been channeled into romance plots, which culminated in fantasies of living happily ever after as they merged their identities into those of the men whose affections they were lucky or crafty enough to win. The adult women around me when I was growing up had designed their lives as romance plots. Nancy Drew lived a quest.[7]

Reading the books today, I cannot help but cringe at the racist stereotypes, antisemitic asides, and assumptions of class superiority that exist side by side with the vivid portrait of Nancy. After 1959, the series publisher began to issue revisions of the original stories, removing their most offensive aspects. Sadly, these revised versions also portray a less spirited and independent Nancy. By the time these newer books came out, I had moved beyond Nancy Drew. But the original Nancy had left me with a narrative for a female life I had not known before I encountered her: a story in which a girl who could do almost everything wielded her power in the cause of truth and justice.

An Extraordinary Document of Adolescence. There it is right on the cover. And above that a young girl's face in a photograph so like the ones we had taken each year at school and exchanged with our friends. Her hair neatly parted and bunched at one side of her face with an invis-

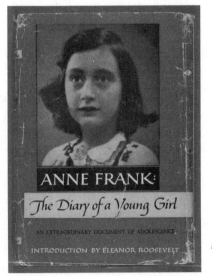

My copy.

ible barrette. Her eyes staring just beyond me. She looked as if she might be my friend, and that is what she became when I opened *Anne Frank: The Diary of a Young Girl.* I still have the book, with my name inscribed inside in my awkward child's handwriting.

I am certain that this was a volume I selected for myself, perhaps on one of the trips to Scribner's Fifth Avenue bookstore that we looked forward to whenever our New Jersey grandparents took us on an outing to New York. The store seemed to me like an enormous church, a single, huge two-storied room with a wrought iron balcony looking out above the main floor. Books for young people were at the very back and down a few steps. My mother would admonish us not to disturb the other customers or run through the tables stacked with books in the main section of the store in our eagerness to amass a pile of reading matter to take back to Virginia.

From the time I was nine or ten, I was an aspiring adolescent, so the notion of discovering a pathfinder to guide my way had a powerful appeal. "I hope I shall be able to confide in you completely, as I never have been able to do in anyone before," Anne wrote to her diary.[8] But it was as if she were writing directly to me.

I had never, at least as far as I knew, met a Jewish person. With one or two Catholics as exceptions proving the rule, everyone in my school was Protestant—and overwhelmingly Episcopalian to boot. I remember being stunned when I was looking at an encyclopedic book on world religions shelved in my elementary school classroom and saw that Episcopalians did not even make up a sliver on the pie chart. It was a shock to realize that my world was so unlike what surrounded it. I knew little of the Holocaust, except that it was one of the evils our Nazi enemies had perpetrated. But what I came to see as I read the diary reinforced my conception of World War II as a moral combat, as a clash of evil and righteousness. Anne became much more than an emerging adolescent; she was an embattled champion of the true and the good.

By the end of the twentieth century, Anne Frank's diary had sold more than twenty-five million copies worldwide. It had been made into an American movie (1959) and more than one play, including a Broadway hit (1955). It had also generated controversies, critical debates, and even lawsuits. Holocaust deniers insisted it was a fake until the Netherlands Institute for War Documentation and the Netherlands Forensic Institute, in an effort to settle the matter, performed an exhaustive analysis of glue, paper, ink, and handwriting and confirmed it had indeed been written by Anne. Others argued about how much the story should be regarded and presented as Jewish and how much as universal, how to weight the World War II dimensions of the story in relationship to the portrait of a young girl growing up. Some insisted that this was not a Holocaust story at all because it was only after the diary ended and Anne was transported to Auschwitz and then Bergen-Belsen that she could have truly understood the magnitude of Nazi brutality. As one critic wrote with some scorn: the diary was so popular because it represented a "Holocaust without tears."[9]

I was drawn to the book by its subtitle: *An Extraordinary Document of Adolescence*, clearly intended by a savvy publisher to universalize the diary to make it appeal to young girls like me. I was not looking for a story of the Holocaust. But I got one, and it came with plenty of tears. Anne seemed like me in so many ways, and yet she had been tortured and killed simply because she was Jewish. For me, with my obsession about what was and wasn't fair, this was unbearable and intolerable. Through the universal aspects of her narrative, I was drawn into new revelations about the particularities of her tale. Judith Miller has written, "We must remind ourselves that the Holocaust was not six million. It was one, plus one, plus one . . . Only in understanding that civilized people must defend the one, by one, by one . . . can the Holocaust, the incomprehensible, be given meaning."[10] I started with the one who was Anne Frank, and her diary confronted me with the reality of six million.

The poet and critic John Berryman hailed the diary as an exemplary chronicle of "the conversion of a child into a person." When I first encountered the book, I was also a child and, more specifically, a girl, myself striving to metamorphose into a person. "Every day," Anne wrote, "I try to improve myself, again and again." She was confident of what she regarded as the most "outstanding trait in my character . . . my knowledge of myself," which enabled her to "watch myself and my actions, just like an outsider."[11] She seemed to invite me to join her in that exploration and encouraged me to emulate her by turning a similar gaze on myself.

I was, of course, not Anne, not faced with war and extermination, not compelled to hide in an attic. But I resonated with her description of her struggles with her parents: "I'd really like to be rid of them for a while!" Most often it was just her mother who was the target of her resentment. Her mother was "short-tempered" in contrast to a father far more "kind and patient," who Anne feared might not love her enough—and even prefer her sister: "I adore Daddy. He is the one I look up to. I don't love anyone in the world but him. He doesn't notice that he treats Margot differently from me. I have always been the . . . ne'er-do-well of the family." Anne, an avid reader and aspiring writer, shared with her father a love of the life of the mind, and she found she could "discuss things and argue better than Mummy . . . I feel superior to her over a great many things." Determined that her adult future must be different from that of "ordinary housewives," she could not imagine growing up to be like "all the women who do their work and are then forgotten. I must have something besides a husband and children, something that I can devote myself to!"[12] Anne felt herself to be the disfavored, failed child, the troublesome one in comparison to her sister, the perfect Margot. This all seemed so familiar to me: I, too, resented and quarreled with my mother and scorned the life she had chosen. I, too, felt a failure in meeting my parents' expectations.

After one dramatic confrontation, Anne proclaimed herself motherless. "I have to be my own mother," she wrote. She determined to free herself from any assumption that she could rely on her parents; her sense of disappointment would propel the conversion Berryman described. "Although I am only fourteen, I know quite well what I want," she proclaimed, "I know who is right or wrong, I have my own opinions, my own ideas and principles, and although it may sound pretty mad from an adolescent, I feel more of a person than a child, I feel quite independent of anyone."[13]

She was in fact completely dependent on everyone around her: on her fellow occupants of the Secret Annex to be silent while the unknowing office and warehouse workers toiled every day below the stairs; on her parents and their dwindling financial resources to fund the costs of their confinement; on the several Dutch citizens who forged ration cards, procured food, and hauled supplies to the attic under cover of night. That Anne could establish such a strong sense of self under these circumstances seemed at once reassuring and challenging. Perhaps I, too, could succeed in becoming a person.

Other reading offered me stories set closer to my own experience. As with so many young girls of my generation and beyond, I consumed a steady diet of what have come to be called "pony books." Although for many readers, these books substituted for the pony itself, I lived in a world of horses. But the books still represented a kind of wish fulfillment—about my most expansive aspirations for what connection to an animal might come to mean. I read dozens of these books. *Black Beauty*, published in England in 1877, might be seen as the origin of the genre. I found the horse's own narration of its mistreatment agonizingly sad and upsetting. This horse with a voice and a point of view that could be understood by humans had launched a movement for animal welfare in Victorian Britain, and it reinforced what I already knew: animals—our five dogs and our ponies, the orphan lambs I rescued and bottle-fed in the basement, the steers I raised in 4-H—were significant others in my life. They taught me to listen with more than just ears, to observe and to empathize. Pony books offered examples of cross-species communication that explored these possibilities in ways that seemed and sometimes even were magical.

My very favorite was not the Black Stallion series, or *National Velvet*, or the Marguerite Henry tales of the ponies of Chincoteague, though I read them all. For me, the best was *Silver Snaffles*, published in England in 1937, in which Jenny, who is longing for a pony, is given a secret password that transports her through the Dark Corner of a stall into a stable of talking mounts who teach her how to ride. Ultimately she, on horseback of course, rescues one of the ponies who has been kidnapped and taken to the "Land of the People Who Had No Horse Sense"—people who stroke horses' noses with "white wooly gloves," who regard ponies as status symbols, who smack their mounts incessantly with hunting crops, who gallop them on hard-surfaced roads. This wasn't quite the cruelty Black Beauty had been subjected to, but it required intervention nonetheless. Jenny's bravery sets the world right again. The book ends with Jenny reflecting on "all that the ponies had taught her," as her father recognizes her passion for horses and gives her a pony of her own.[14]

Another of my favorite pony books opens with a young girl too scared of horses to want to learn to ride. Pam is visiting her grandfather when a new foal is born to a mare too sick to nurse it. Forgetting her fears in face of the necessity of caring for the needy baby, Pam feeds the filly with a bottle in the family kitchen. As Pam and little Frosty bond, the girl develops new trust in horses, becomes an expert rider, and, over a nearly five-year period, trains and schools Frosty to be a champion. The book is detailed enough about how Pam works with Frosty to serve almost as a training manual in itself. It left me with no doubts as to Pam's skills and determination and Frosty's acumen. In the tradition of *Black Beauty* and the Land of the People Who Had No Horse Sense, the book includes characters who demonstrate how horses should not be treated—ridden too young or too hard, schooled through negative reinforcement, treated too inconsistently. But the power of *Pamela and the Blue Mare* is its portrait of the girl and the horse who grow up together—and grow up *because* of each other. Together they find confidence and, at the horse show that closes the book, triumph.[15]

Horse riding provided the occasion for risk taking, physical strenuousness, fearlessness, and the display of skill—opportunities not otherwise readily available to girls during my childhood. When I cantered across a field on my pony, Black Twig, or guided her through the woods, carefully ducking to avoid low branches, I felt powerful, free, in control. Somehow prevailing gender rules were relaxed in the stable, and women could openly display proficiency, strength, and independence—not to mention wear pants. Women could literally seize the reins. Yet with horses and other animals, one needed more traditional feminine attributes as well—to be a nurturer, to feed and groom and care for these dependents. I could confide in animals and they, unlike so many humans, seemed to understand. It was a world apart from the rest of my life. To the question "Most likely to be found?" posed to each member of my class in my eighth-grade yearbook, my answer was "In the barn."[16]

I left Virginia for boarding school in New England just weeks after *To Kill a Mockingbird* appeared in the summer of 1960. The book would soon become a publishing phenomenon, winning the Pulitzer Prize, selling more than a million copies a year for the next four decades, and regularly appearing on school reading lists across the country. It quickly drew the attention of my ninth-grade teachers. The story of the moral and psychological growth of a young girl combined with the book's central themes of racial justice to make it seem almost required reading in a girls' school located in Concord, Massachusetts, a nineteenth-century hotbed of antislavery activism. I was one of very

With my first dog,
c. 1950.

In the barnyard
with my steer
Ferdinand, 1960.

few girls in the school from south of the Mason-Dixon Line, and I remember my English teacher being particularly eager that I read the book and share my reactions. My classmates found it an eye-opening portrait of an alien world. I saw in Maycomb, Alabama, many of the attributes of the Virginia community I had just left behind.

I was captivated by Scout. It seemed like a long time since I had been eight years old, and the 1930s were the ancient past. But there was so much about her life that rang true and so much about her that was entirely sympathetic. Like many girl heroines, she had no mother to insist on indoctrinating her into ladyhood. She preferred overalls to dresses because of the freedom they allowed. She knew that when her brother reminded her she was a girl, it was to exclude or diminish her. Scout was a fighter—in a literal not just a figurative sense: she punched those who tormented her at school and kicked full-grown men in the groin. But her physicality was accompanied by a deep and mature reflectiveness expressed in her narrator's voice, a capacity that has been criticized as installing an inconsistency in point of view at the heart of the book. Like her father and her brother, though, Scout was a thinker and an avid reader—for which she was rebuked by a first-grade teacher who shared the views about early reading held by my own elementary school headmaster. Scout took the racial arrangements of her world for granted, including the devoted presence of Calpurnia, a Black woman who cared for the children. That Calpurnia might have a "separate existence" outside the Finch household and apart from her relationship to them seemed to Scout unimaginable. It "had never dawned on me," she confessed.[17] I had grown up with the same blindness.

Much of the book's enthusiastic reception centered on Scout's father, the lawyer Atticus Finch, and his heroism in defending—unsuccessfully—a Black man accused of rape in Depression-era Alabama. The wildly popular film made from the book in 1962 portrayed him in even more admiring terms, and his image was further enhanced by Gregory Peck's appearance in the starring role. But I was not all that interested in Atticus. I was envious of his closeness and deep devotion to his children. I would have welcomed that level of fatherly attention. But other aspects of Atticus seemed conventional and even predictable. He had few doubts about the social hierarchy that structured white as well as Black society. As Scout's brother, Jem, explained with some bitterness, he had learned that there were "four kinds of folks in the world": those with "background" like the Finches and their neighbors in town, the hardworking white folks who lived out in the woods but could hardly read or write, the "low-grade" white trash, and "the Negroes." Atticus embraced a noblesse oblige that dictated civility to all and underscored his duty to preserve the accepted foundations and values of the prevailing social order. He lived by prescriptions of manhood that required courage in defense of that world. His children had not ever known him to fire a gun, but it was Atticus who proved to be a dead-eye shot when called to eliminate a rabid dog menacing the town. He did not flaunt his superiority; he was a gentleman.[18] My father, it seems, was not the only southern man compelled to shoot a dog.

In 2015, HarperCollins issued a long-awaited second Harper Lee novel that caused an uproar. Written before *Mockingbird*, *Go Set a Watchman* takes place some twenty years later. Scout is now an adult and discovers on a visit home that in civil rights–era Alabama her father has become a leader in the White Citizens' Council, an organization that proliferated in the South in the 1950s and '60s and has sometimes been described as a kind of uptown Ku Klux Klan. Atticus proves to be a staunch defender of the southern way of life against demands for racial change. Generations of readers who regarded themselves as Atticus's devoted fans rose up in dismay. Those who had watched the *Mockingbird* movie dozens of times, had decided to become lawyers to follow in his footsteps, and had named their dogs or even their children after him refused to accept this portrait of their hero, and joined a chorus charging that the book must have been published without eighty-nine-year-old Harper Lee's full awareness and consent. But three women who had grown up in Alabama in the 1950s and '60s—one a journalist, one a Pulitzer Prize-winning historian, and the third the actress who played Scout in the 1962 film—insisted otherwise. The Atticus of *Watchman* was the "Atticus we always knew." The journalist explained, "The disillusioned readers . . . were confronting what we had discovered in the course of growing up, leaving home and looking back on a world that compromised every white person who lived in it."[19]

It was Scout, not Atticus, who represented the beacon of hope and possibility in *Mockingbird*. It was children who might be able to change the southern future. It was Scout who confronted the angry would-be lynch mob on the jailhouse steps and brought them to their senses. When Jem sank into despair in the days after Tom Robinson's conviction for rape, proclaiming to his father, "It ain't right," Atticus simply agreed.[20] He had learned to accommodate. But Jem and Scout and their friend Dill were sickened by the miscarriage of justice represented by the trial. They had not understood the world to work that way; they were compelled to recognize the hypocrisy and denial fundamental to the lives of the adults around them; they were not yet compromised. In Scout, I found another example of a child seeing clearly, a child who believed in her responsibility to the world, who wanted to defend the values she had been taught—even as she came to see them mostly honored in the breach. Had she been a little girl in 1957, I thought she might well have written to Eisenhower, too.

But will the children be able to retain their clarity of vision, their uncompromising sense of right and wrong? *Mockingbird* leaves that question unresolved. When Dill was reduced to weeping and vomiting by the trial, the town outcast—a white man who readily acknowledged his mixed-race children—at once warned and reassured him that he would not always react to injustice in this way: "Let him get a little older and he won't get sick and cry. Maybe things'll strike him as being—not quite right, say, but he won't cry when he gets a few years on him."[21] Would Scout just become a lady and fully embrace the racial mores of rural Alabama, with its everyday cruelties and indignities punctuated by regular episodes of violence and terror? I chose to believe that somehow she would not; I chose to have faith that what she had learned in the course of the book would enable her to continue to see through the hypocrisies that surrounded her and persist in the battle for right against wrong. I was betting on Scout.

I was invested in Scout's future and in the possibility she seemed to represent. Children did not have to see things exactly like their parents; they did not have to grow up to be their parents. They had not yet been co-opted and corrupted by evils that surrounded them; they took risks because they did not even understand they were doing so; their innocence was their power. When I read *Mockingbird* in the fall of 1960, I had long known about the children bravely integrating southern schools. I knew, too, about the children who had fought in the Hungarian Revolution. I had learned the preceding February about students sitting in at lunch counters in Greensboro, North Carolina. *Mockingbird* provided me with another model of a warrior for justice. These girls who dared—Nancy, Anne, Scout—were daring me.

7

FRIDAY FOR REVOLUTIONS, WEDNESDAY FOR LIFE

Have the courage to be disturbed.

—ELIZABETH B. HALL[1]

I left Virginia for New England to become a boarding student at Concord Academy three days before my thirteenth birthday. The school occupied a row of picturesque late eighteenth- and early nineteenth-century clapboard houses that stretched along the town's Main Street. Behind them, a few other buildings dotted a campus that stretched down to the Sudbury River. It looked like an illustration for *Little Women*, which had been written just across town less than a century before. I was assigned a room under the eaves on the third floor of Tucker House at 62 Main Street that I was to share with two girls from older classes. Concord believed in mixing up students of different ages—and in having everyone shift rooms entirely three times a year. The mother of a friend thought this a terrible idea, as she was sure we would come to expect to change husbands with equal frequency, but I appreciated the chance to get to know so many people from every class so well. And it was good for me to have those older and wiser roommates as I began to establish a new life away from my family.

When my birthday arrived almost as soon as we had moved in, my new roommates surprised me with one of Concord's legendary "Stuffs." When the house grew quiet after Lights Out, they began to extract boxes and bags from under their beds—roast chicken, brownies, cookies, potato chips, sodas. A half dozen other pajama-clad residents quietly slipped in from down the hall with their own contributions. We must have made enough noise to alert the housemother to our illicit gathering, but there were no heavy footsteps on the stairs to send us scattering to our beds. Looking back, I think the housemother probably put the idea in my roommates' heads in the first place as a way of making a very young new student feel at home. I felt I belonged at Concord Academy from that day forward.

Concord was something of an unusual school in the early 1960s. All girls and less than four decades old, it did not have the history or the financial resources of some of its more established sisters—Miss Porter's or Emma Willard or St. Timothy's—not to mention its venerable and richly funded male counterparts, schools like Groton, Andover, Exeter, or St. Paul's. And it differed from them in philosophy as well. "This is not a 'strict' school," the headmistress, Elizabeth Hall, explained to students, "but it is a hard school . . . It is hard because finding out for yourself is far more difficult than following directions . . . It is hard because you are forced to meet yourself face to face . . . Rules would have given you an escape from thinking."[2]

I remember recognizing the uniqueness of the school culture when I first visited as a prospective applicant and learned that the penalty for lateness was not an accumulation of demerits or other dread punishment, but the requirement that you saw a log of wood for one of the many school fireplaces. It was annoying enough to have to do this task—especially in the cold of winter—to motivate you to try to be on time, but if you weren't, your sin was quickly expiated, and the campus was supplied with firewood. We made ourselves useful as we atoned for our tardiness.

Compared with other girls' schools of the era, Concord gave us enormous freedom. We could go into town—a few minutes' walk away—any afternoon after classes; we could take a bus to Cambridge or Boston on Saturdays or Sundays or spend weekends away from campus whenever we liked, as long as our grades were acceptable. This was not the norm at most boarding schools, for girls or boys.

One of my contemporaries remembers how her brother was "locked up" at Groton, while she roamed "free" at Concord. "They trusted us," she recalled.[3]

Dear Mrs. Hall,

could you please talk about revolutions on Friday.

On Wednesday could you talk about life.

Thank you

When Mrs. Hall asked what subjects we would like her to address in her chapel and assembly talks, this was one response.

For me, the sense of liberation was almost overwhelming. I was no longer isolated on a farm, but once again in a New England village like the one I had relished during the summers with my grandparents. And, like Scout or Nancy, I no longer had a mother scrutinizing and, as I perceived it, criticizing my every move. I was in a school where girls were what mattered, and where their intellects were reinforced and rewarded. I wrote a letter to my parents about once a week, and I would take my turn on the phone in the hall of the dormitory to call once or twice a month. From that time onward, my parents knew and understood little of my life. For the most part, it was not that I intentionally hid or kept things from them. It was that they had become almost irrelevant; they represented a constraint I had to manage and sometimes resist, but no longer the same challenge or looming emotional force.

But Concord was not without its own complexities and contra-dictions, and many of these were embodied in the personage of its extraordinary headmistress. Mrs. Hall had run the school for more than a decade when I arrived and was credited not only with dou-bling Concord's size but also with having transformed it from mostly a local day school into one with a national reputation. Yet Mrs. Hall put on no airs. She often referred to herself not as headmistress, but as "Head Mischief," an example of the gently self-mocking approach to life she called being "simply true."[4] It was the same outlook that led her to request we sing "Nearer My God to Thee" to her every year on her birthday. Even a half century later, my schoolmates speak of the impact she had on their lives. At a time when most of us came from families in which women did not pursue careers, here was a woman of such commanding presence and professional accomplishment that we were at once intimidated and entranced.

Concord's charismatic headmistress Elizabeth Hall renovating a historic house, mid-1950s.

Elizabeth Hall had entered Radcliffe College during World War II as a freshman at the age of thirty-two with four young children, two Nova Scotian maids, and a husband in the South Pacific. She commuted to Cambridge from suburban Weston by bicycle, train, and subway; nursed her children through measles, mumps, and chicken pox; and graduated in four years, magna cum laude and Phi Beta Kappa. Hired at Concord first as a teacher, she was soon elevated to be headmistress. In pearl necklaces, tweed suits, and sensible shoes, she strode across the campus followed by a string of miscellaneous dogs, who attended chapel and assembly with the rest of us. It was hard to imagine what she could not do. During her first year running the school, she drove a tractor named Beulah to clear away brush for a skating rink and a new athletic field. A few years later, she and a team of faculty and students dismantled an old Freewill Baptist Meeting House in New Hampshire and hauled it board by board to reassemble as the Concord Academy chapel. When the school later decided to name the building after her, she observed that the Hall Chapel would relieve the school of having to name something Hall Hall. She insisted that before we graduated, we needed to know how to change a tire, master Robert's Rules of Order, and execute the piercing whistle that she herself, fingers in mouth, often used to get our attention. I never accomplished the last of these and have had many occasions over the years to regret it. A skilled woodworker, she carved what she called the Ten Deadly Virtues into a plaque that hung outside the assembly hall, then proceeded to lecture us on each one in turn: Citizenship, Friendliness, Responsibility, Perseverance, Initiative, Cleanliness, Consideration, Generosity, Honesty, Self-Respect.[5]

Mrs. Hall's talks transfixed us. She took us seriously, urged us to think about Big Questions, and recruited us into a moral strenuousness intended to be the basis for a considered life. She seemed a combination of Socrates and General Patton. "Function in adversity. Finish in style," she charged us.[6] We were eager to know what she thought about democracy, freedom, sex, love. She once recalled a scene involving two fifteen-year-old students who asked for an appointment to see her. They came to her office and began to exchange pleasantries about the weather, settling uneasily into their chairs until the braver one finally said something like "We wondered if you could tell us why life is worth living?" "How much time do you have?" Mrs. Hall replied. "Ten minutes," came the answer. Preserved in the collection of her papers at Radcliffe's Schlesinger Library is a penciled—and unsigned—note from a student: "Dear Mrs. Hall, Could you please talk about revolutions on Friday. On Wednesday could you talk about life."[7]

We were terrified of her, yet we aspired to be like her. She seemed a living example of the qualities and virtues she spoke to us about. We desperately hoped for her approval, or at least her attention. I remember one evening after dinner during my first year at the school, she took me aside in the coatroom of the dining hall and told me I might make something of myself if I would just put my mind to it. Those were certainly not her precise words, but it was definitely her meaning. I must have done something that had not entirely pleased her. She didn't chastise me for what I had done—but rather for what I had not yet done and what she thought I might do. The impact of that moment on my life was enormous, not so much because of what she said, but because she had noticed me. When two years later I was elected president of the senior class, it was her congratulations that mattered most. She had challenged me and respected me. Most important, she had expected something of me.

And yet. She was no revolutionary and very much the product of her background and her time. Her father had been enormously rich—a "Wizard of Wall Street"—and she took for granted both her privilege and ours.[8] She assumed we would never need to worry about making a living and would always enjoy material prosperity. "You, who are possessed of much," she addressed us as she urged a noblesse oblige founded in a sharp sense of social hierarchy. "Much more is expected of us than is expected of others."[9]

She embraced hierarchies of gender as well. "Ladies, be ladies," she exhorted us, even as she drove a tractor, dismantled a building, ran a school, and held everyone around her in her thrall. She admitted to having been a committed tomboy and having bridled at such demands. Finally, she was sent away to school by her parents "to acquire more conventional graces." She acknowledged that to ask us to be ladies might sound like asking a girl to impersonate her great-grandmother. But the archaic term, she continued, connoted "womanly excellence," the fullest realization of our feminine selves, to which we should all aspire. A woman's femininity, she explained, "is proven by her willingness to sacrifice personal advancement in behalf of making the labor of man meaningful in terms of his noblest aims." What she told us in her beloved chapel and assembly talks seems from today's vantage point completely at odds with what we saw her doing before our eyes. "I do not think women are the equals of men," she baldly declared; in her view they were complementary. The struggle for political equality, she believed, had "forced the exaggerated claim that women were equal to men in every way and therefore should have every possible equality of opportunity and privilege." To have them compete would be, as she put it, "as ridiculous as it would be to put the wind instruments of the Boston Symphony Orchestra in competition to see which could produce the loudest music, or get first to the end of the score."[10]

Because men and women occupied different places in the world, this meant in her view that very few women would or should expect to pursue careers. It makes me sad these many years later to read words I must have heard long ago as her prescription for a woman's life. She expected us, she said, "to have the humility to accept the fact that it will be given to very few of us to accomplish anything in our lives to which we can refer as a measure of our success. This is . . . especially true of women, for most of whom the luxury of defining a specific accomplishment is over when they complete their formal education . . . From then on, for most of us, life is an unending series of small tasks,

usually well within our means to accomplish, and of continual inter-
ruptions." Did she really mean that? Was that all we could expect
from the future? Did she see herself as the exception? Did we actually
take this in? What did we do with such advice from one we respected
so deeply?

She failed at teaching us to be resigned to lives characterized by
unending series of small tasks, and I suspect that on some level she
intended to. "All of us have an overwhelming need to feel that our
lives amount to something," she continued just a few phrases later.
At the same time that she was telling us what we shouldn't do—
compete directly with men, pursue careers, think we were equal to our
husbands—she offered us what she cast as a more transcendent realm
of accomplishment. Men took care of life's practicalities; women were
responsible for "the keeping of society"—upholding ethics, defining
and transmitting values, calling the world to account. "Freed of the
necessity of competing in the economic sphere, woman, far better
than man, can define the idealistic goals for which we strive."[11]

I remember my initial encounter with this message, in a vespers
service my first week at the school. Mrs. Hall's ostensible subject
was clothes, an obvious preoccupation of adolescent girls. But she
quickly transformed the question of what we chose to wear into a
much broader consideration of our "attitude toward life." She could,
she said, "make no case for those who do not care about good . . .
those who have no value sense . . . no idea of justice . . . of what is
fair or unfair . . . of truth or falsehood . . . of beauty or ugliness . . . of
strength or weakness . . . of mercy or meanness . . . of love or hate . . .
of RIGHT or WRONG." This was a message that had a lasting effect on me—justice, truth, mercy, love: these were meant to be my
purposes and the purposes of my education. Mrs. Hall and Concord
would hold us to the highest standard—not of individual achievement
but of values and service. It was our job to make a better world. The
implication was that we were the carriers of justice and truth, while
those boys down the road at Middlesex or Belmont Hill were wor-

rying about careers and college. She charged us not to be "victory addicts"—those "whose each successive victory creates a craving for another."[12]

Many of Mrs. Hall's comments about women's place and duties sound to me now distressingly like pronouncements from the mid-nineteenth century. She was born just nine years into the twentieth, so perhaps these actually were views her parents had embraced and passed on to her. Historians of nineteenth-century white women have described an ideology of gendered "separate spheres," in which middle- and upper-class men inhabited a bustling public world with responsibility for politics and making a living. By contrast, the True Woman belonged at home, with the duty of enshrining a higher morality through domesticity and child-rearing. Scholars have pointed out, however, that this allocation of roles turned out to be something of a double-edged sword. To give women control over morality, truth, and the transcendent, as well as the character of future generations, was no meager assignment. Work in women's history over the past five decades has traced how women used this allocation of responsibility to propel themselves into the nineteenth century's myriad reform movements, from abolition to temperance—the latter a cause that, in an era in which respectable women did not drink, represented a direct assault on male prerogative. The sphere into which woman had been relegated turned out to give her considerable potential power—power that often came to be exercised well beyond the domestic realm in which it was expected to operate.

In Mrs. Hall's life, much the same transformation and turbocharging of the ideology of separate spheres took place, though I doubt she ever fully recognized the contradictions between her words and her deeds. She simultaneously embraced a deference to men and the conviction that women actually do the most important things in life. And she believed that education should be about those genuinely important things—not about what college you got into or what honors you might achieve (significantly, none were awarded at Concord) or what career you might pursue. Our education was to be about the Big Questions that she so regularly addressed with us. "Have the courage to be disturbed," she told us.[13]

The environment of a girls' boarding school was intense, especially during the interminable cold New England months that turned the community inward as the days shortened and the snow fell. Striving to live up to the standards Mrs. Hall had set for us could seem a bit like living in a version of *The Pilgrim's Progress*, with the Slough of Despond beckoning on every side. But our moral strenuousness was rehearsed and reinforced in the chapel and assembly talks we heard several times each week and in our conversations after Lights Out when roommates together explored the Meaning of Life. The 1960s had begun, and increasingly we aimed our reflections not just at ourselves and our innermost hopes and feelings but also at the realities of the world around us.

On January 20, 1961, my biology class was permitted to skip science for the day. We crowded instead into a housemother's apartment to watch John F. Kennedy's inauguration on her little black-and-white television. I remember an elderly, white-haired Robert Frost blinded and bedazzled by the reflection of the winter sun off the newly fallen snow, unable to read the poem he had composed for the occasion and reciting another from memory instead. And I remember the young president exhorting a new generation in a language of duty and responsibility. I heard his words as in many ways only a more rhetorically powerful version of messages we were used to receiving on a regular basis. "Ask not" what can be done for you, but what you can and must do for others. The world was waiting for us to make it better.

Our own little world at Concord could have benefited from more rigorous scrutiny. I reveled in this new environment of intellectual rigor, openness, and challenge, of empowered females and high expectations. But the school was overwhelmingly homogeneous; it was essentially a community of well-off white Anglo-Saxon Protestants.[14] My favorite history teacher could, sixty years later, list by name the

Jews at the school during our time there—he and one other teacher, fewer than a handful of students.[15] And I was living as well in a world even more racially segregated than the one I had left in Virginia. Segregated de facto rather than de jure, to be sure, which reinforced a certain moral complacency on the issue. Concord had not a single Black student until my senior year and no Black faculty or staff. The school was not especially unusual in this regard. Andover and Exeter—large, rich in scholarship funds, and cosmopolitan in outlook—had admitted a few Black students since the mid-nineteenth century, but the smaller boarding schools were more like Concord. Middlesex, Milton, Miss Porter's, and St. George's had no Black students in the fall of 1960. My brother Tys, who would graduate from St. Paul's the following spring, had no Black—or Jewish or Catholic—classmates and went on to Princeton, where only one member of his class of 1965 was African American.[16]

As the civil rights movement gained momentum in the early years of the 1960s, a few of us at Concord began to press to integrate the school and to push for more Black visitors to campus. But this was not yet anything like an era of student activism or student demands. We asked respectful questions and initiated polite discussions with our teachers and school administrators. We were pleased when at last one Black student arrived on campus in the fall of 1963 and when the following spring the Reverend John T. Walker, the first Black teacher at St. Paul's and later the Protestant Episcopal Bishop of Washington, a champion of social and racial justice, was invited to be our commencement speaker. Students greeted these changes with enthusiasm and perhaps a bit of over-solicitousness. When I learned that a Black student would be enrolling my senior fall, I asked if I could room with her but was told that assigning her to the president of the senior class might seem to focus too much attention on her arrival. Concord would be no Little Rock.

I was in the North, living in a town that had, a little more than a century before, been a stronghold of antislavery sentiment. The Concord residents Ralph Waldo Emerson and Henry David Thoreau became outspoken opponents of human bondage, and the revolutionary John Brown relied on the town for financial support for his raids in Kansas and his ill-fated 1859 effort to raise a slave rebellion at Harpers Ferry. A Concord schoolmaster was seized by federal marshals as one of Brown's "Secret Six" co-conspirators and rescued only when 150 townspeople rushed to his defense. Yet the flame of racial justice seemed to have flickered in the subsequent century. By custom and economic circumstance, twentieth-century Concord Academy was as segregated as the Virginia community in which I had grown up. But there was an important contrast. Although an ideology of racial difference and white superiority might well have lived somewhere deep within the hearts and minds of those around me, I never heard it articulated or justified. In fact, the opposite was true. We earnestly discussed *To Kill a Mockingbird* with our English teacher; we read of the violence against the Freedom Riders with horror and anger; and like so many other white Americans, we began to look on Martin Luther King, Jr., as an American hero. This gap between rhetoric and reality might justly be seen as rank hypocrisy. But it was neither blindness nor denial. And it also proved a foundation for change and possibility.

In February 1963, the headmaster of Groton School, John Crocker, extended an invitation to Concord Academy. An Episcopal minister, Crocker had long been dedicated to civil rights and had admitted the first Black student to Groton in 1952. He had come to know Martin Luther King, Jr., during King's years as a graduate student at Boston University and had persuaded him to spend two days at Groton, meeting with students and delivering a speech at an event that would include guests from nearby schools. We were told we could sign up if we were interested. On a cold winter night, a yellow school bus carrying about twenty Concord students drove the hour to Groton. It was six weeks before King would be jailed in Birmingham; it was six months before the March on Washington for Jobs and Freedom and the "I Have a Dream" speech, and two years before the Selma march. Yet in my eyes he was already a Great Man.

He was also a great orator. In his address to this gathering of students, King spoke more as the scholar than as the Black preacher who would rivet the crowd in Washington the following August. He cited anthropologists, philosophers, Shakespeare, John Donne, and the Bible. He educated us about the structure of syllogisms and the variety of Greek words for love. But the cadences of his speech, the poetry of his words, and the moral force of both the message and the man carried an emotional power that was captivating. We were seated on folding chairs in the school library, with the younger Groton boys graciously ceding their places and settling cross-legged on the floor for the fifty minutes of his talk. One Groton student secretly made a recording of the event that reinforces what I remember: we were so still and quiet as we listened to him that we hardly breathed.[17]

"America is essentially a dream," King began, but "a dream yet unfulfilled." He confronted us with the "sublime words" of the Declaration of Independence and the "strange paradoxes" of institutions like slavery and segregation that defied them. Throughout the speech, he repeated his call for "people of good will" to make the American dream a reality. He spoke of colonialism and its imminent end and urged us to take a world perspective on justice, not just because it was necessary to defeat communism but because it was right. He challenged the notion that there were superior and inferior races, insisting that different life outcomes were the results of differences of circumstance. He offered examples of accomplished "individuals in the Negro community" like Marian Anderson, George Washington Carver, Ralph Bunche, and Booker T. Washington as evidence of Black capacity. And he called for legislation and nonviolent direct action as necessary means to achieve justice and equality. He attacked what he called the "myth of time." Insisting that patience would yield change, he argued, would delay progress for decades if not centuries. Nor would education in and of itself solve the problem of racial injustice. Laws were necessary; they might not "change the heart but they could restrain the heartless." And the Gandhian method of nonviolent direct action could work on the conscience of the oppressor to compel genuine transformation. Moral ends must be pursued through moral means. Racial injustice, he reminded his Massachusetts audience, was not confined to one part of the country; housing and job discrimination flourished in the North just as segregation did in the South. This was a struggle to "save the soul of our nation," which was profoundly threatened by the "appalling silence of good people."[18]

King's talk was well calibrated for his young and idealistic audience. We recognized ourselves in his words—complacent residents of a region that did not feel the urgency of Georgia or Alabama. We wanted to see ourselves as among the "good people," but we had to recognize what had up to now been our "appalling silence." In less than an hour, King had not only explained the political, philosophical, and religious foundations of the civil rights movement but also charged us to join him. Here was a powerful response to John F. Kennedy's question, a compelling answer to the question of "what you can do for your country."

But that evening, on the bus ride home, what we did most immediately was to try to sleep or to finish the homework we had neglected in order to make the Groton trip. For me, the academic rigor of Concord was a joy and a constant pressure. Looking back, I realize I had no adequate science education there at all—a general science course in ninth grade and a biology course in twelfth—but my history, language, and literature courses were bracing. I took three languages and, though I eventually abandoned Latin, was able to enroll in advanced classes in both French and German when I got to college. Mr. Scult, my European history teacher junior year, urged us to always "think otherwise," to challenge ideas and assumptions. We relished the lively classroom debates that resulted even as we strived to master our seemingly endless assignments, including a requirement that we read the 1,225 pages of *War and Peace* over the Christmas holidays. I was supposed to be adjusting to contact lenses during the vacation, but they made the print blurry. Tolstoy won, and I continued to wear glasses. Mr. Scult took us through each step of writing a term paper, from research, which had to be based on primary sources, to drafts to final presentation. I applied these same lessons in my American history course my senior year to produce a condemnation of the House Un-American Activities Committee, its origins and outrages. My teacher, who had at one time been an FBI agent, awarded the paper a fine grade but suggested I might want to wait till the second semester of college to start my anti-HUAC campaign.

The most important thing I learned at Concord, however, was how to write. I am not sure quite how it happened, but I know it was in Miss Mendenhall's English class and had something to do with her painstaking attention to every word and phrase and paragraph of the papers she assigned so regularly. By the end of the year, it was clear to her and to me that my essays were far better than those I had been submitting in the fall.

There was a certain rhythm to intellectual growth at Concord— or at least to mine. Every September, I encountered a new crop of teachers who more or less humiliated me with lackluster grades and mediocre comments at half term. This had the effect of concentrating the mind—as in Samuel Johnson's oft-quoted remark about hanging. Mild panic would ensue until I clawed my way back to some level of respectability—by which point I would be able to see I had truly learned something. The school embraced the highest standards for our intellectual as well as our moral development. I was blessed not to grow up in the era of grade inflation.

The routines of classes and homework, chapel and assembly, athletics and chorus constituted what Mrs. Hall referred to as the "dailiness" of Concord life.[19] On some weekends, it was possible to sign up for a mixer at one or another boys' school and take the bus to St. Mark's or Exeter or St. Paul's for a dance. Students were paired up as "dates," assigned on the basis of height—tallest girl to tallest boy. I was very tall, so it seemed I often got a gangly basketball player or a boy who had shot up without gaining an ounce of weight and so looked like an emaciated crane. If you liked someone you met, you haunted the mailboxes the following week hoping for a letter. (The boy, of course, had to write first.) Wednesday was the critical day, and after Friday you more or less gave up. If the correspondence went well, you might be invited to a Spring or Fall Weekend—a dance, athletic contests, perhaps a concert, and a well-chaperoned overnight—at the boy's school.

Some girls developed relationships with conveniently located boys from nearby Middlesex, and that meant they could meet in the village and see one another more than once or twice a term. But for me, and for most boarding students, Concord was a female world in which our crushes and romances with absent males existed more in the realm of fantasy than reality. We spent far more time discussing these relationships with our roommates than we did interacting with the boys themselves. Does he really like me? Why hasn't he written? Did he meet someone else at another dance? Was I too forward answering his last letter? Did I respond too quickly? How hard-to-get should I pretend to be? How far should I let him go when I see him again? Would I ever find the perfect boyfriend? Would I ever find someone who wanted to marry me, or would I be consigned to living my life as an Old Maid?

Events beyond the school's walls had a way of pulling us back to a reality more consequential than our own adolescent lives. The Cold War was escalating and all too close to becoming hot as Kennedy raised the stakes with the Bay of Pigs invasion just weeks after his inauguration. The summer of 1961 saw the construction of the Berlin Wall and a speech from the president that urged all Americans to build fallout shelters. When, in October 1962, news broke of Russian missiles installed in Cuba just ninety miles from the Florida coast, direct nuclear confrontation seemed all but inevitable. I remember gathering with a handful of friends one evening in an empty room, sitting atop the desks we usually occupied for history class, and imagining the end of the world. What would we most regret not having experienced if our lives ended now? We were at once genuinely terrified, yet disbelieving that something so unthinkable could occur. And the security that accompanied that disbelief permitted a frisson of excitement about living in such a critical moment. Given what we now know about how very close to disaster the world came, it is clear there was little reason to temper our fear.

Kennedy took office my freshman year and was killed in the fall of my senior year, bookending an era in my own life as well as in the country's history. I was dissecting a crayfish in biology lab when someone burst through the door with the news of his death. Almost automatically we all drifted to the chapel. I assume there must have been teachers who sought to console us with speeches and prayers, but I have no recollection of them. The days that followed were a haze—of numbness, of incredulity that such things as assassinations happened in enlightened twentieth-century America, of grief intensified by television portraits of a widow in a bloody suit, of a riderless horse with boots backward in stirrups, of a flag-draped caisson, of two children tailored for this unthinkable performance in their brave and stylish matching coats. A great many of us thought it the most terrible occurrence of our lives.

In fundamental ways, Concord was a bubble. A bubble of privilege, to be sure. A bubble for white Anglo-Saxon Protestants. A bubble in which men were scarce and women ruled. But we could hardly hide from the world and the accelerating changes and crises all around us. The school urged that sense of responsibility on us, and the state of the world made it seem imperative. A few weeks after I returned from Groton uplifted by the words of Martin Luther King, Jr., I came across a flyer in a pile of materials collected by a school administrator into a folder labeled "Summer Opportunities." It described study trips to Russia and Eastern Europe, during which participants would meet with their counterparts behind the Iron Curtain to discuss foreign affairs and the means to avoid world war. If I was concerned about "the cold war and the tensions that divide the world," it proposed, I could join other young Americans and get to know those often considered our "enemies" as friends. I was invited to make "an investment in peace." The organizer, a man named Dick Hiler, had long worked with the American Friends Service Committee in Philadelphia. Although these were not officially AFSC trips, they were infused with Quaker values and purposes, and all the groups were interracial. One of the trips focused on East Germany, Czechoslovakia, and Yugoslavia, so I would be able to practice my German-language skills at the same time that I was working for world peace. For "youth . . . tired of having to sit by while bitterness and hatred threaten to engulf us all in war," this would be an opportunity to "do something *now* to see that we reach a peaceful settlement."[20]

I was one young American tired of sitting around waiting for one side or the other to decide to blow up the world with a nuclear strike. The anxieties of the Cuban missile crisis the preceding fall had only underscored the sense of helplessness that had gripped me from the time of the Sputnik launch and the Hungarian Revolution. But perhaps my generation could begin to fix this dangerous world our elders had created. We could help to end the threatening standoff between East and West by getting to know and understand one another, by forging ties that could serve as a foundation for a different world order. I knew I had to make this trip.

8

ACROSS FRONTIERS

Travel is fatal to prejudice.

—MARK TWAIN[1]

I find it hard to imagine why my parents let me go. The left-liberal Quaker politics that suffused the whole venture were far from theirs, and the racially integrated nature of the group must have troubled them, too. The very assumptions on which the trip was based flew in the face of two foundational doctrines with which I had grown up: segregation and anti-communism. But characteristically leaving child-related issues to my mother, my father ignored the matter of my summer plans. My mother, in turn, was reassured by the fact that I had learned about the program through my school—seeing this as some sort of at least tacit approval of the undertaking. Propriety rather than politics tended to be at the heart of her concerns about my activities in any case. But I recall my acute embarrassment when she insisted upon traveling to Philadelphia to interview those who would be in charge. She wanted to check out the chaperones.

Dick Hiler had founded the sponsoring organization, East-West Travel Seminar, and he sent two or three student trips to Eastern Europe and the Soviet Union each summer. Although he ran the overall operation, he was slated to lead a different trip from the one I chose in 1963, but he and Fritz Kempner, our senior leader, were both associated with reassuringly respectable Friends' schools and organizations. Somehow, they sufficiently allayed my mother's fears to persuade her to let me participate. I cannot help but wonder if, just two and a half years distant from her death—and already ill in ways none of us yet recognized—she was beginning to lose some of the strength of will required to control my life. It would be more charitable to think she had begun to acknowledge that I was my own person and had to make my own choices. I never saw convincing evidence of this, however, and we continued our battles to the very eve of her death. But, for whatever reason, she let me go.

My passport picture, 1963.

From late June till late August 1963, I traveled seven thousand miles in West and East Germany, Czechoslovakia, and Yugoslavia, as they were then known, in a Ford Microbus—a vehicle the size of a VW van—with six other high school students and two group leaders. We crowded in, three to a row, sometimes for drives of ten and twelve hours. As we sped along, we sang; we told jokes; we talked about our schools and families; we listened to Fritz tell us about growing up in Berlin before he fled Germany in 1938 in the face of rising antisemitism. Sometimes we staved off boredom by starting food fights or by upending our water thermoses over one another.

Five of us were male, four female; three of us were Black, one was Asian American, though this was not a category any of us recognized then. Beverly, daughter of a Japanese father and a German mother,

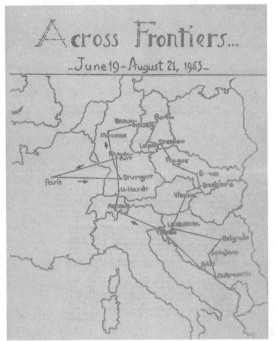

The cover of
the mimeographed
report from our trip,
summer 1963.

remembers that everyone we encountered simply "read me as white." They also read her as beautiful and regularly fell in love with her. One trio of young men we met in West Germany were so captivated both by Beverly and by the world of American jazz and folk music to which Chuck Lawrence, who was African American and an avid banjo player, introduced them that they drove a thousand miles to find us again on the Adriatic in Yugoslavia. At fifteen, I was the youngest participant, and I, too, was taken by what I saw as the sophistication and worldliness of the older members of our group. Music, fashion, progressive politics: these were realms of knowledge and experience that had made scant appearance in my cloistered girls' school life. I knew I could never be as cool as Chuck and Bev, and I was awed to be in their company.[2]

During an initial week of orientation in West Germany, we met with local high school students and began to immerse ourselves in the

Beverly Mikuriya
in Czechoslovakia,
summer 1963.

specifics of East-West politics. The Oder-Neisse question, the Hall-stein Doctrine, the Globke affair—I no longer even remember what they were. But, ever the eager student, I took pride in my new mastery of the details of the Eastern European situation and my ability to discuss it knowledgeably with young people on both sides of the Iron Curtain. Even if I could never succeed at being cool, I knew I was good at being smart.

On June 26, not long after our arrival in Europe, we watched on a television in a Stuttgart youth hostel as President Kennedy delivered his famous *"Ich bin ein Berliner"* speech to a crowd of more than a hundred thousand in West Berlin, just six hundred kilometers away. Twenty-two months earlier, in August 1961, the East German government had erected a concrete-block wall twelve feet high and almost a hundred miles long, snaking through the city to separate East and West and to stem the tide of disgruntled East Germans fleeing communism for freedom. Three hundred guard towers, barbed wire, searchlights, police dogs, minefields, and soldiers with shoot-to-kill orders made the barrier a vivid symbol of repression and cruelty. Within days of the wall's completion, the import of these orders—*der Schiessbefehl*—was made clear to the horrified eyes of the world: anyone endeavoring to breach the wall was summarily shot.[3]

By the end of 1961, twelve would-be escapees were dead; by the end of 1962, there were twenty-two more. We would see the white crosses erected by West Berliners at spaces along the wall to mark where people had been killed. These gruesome deaths—almost executions—were highly visible, described and photographed for newspapers and broadcast on televisions around the world. One story, involving a boy close to me in age, filled me with particular horror. Almost exactly a year after the wall was first erected, Peter Fechter, just eighteen years old, was shot as he endeavored to climb to freedom. He fell wounded in what was known as the "death strip" adjacent to the East German side of the wall. In full view of observers from both West and East, Fechter lay screaming for almost an hour as he bled to death. The East German guards had been ordered not to help him and to shoot anyone who did.

The wall offered the Free World a powerful symbol and propaganda tool in its characterization of soulless communism, and Berlin became the front line in the Cold War. Watching Kennedy on TV reinforced my sense of the significance of where we were headed for the future of peace and liberty in the world. "All free men," the president declared to the enormous crowd, "are citizens of Berlin." Berlin, and the unyielding wall built at its center to impede freedom, stood as the symbol of the real meaning of communism. Abandoning his carefully and diplomatically prepared remarks, Kennedy delivered a much more bellicose speech than his advisers had recommended, identifying the United States with the city now physically enclosed within the Eastern bloc. The American president almost taunted his enemies with the repeated phrase *"Lasst sie nach Berlin kommen."* If

there are those who don't understand "the great issue" between freedom and communism, if there are those who believe in compromise,
if there are those who think we can "work with the Communists . . .
let them come to Berlin." They would then understand why no concessions were imaginable. But our little band did hope for peace, rap-
prochement, and compromise, and Berlin was where we were going.

The Cold War rhetoric I had grown up with made me feel some
apprehension about coming face-to-face with communism. As we
met with groups of West German students and conversed with our
host families, we heard stories of acquaintances and even relatives
shot and killed as they had tried to flee over the wall. Others gave
accounts of friends within East Germany—officially, the Deutsche
Demokratische Republik—arrested and even jailed for speaking out
against the president, Walter Ulbricht, and his regime. One group of
boys in school in Stuttgart told us why they had decided to flee East
Germany the very day before the wall was erected. On one of our last
evenings in the West, we gathered at the house of their teacher. He
had invited a student who had recently escaped from East Berlin to
join him in warning us that our notions of peaceful ties with the DDR
were naïve and even dangerous. People will not speak honestly to you,
the student reported, because they always fear informers. Phones were
tapped; residences were bugged. We would be watched, and so would
those with whom we came in contact.[4]

These descriptions and admonitions seemed frightening but a bit
unbelievable. This was the stuff of spy thrillers. Why would anyone
bother with us? Surely our hosts were overstating things. Chuck Lawrence, judging the evening, observed, "These people were too close
to the situation." We were not caught up in the immediacy of the
conflicts the way they were, and our greater objectivity, we presumed,
would enable us to make our contribution to East-West reconciliation and peace. "Can we deal with this situation by continually telling
ourselves how bad it is and feeding the flames of fear and hate? I
think not," Chuck concluded.[5] We were determined to penetrate the

abstractions of communism by connecting with real human beings and their lives.

Of course, our hosts were exactly right. With the wall in place, the DDR's notorious Ministry for State Security—the Stasi—was perfecting the East German surveillance state. Not only was there one Stasi agent for approximately every sixty-three citizens, but thousands of other East Germans were also recruited to report regularly on relatives, neighbors, and friends. If these part-time informers are included, it's been estimated that there was 1 agent for every 6.5 inhabitants.[6] To an innocent and idealistic group of Americans in 1963, such realities seemed unimaginable. But our innocence would have its consequences.

The prospect of crossing the frontier of the Free World was disquieting, but I was apprehensive as well about other new experiences. I had never lived as closely with Black people as I was going to that summer, and never in conditions of community and equality. I affirmatively wanted to do this; I had sought out this opportunity. But I worried about the baggage I brought with me. What terrible and humiliating assumptions had I imbibed that I would unwittingly reveal? Would I make my interactions with my Black traveling companions feel stilted and awkward? How much was I a captive of what we today might call implicit biases? Could I succeed in making Black friends? I had never before even been in circumstances that made such relationships possible.

The African American members of our group were accomplished in ways that underscored the absurdity of any ideology of white superiority. Madelyn Nix had been one of the nine students who had integrated Atlanta's public schools two years before. Chosen from more than a hundred who volunteered, Madelyn had been tested by school authorities for academic and psychological qualities, and selected for her intelligence and equanimity. As she later explained, they wanted "candidates whom they saw as smart, low key, slow to anger, and focused . . . I loved education, so I did not feel a lot of pressure and I kept my anger to myself."[7] Madelyn was the daughter of the dean of students at Morehouse College, a prominent individual in the city's Black elite and a part of the Black educational consortium that also included Spelman College and Atlanta University. Her mother had been a college valedictorian and worked as a teacher. Hers was a family considerably better educated than mine.

Madelyn Nix in Berlin, summer 1963.

Atlanta was seen as more moderate on racial issues than much of the rest of the Deep South, but the officials responsible for school integration had felt compelled to prepare for the kind of violence and upheaval that had erupted elsewhere. A biracial coalition had undertaken months of planning to ready the nine students for what they might confront at the four schools in which they were scheduled to enroll. Members of Atlanta's Quaker community served as coaches to the students during the summer before their matriculation, preparing them for the opposition and hostility they were likely to face. Robert Coles, a Harvard psychiatrist, met regularly with the students, who would ultimately serve as subjects for *Children of Crisis*, his study of youth resilience.[8] As the opening of school approached, the Atlanta Nine were barraged with threats—facilitated by the Ku Klux Klan's distribution of their names and addresses. On August 30, 1961, Madelyn—sent off from home in a police car surrounded by cheering Morehouse students—entered Joseph E. Brown High School, named for Georgia's Confederate-era governor. There was no violence at any of the four newly integrated schools. "Last week," *Time* declared, "the moral siege of Atlanta ended in spectacular fashion with the smoothest token integration ever seen in the Deep South."[9] President Kennedy congratulated the white citizens of Georgia on their restraint but, tellingly, offered no words of praise or appreciation to the courageous Nine.

Integration in Atlanta may not have produced violent confrontations, but it could not have felt frictionless to those in its midst. For the remainder of the school year, Madelyn endured daily racial insults. Teachers refused to call on her, and her classmates either ignored her or played what she, with characteristic composure, dismissed as "pranks." When spring brought the customary senior trip, the principal called Madelyn to his office. The venue selected for the outing was segregated, he explained, so Madelyn could agree not to go and let everyone else enjoy themselves, or she could insist on being included and see the trip canceled. Madelyn stayed home.

But she remained undaunted. "'Try' is my favorite word," she later explained. Raised in the heart of Atlanta's civil rights community, Madelyn witnessed the sacrifices and struggles of her neighbors, individuals like Morehouse's president, Benjamin Mays, or her family's pastor, the Reverend Martin Luther King, Jr. She explained her own decision to become one of the Atlanta Nine: "We were dedicated to excellence and willing to participate in any way that we could because we wanted a better world for those yet unborn." Madelyn was a girl who dared. She was one of those students whose courage and commitment I had been admiring since I first read about Little Rock. I felt privileged to hear her story and to spend nine weeks in her company. The unflappability that had made her such a good choice for the Atlanta schools made her an ideal traveling companion. "We have great coping skills," she said of the Atlanta Nine.[10] These skills served as a model for our Traveling Nine as well.

At twenty, Chuck Lawrence was older than the rest of us and officially a co-leader of the trip. A rising junior at Haverford College, he was one of only two African Americans in his class. Tall and handsome, with a deep voice and a ready laugh, Chuck exuded energy and always seemed poised for action—about to take off from the blocks like the track star he was. But he had a gentle side, too, and took pains to pay close attention to us, his charges, and respond to our thoughts and moods. The banjo he had brought with him drew our group more closely together and brought strangers to us as well. I have many images of him in my mind's eye—on the Charles Bridge in Prague, on a dock beside the harbor at Dubrovnik, at a rest stop on the Autobahn—surrounded by curious onlookers enveloped in a community of song.

Like Madelyn, Chuck was from an academic family. His father had studied with W. E. B. Du Bois and was a professor of sociology at Brooklyn College for thirty years. His mother was a psychiatrist and a professor at Columbia Medical School. They had begun breaking barriers a generation before *Brown v. Board*. Chuck's father was one of the most prominent Black lay leaders in the Episcopal Church and would spearhead its later efforts against South African apartheid. His mother, Margaret Morgan Lawrence, was the only Black undergraduate at Cornell University when she entered in 1932, and when the university's medical school rejected her because of her race, she became the third African American admitted to Columbia Medical

School. Chuck had grown up in New York City and nearby Rockland County in what he described as "very white spaces and schools." He frequently found himself, he reflected, with people "where it was their first experience with Blackness." Chuck's freshman roommate at Haverford, he recounted, was from Virginia, and "I was the first Black person that he knew at all other than servants who worked in his house." Chuck was accustomed to the likes of me.[11]

But he and Madelyn and Shirley Bradford, the other Black member of our group, were not accustomed to what greeted them in Eastern Europe. Many inhabitants of the countries we were visiting had never seen a Black person, and they looked upon them with wonder, often sidling up to touch their skin or feel their hair. Chuck remembered a man in an East Berlin restaurant who loudly remarked to his son as they rose to leave, "Wait until we tell your mother we talked to a Negro today." Madelyn recalled a curious onlooker asking her if she could rub her skin color off.

Race was prominent in the minds of nearly every group we met behind the Iron Curtain because anti-American propaganda made racial injustice and unrest central to the critique of capitalism and the West. The Kennedy administration, Chuck reported at the end of the summer, had been represented to the inhabitants of the Eastern bloc "in such a way that it might well have been mistaken for the K.K.K." Dr. King's 1963 Birmingham campaign, taking place nearly five thousand miles away, produced a stream of horrifying images of children under attack from police dogs and fire hoses that our communist hosts shared with us regularly. "If you ask East Germans about freedom in Berlin they ask you about freedom in Birmingham. If you ask Czechs about freedom in Prague they ask you about freedom in Jackson, Mississippi," Chuck wrote. "We always tried to respond in a way which would counteract these biased reportings without in any way hiding the truth." But our best argument was ourselves. "No one could honestly look at our group," Chuck concluded, "and still feel that every white American was a bigot." Madelyn agreed: "There was no racial prejudice among our group. This . . . amazed and impressed quite a number of the people we came in contact with."[12] For me, it was life-changing: a proof of what I had professed to believe, a realization of what I had before understood only as an ideal and an abstraction.

On July 7, we crossed from West to East Berlin through Checkpoint Charlie, already legendary in Cold War annals. "You are leaving the American Sector," a large sign reminded us. It was, in the words of one historian, "the most dangerous place on earth," and would be "the epicenter of global conflict for nearly three decades."[13] Only a few yards away was a site we had visited and photographed—the section of the wall where Peter Fechter, so close to us in age, had bled to death just a year before. I worried that once we entered East Germany, even we American citizens might find it more difficult to leave than we expected. If people were trying so hard to get out, what was I doing attempting to get in? It felt a little like we were crossing into a prison. A large sign reminded us in four languages—English, French, German, and Russian—"You are leaving the American Sector"—as if the barriers and bunkers and watchtowers would let us forget. Armed soldiers with forbidding expressions stood guard on both sides of the dividing line as we waited to have our documents scrutinized—first by the Americans, then by the East Germans. Restless and not a little anxious as we stood alongside our van, we began to dance. The preceding fall, the Motown star Marvin Gaye had released a hit single called "Hitch Hike," which had inspired a similarly named dance. Thumbs raised, bodies swinging to our own vocal rendering of the song, we decided to Hitch Hike our way across the Iron Curtain. American and East German guards seemed equally disapproving— here was one thing they could agree on—but in rhythm, in harmony of voice and movement, and in fun, we tried to contain our nervousness about what lay ahead in a country we had been taught to regard as the enemy.

Dancing the Hitch Hike at Checkpoint Charlie, July 1963.

As soon as our minibus rolled through the barrier that officially marked the border of East Berlin, we were greeted by a young man with dark hair, large glasses, and a briefcase who introduced himself as our guide. Roland was a student at East Berlin's Humboldt University, assigned to us by the Department for Youth Tourism to Foreign Countries of the German Travel Bureau of the German Democratic Republic. He produced a detailed itinerary of how we would spend our time during our stay, with, of course, his constant accompaniment. He was to be our minder. He introduced himself with a lengthy speech, which I summarized in our end-of-trip report: "West Germany was a fascist state which aroused militarism and anti-Semitism in the people. The United States had no free elections and its claims to democracy were merely a farce, for the whole government was run by Rockefellers and Morgenthaus who had bought their way to power. The DDR, on the other hand, was a state run by the people who enjoyed all freedoms because they were given all possibilities for development."[14] We bombarded him with objections and counterexamples, and strengthened our case as in the following days we encountered more and more instances of repression of speech and movement. The incontrovertible existence of the wall made his position a difficult one to defend. But he struggled valiantly.

Roland loved arguing with us—and we with him. Determined to demonstrate the benevolence and flexibility of the East German state, he gradually began to permit us to deviate from our mandated schedule. Fritz had old childhood and family friends who had ended up in the East when Germany was divided, and he arranged for us to visit and talk with them, which gave us a clear-eyed view of the repression and hardship that characterized life in the DDR. Citizens stood in long lines for basic groceries; shortages of butter, meat, and fresh vegetables were routine. Travel was restricted, and prohibited outside the Eastern bloc; Western books and newspapers were forbidden; it was dangerous—even within the walls of one's own house—to speak against the regime. Fritz's friends communicated in whispers, by indirection and innuendo, pulled the shades, turned the radio volume up, and urged us not to repeat to Roland what they'd said. Hearing our hosts describe the oppressions and deprivations that characterized their daily lives and witnessing their very real fears made an impression that similar stories delivered in the safety of West Germany had not.

But I also developed a certain appreciation for Roland's idealism about the socialist project. He proudly toured us around a collective farm and extolled the possibilities for both greater equality and greater productivity in communism's agricultural organization. We visited a calisthenics festival at a huge stadium in Leipzig and learned details of the DDR's system of free education, up to and including Roland's own university studies. No one in East Germany was unemployed; no one went hungry; everyone had free medical care. I began to understand that when East German communists used—as they often did—the word "freedom," they meant something quite different from what I had come to understand. "Freedom" in my mind had meant exclusively "freedom from": freedom from censorship, from restrictions of movement, from governmental dictates or oppression. It was a revelation for me to hear East Germans speaking of a "freedom to": freedom to be educated, to get health care, to work. Personal freedoms, freedom of the press, freedom of movement, they argued, could all be sacrificed—or, Roland often insisted, just postponed—in pursuit of the Marxist goal of freedom from economic oppression. Freedom began to seem a much more complicated matter than I had appreciated. Sacrificing "freedom from" still seemed to me an unacceptable trade-off, but I gained a glimmer of insight into what the world might look like through a dedicated communist's eyes. I had to confront the limits of my own thinking.[15]

On our last night with Roland, he accompanied us to Dresden's Freundschaftsball—five hundred or so students, including foreign delegations from Russia, Poland, Bulgaria, Cuba, and Czechoslovakia, all introduced to rousing applause. When our turn came, we were greeted enthusiastically, too, and young people from across the globe crowded around us. A high school rock-and-roll band took the stage, and soon we were leading this panoply of world youth in the twist. With Chuck and Shirley joining the band for vocals, the Freundschaftsball became something more like an exuberant American rock concert. As Chuck wrote, "With the gyrations of many pelvises and the wrenching of many backbones, the iron curtain came tumbling to the floor."[16]

Roland was reflective about his time with us, admitting on this last night together that we had influenced him to see things a bit differently. "I trust Ulbricht and Khrushchev," he affirmed, "and I believe in what they are trying to establish for the worker. I also now trust you and believe that you will not try to force your system on us. This is all we ask—time to try to work socialism out."[17]

Ulbricht's government, though, seemed no longer to entirely trust Roland. Fritz dropped in on Roland a few weeks after our trip ended and found our guide had "paid a price." He was no longer to be permitted to lead Western traveling groups and had been assigned a job as a dishwasher in a youth hostel until the university opened in the fall. Roland assumed that a Communist Party member listening to one of our many discussions had reported him. Fritz brought another student group to the DDR the following summer, but after that he was refused entry: "You are not welcome among us!" he was officially told. Only when the wall fell would Fritz be able to travel in eastern Germany again.[18]

We were probably lucky not to get into more trouble. I had developed a friendship with a student we met in Leipzig, and after several encounters he took me aside and told me of his plans to try to escape to the West. He hoped I might help him. Was he sincere? Was his approach an effort at entrapment? Either way it was dangerous, so did it matter? I couldn't imagine what I could do that would be useful, but it was my sense of incapacity, rather than what would have been an appropriate level of caution, that prevented my taking any action. Roland, it turned out, had in some sense succeeded in making us regard the DDR as less menacing and repressive than in fact it was.[19]

Prague was no more than a two-hour drive from Dresden, but as we passed through the barbed-wire boundary between East Germany and Czechoslovakia, we felt ourselves not just in a different country but in a different world. Our time in the DDR had been intense— partly because Berlin had become such a worldwide symbol and focus of East-West hostility, partly because Fritz had connected us with friends who revealed their deep opposition to the Ulbricht regime, and partly because the reality of the wall underscored the repressiveness of the East German state. Several of us, including me, had German-language skills good enough to enable us to operate, to a degree, outside the bubble our guide had been instructed to construct for us. None of us spoke a word of Czech, however, so we would become dependent on our new guide, Eduard, and the portrait of his country he hoped to convey. He described, and we thought we saw, a greater degree of openness, even in what we knew was a totalitarian regime.

We had visited the DDR at a time of rising repression and international tension in the aftermath of the erection of the Berlin Wall;
Czechoslovakia, by contrast, was at a moment of emerging liberal-
ization. The forces that would erupt in the democratic demands of
the Prague Spring five years later were starting to be felt. Economic
stagnation in the early 1960s had prompted widespread criticism of
state centralization and a push for the incorporation of more market-
oriented elements into Czech life; restrictions on travel outside the
country were loosening; artists and writers began to insist on free
expression, and the internationally influential New Wave cinema had
appeared. Just a few months before our arrival, a festival celebrating
Franz Kafka marked the end of an official ban on his works.

I was only vaguely aware of all this, but I noticed a real contrast
with the atmosphere in East Germany. In 1968, the Prague Spring
would be crushed by Russian tanks, and the newly imposed regime
of subjugation and censorship that followed persisted until the Velvet
Revolution of the 1990s. But I had little inkling of the stops and starts
Czechoslovakia would experience in its movement toward democracy.
I simply saw it as further along than the DDR on what I assumed to
be an irreversible route toward Western-style freedom.[20]

In recent decades, as Prague has become one of the world's most
visited tourist destinations, attractions like the Charles Bridge and
Wenceslas Square are jammed at all hours of the day and night.
Communist Czechoslovakia was something of a magnet for travelers
from the Eastern bloc, but this was a limited tourist trade, and we
had access to the city free from the crowds that have now become
constant. We spent far less time meeting with youth or school groups
and discussing world issues than we had in the DDR. Eduard chose
sights and activities that he thought would entertain us and show
off Czechoslovakia's beauty and storied past: a castle, a boat ride on
the Vltava, an outdoor staging of *Aida*—with performers singing in
three different languages. Eduard's one ill-considered choice was to
take us to a brewery where tastings of legendary Pilsner left several of

our group—almost all underage and inexperienced drinkers—quite inebriated.

In Prague and in Brno and Bratislava, our other two stops, we stayed in youth hostels where we met young travelers from parts of the world we had little direct knowledge of: the Soviet Union, non-aligned African countries, even Red China, as we knew it then. Once again, the twist proved a key instrument of international diplomacy. I began to think that what these new friends seemed to envy most about America was not so much our political freedoms as rock and roll and, especially, our blue jeans. We were in communist Eastern Europe, but these interactions gave us a sense of a much wider non-Western world and introduced us to students from every part of the globe who, like us, worried about a future of international polarization and conflict.

Yugoslavia was even more different from Czechoslovakia than Czechoslovakia had been from the DDR. Under Tito (Josip Broz), Yugoslavia had determinedly forged its own independent path as a communist nation, declaring itself assertively nonaligned and refus-ing to ally with Russia or join the Warsaw Pact. Tito had led what has been seen as the most successful resistance movement in Europe against German occupation, and his wartime prestige fueled his post-war power. Breaking away from Stalinist control in 1948, Tito sought to create a united Yugoslavia out of the ethnic divisions that would ultimately destroy it. When we crossed the border headed toward Ljubljana, he had been in power for nearly two decades, and the pre-ceding spring he had been named president for life. His more market-oriented version of communism had already achieved a dramatic increase in his country's standard of living and personal consumption, and Workers' Self-Management policies devolved power to the hands of the people. Tito's authoritarianism was tempered by a greater toler-ance of individual freedom than in the DDR. We were not required to have guides or minders and could explore as we liked; we succeeded in tracking down a current copy of *The New York Times* in Belgrade; we could see religious observances flourishing in every city we visited.

We also witnessed genuine enthusiasm for the Yugoslav nation on a visit to a Youth Brigade Workcamp charged with building part of a road from Belgrade to Dubrovnik. Beginning in the last days of World War II, the Yugoslav Communist Party recruited students to spend their summers helping build roads and railroads in a country that had infrastructure more appropriate to the nineteenth century than the modern world it wanted to join. Before the war, there had been fewer than a hundred kilometers of paved roads in the entire country, but patriotic youth were now challenged to construct a new Highway of Brotherhood and Unity that would help revolutionize not just transportation but citizens' lives as well.

The writer Aleksandar Hemon has chronicled the transformation in his parents' circumstances as they, like so many other Yugoslavs, moved from rural deprivation into solid middle-class existence in the years after the war, and he recounts as well his mother's participation in road-building youth brigades. Born in 1937, she was an enthusiastic and idealistic volunteer in what Hemon has described as the "common project" that was socialist Yugoslavia. As our group came to see firsthand, road building was about a great deal more than roads. Shoveling stones, digging into hills to flatten the grade, we toiled alongside Yugoslav teenagers who sang of the joy of working, the greatness of Tito and Yugoslavia, and the noble deeds of the partisans who had defeated the Nazis. When we returned from the labor site at day's end, the singing turned to dancing as we joined hands and circled the camp.

As a boy in the 1970s, Hemon rejected his mother's youthful ideals and dedication. Yugoslavia had begun to seem to him less an ambitious project than a "failed experiment," and Aleksandar's generation embraced cynicism over nationalist fervor. His mother's Highway of Brotherhood and Unity was in his view the "Highway of Youth and Foolishness."[21] But in 1963, among our Yugoslav counterparts, Hemon's mother's enthusiasm still represented a level of grassroots support for a communist state that I had not previously encountered.

Eastern Europe was not simply about repression. Here were expressions of dedication and civic-mindedness that made my Americanism seem in many ways shallow and wanting. I had never shoveled stones for my own country, yet here I was in my own youth and foolishness endeavoring to move mountains on the other side of the world.

Dubrovnik, summer 1963. Me, Shirley Bradford, Beverly Mikuriya, Chuck Lawrence, Fritz Kempner, and Chuck and Bev's German fan club.

We endured Yugoslavia's roads and mountains firsthand during two ten-hour days of driving through the rugged slopes of the Dinaric Alps to an International Youth Camp in Dubrovnik, an astonishingly beautiful city of medieval buildings and alleyways perched on the Adriatic. We found ourselves in a kind of mini–United Nations, with special emphasis on the nonaligned states. In this setting, divisions of East and West, of communist and capitalist, faded in the face of far more complex allegiances. National identities dimmed as we made connections that transformed individuals into friends rather than Egyptians, Ghanaians, or Poles. My time in Yugoslavia upended many of the assumptions I had held about the polarizations of the

Cold War and the unmitigated repressiveness of a socialist state. Yugoslavia, in all its complexity, was unlike any nation I had seen or imagined. It would be hard for me to envision the world in binary East/West, communist/free terms again.

Dubrovnik was also a place that fit uneasily into a narrative of socialist discipline and unrelenting dedication to political or national purpose. It had not yet become one of the most prominent resort destinations in Europe, but the setting on the Adriatic, with its crystalline waters, invited a kind of sybaritic indulgence in sun and sea. We put aside the earnestness that had prevailed for eight weeks and just had fun—with each other, with the West German friends who had showed up in search of Chuck and Bev, and with the other denizens of the youth camp. We swam, we sang, we danced, and we talked endlessly. One evening I accepted an invitation from someone who introduced himself as a Nigerian prince to come to his royal tent for refreshments. Chuck was dubious about the arrangements and wary about this man who was so much older than I. He probably also had figured out how clueless I was about men—and even boys. Chuck lurked protectively nearby while I had an awkward but memorable evening parrying the prince's advances. I felt—both proudly and a little nervously—very far from home.

My 1963 trip was a journey to three countries that no longer exist. A divided Germany has since been reunited, a united Czechoslovakia has since divided, and Yugoslavia disintegrated into cruel ethnic warfare before emerging as multiple new states. The nationalist enthusiasm we had seen in the Youth Brigade Workcamp turned out to be a somewhat desperate effort to create not just a highway but an elusive nation of Brotherhood and Unity. And the multilanguage performance of *Aida* we attended in Bratislava might have offered us a clue about the divisions roiling beneath the surface of a forcibly united Czechoslovakian state.

I could only hope for, rather than truly envision, the end of the Cold War, which took nearly three more decades to arrive. But we thought we were at least doing our small part to accelerate that day. Asked by Fritz to write about the most memorable part of the trip, I responded, "For one who has not been with us this summer, it is easy to be cynical and to laugh" at our ambitions to "bring about a better understanding among the cold war participants." But, I continued, "it is not often, I think, that one lives in such an atmosphere of learning and examining, conscious always of a sense of purpose."[22] Learning and examining, suffused with a sense of purpose: this, I recognized, was how I hoped to live the rest of my life. I had spent nine weeks in an atmosphere I hadn't known existed.

We arrived back in the United States on August 27, 1963, the day before the March on Washington for Jobs and Freedom. We had heard almost nothing about it in the isolation of our travels. Perhaps if we had known more, Madelyn later mused, we could have made it our final destination.[23]

9

CATCHING UP WITH THE REVOLUTION

No American is without responsibility.

—MARTIN LUTHER KING, JR.[1]

I heard from Dick Hiler not long after I returned and had settled back into my Concord routine. He had an idea for a different sort of trip for the following summer, and he wanted me to come. Peace was not only an international challenge. The events of 1963 in Birmingham and the contagious energy of civil rights protests across the South had underscored the deep fissures of race and politics in our own country. "Here too," in the United States, Dick's brochure for his new program would read, "there are areas of conflict and tension which need to be understood before they can be resolved." Violence could not be the answer; the "real solution must be born out of understanding, humility and a respect for all men, even those with whom we disagree."

Dick proposed to assemble a group of fifteen high school and college students and three adult leaders to travel to sites in the South "in an effort to learn more about the people, the problems and the possibilities of our nation."[2] His work in the high school program of the American Friends Service Committee had connected him to residents—and particularly young people—in places throughout the South where the AFSC had been working to build bridges across racial divides, to enhance communication between whites and Blacks, and to support struggles for civil and human rights.

The commitment to reasoned and informed discourse with one's enemies had attracted me to the Eastern European trip, and these

Dick Hiler and
his wife, Heide. Dick
organized the summer
programs in Eastern
Europe and the South,
and accompanied us
on our civil rights
journey, summer
1964.

instincts had only been reinforced by a summer's deep immersion in Quaker values. Applying these principles to the South's racial conflicts was even more appealing, perhaps because those on the other side of the debate were people like my own family. It was hard for me to dismiss all white southerners as irredeemable enemies. And talking, discussing, and exchanging perspectives in the hope of persuading and enlisting others was my favorite form of action, uniting as it did the realm of ideas, which I loved, with my fervent desire to help fix what I saw as a broken world.

Looking back now, the idea that we would be able to talk frankly and win the trust of both Blacks and whites at a time of such bitter polarization seems astonishingly naïve, and it would prove to be so from the outset of our journey. Though Dick's brochure stated that we would "plan to view situations as objectively as possible," we were already far from objective or disinterested about what was going on in the South. We were an integrated group, and our feelings were wholeheartedly on the side of the Black freedom struggle. Some of our members had been arrested and jailed as teenage activists in their own communities before they joined us, and they had few illusions about the possibility of convincing so-called white moderates to support change in long-standing racial arrangements. We lived with Black families in the communities we visited; we joined them in rallies, voter registration drives, petition campaigns, and picket lines. We were seen from the start as part of the invading army of "outside agitators" that white southerners feared and decried.[3]

I arrived at the Quaker Fellowship House in Washington, D.C., on June 22, 1964, to begin our orientation. The day before, three civil rights workers—James Chaney, Andrew Goodman, and Michael Schwerner—had disappeared near Philadelphia, Mississippi. There was little doubt they had been kidnapped and likely killed by white segregationists, probably under the auspices of the Ku Klux Klan. The three men had been part of a project called Freedom Summer, organized by a coalition of civil rights organizations to bring students from the North to register voters and combat segregation. The implications of these disappearances were not lost on me or the others in our group, who were all meeting one another for the first time. No one wanted to seem cowardly or lacking in commitment to our own project, but we talked nervously about what we were hearing on the news, sharing the few available details as we speculated about what had actually happened. Dick tried to reassure us by emphasizing that from the beginning he had explicitly ruled out any Mississippi time for us, judging it too dangerous. But that seemed small comfort. I, and others, I would guess, quietly wondered, "Well, is Alabama all that much better?" But no one openly voiced fears or second thoughts. Instead, the sense of risk and danger drew us closer as we were briefed on recent civil rights developments and on what to anticipate in the communities we would visit.[4]

And from our very first evening together, we sang, as we would all summer—while we prepared our meals, when we gathered for meetings or discussions, when we drove southern roads in our two Volkswagen buses. Nearly every memory I have of the summer comes with a musical accompaniment. One of our group leaders, Don Wardwell, was almost a professional musician, with a twelve-string guitar and an endless repertoire of folk songs. "The Cat Came Back" may have been our favorite of those, chronicling the impossible triumphs of a downtrodden feline over every imaginable adversity in verse after verse. Surviving against the odds was a welcome theme. But the songs that meant most to us were the freedom songs we would sing not just with one another but in mass meetings at Black churches and with the many young civil rights activists eager to voice their determination to "let nobody turn me 'round." Singing provided the glue that bound our group together and helped join us to the communities of African Americans in which we would find ourselves.

Several members of our group came from these very communities and were already deeply engaged participants in protests and demonstrations. Eddie Sharperson and Willie Haigler, from Orangeburg, South Carolina, had each been arrested many times—more than a dozen for Eddie alone, he reported. Irvin Walker of Jackson, Mis-

Me, George Crowell, Lorna Rhodes, and the back of Harry Nussdorf's head, at one of our group's regular meetings to discuss our experiences across the South, summer 1964.

sissippi, was preparing to enter Ole Miss in the fall as the first Black student to be admitted without a court order. George Crowell of Birmingham came from a family at the heart of the movement there. Larry Ledeen, who was white, had parents who were leaders in the South Carolina Committee for Human Rights; Linda Martin, also white, was part of a progressive and activist family in York, Pennsylvania. Others of us could claim no such credentials and were simply idealists from communities all along the Eastern Seaboard—from Lincoln, Massachusetts, to Athens, Georgia.

When we gathered in June, Washington had been consumed for months by the final debates over what would become the Civil Rights Act of 1964. Representatives from the Friends Committee on National Legislation, a Quaker lobbying group, updated us on the status of the measure. President Kennedy had introduced the bill almost exactly a year before, but it had been blocked by southern legislators. When he became president after Kennedy's assassination in November 1963, Lyndon Baines Johnson took it up again, focusing on its passage as a necessary tribute to the slain president's legacy. But southern opposition remained strong. A fifty-four-day filibuster had ended when the Senate passed the first successful cloture vote ever on a civil rights measure. On June 19, just as we were arriving in Washington, the bill itself was at last considered. It won only a single southern senator's vote. But that was enough to send it to Johnson's desk, where he would sign it on July 2.

The act would have significant ramifications for our summer. The part of the measure that had aroused the greatest opposition and that seemed most revolutionary in its potential impact was Title II, the section dealing with public accommodations, which prohibited discrimination in hotels, restaurants, movie theaters, and other establishments that were in any way connected to interstate commerce. This was a direct shot at the heart of the legally mandated racial segregation that was pervasive and foundational in southern society. The new measure—and the National Association for the Advancement of

Colored People—would encourage us to join with local civil rights advocates to undertake tests of compliance with the law in stores and restaurants by dispatching interracial delegations from our group to seek service at restaurants and businesses. Life in the company of Black people made the opportunities for direct action and protest almost infinite and almost inevitable. Simply ordering a root beer at the A&W Drive In could be—and was—seen as a threat to civilization as the white South had come to know it.

It seems highly fitting that our first stop was Farmville, in Prince Edward County, Virginia. Not only was this my home state, but Prince Edward had become the symbol and battleground of the campaign for "Massive Resistance" to school desegregation that had been designed and led from my own county by our neighbor Senator Harry Byrd. *Brown v. Board*, he insisted, had to be opposed at any cost; Virginia would close its public schools entirely rather than integrate them.[5]

Twenty-five miles east of Appomattox, Farmville was located about fifty-five miles southwest of Richmond on the route of Robert E. Lee's final retreat. Small-acreage tobacco farmers, both Black and white, provided the county's chief economic activity, and the comparatively high number of Black landowners enjoyed a measure of independence from direct white control that may have contributed to local activism. As early as 1951, students in the Black high school had walked out in protest against educational inequities. Led by sixteen-year-old Barbara Rose Johns, they had demanded facilities equal to those provided the white schools. These bold actions attracted the attention of the NAACP, which urged Black leaders in Prince Edward County to join the emerging legal challenge to the separate-but-equal doctrine. Prince Edward would become one of the five cases ultimately consolidated into the 1954 *Brown v. Board* decision outlawing segregation in public schools.

Whites in the county were outspoken and activist as well, and under the leadership of J. Barrye Wall, editor of *The Farmville Herald*, responded to the *Brown* decision by founding a group they titled the Defenders of State Sovereignty and Individual Liberties—a name taken from the inscription on a local Confederate monument. Senator Byrd offered the Defenders strong backing as Prince Edward emerged as a battleground in the civil rights struggle. Rather than integrating the schools, the all-white county government and school board decided in 1959 to close them entirely. A private "academy," subsidized with tuition grants from the state, was created to serve white students. More than a thousand Black children would be offered no public education for four years. Many parents scrambled to place their children in schools in adjacent counties or send them to live with relatives elsewhere. The American Friends Service Committee, which had long been active in Farmville, created a program to pair teenagers with families in the North, who welcomed them into their homes while they attended local high schools. The experience of these nearly seventy students on the other side of the Mason-Dixon Line reinforced their activism when they returned to Virginia for visits or vacations. During our stay in Farmville, most of our group was distributed among the houses of these students and their families.

The strategy of the NAACP had long been to work through the courts on behalf of racial justice, and both the *Brown* case and the suits filed after 1959 to reopen Prince Edward schools reflected this approach. But a younger generation was impatient with what seemed like a glacial pace of legal challenge and change. Barbara Johns had been an early example of the new direct-action approach to civil rights, and growing militancy in Prince Edward after the schools closed exerted significant influence on NAACP policy. The Reverend L. Francis Griffin, of Farmville's First Baptist Church, was the acknowledged leader of the Black community, and the school reopening case ultimately heard by the Supreme Court in 1964 listed his children as primary litigants. In 1962, Griffin also became the president of the Virginia State Conference of the NAACP and insisted that a purely legal strategy was no longer sufficient. In response to the Birmingham protests of 1963, the State Conference concluded that "for any of the established organizations to play a significant role, it is necessary for them to catch up with the revolution. More specifically, the conservative tactics of the NAACP need to be supplanted."[6] It was also necessary to catch up with the younger generation. When Farmville erupted in protests and marches in the summer of 1963, it was once again people not far from me in age who were in the forefront. And as with Barbara Johns a little more than a decade before, they were girls as well as boys, young women as well as men.

Through that summer and fall, teenagers led almost daily street demonstrations focused not just on opening the schools but also on addressing broader issues, including voter registration and integration of public accommodations. Students mounted sit-ins at lunch counters in local establishments like Southside Sundry, J. J. Newberry's, the College Shoppe, and Owen-Sanford Drug; pray-ins at white churches; and try-ins at Leggett's, a department store that had prohibited Black customers from using fitting rooms. Arrested protesters filled the Farmville jail.[7]

As the suit demanding reopening of county schools wound its leisurely way through the court system, the lengthy denial of education to Black children became a growing public embarrassment for the entire nation. President Kennedy had noted in a 1962 speech that there were four places in the world where children were denied the right to attend school: North Korea, North Vietnam, Cambodia, and Prince Edward County. As I had learned from my travels in Eastern Europe, this carried implications for the Cold War as well as for domestic civil rights. The protest-filled summer of 1963 and its culmination in the August 28 March on Washington led the Kennedy administration to feel it had to ensure some sort of access to education for Black children in Prince Edward in the fall. In September, the Prince Edward Free School Association, organized in large part by Kennedy administration staff and supported by philanthropy that included a $10,000 gift from the president himself, opened access to education to all children in the county. Although a few whites enrolled, the Free

Schools overwhelmingly served the Black residents who had been without educational opportunities for so long. Students returned to the classrooms, and the demonstrations were paused.[8]

In May 1964, the Supreme Court ruled on *Griffin v. Board of Supervisors of Prince Edward County*, declaring the school closings racially motivated and therefore unconstitutional. Public schools would open in the fall. The previous summer's demonstrations and upheavals would not resume. The Court had spoken definitively and at last. But the battle over educational equity and racial justice in Prince Edward was far from over. Just as we arrived in Farmville in late June, the Board of Supervisors had figured out that if it could not close the schools, it could starve them, passing a budget that was a fraction of the funds requested for public education, but at the same time

Because the schools of Prince Edward County were closed for four years, the children of the County must have excellent educational opportunities offered to them.

We believe that the $189,000 of local funds appropriated by the Board of Supervisors of Prince Edward County on June 23, is an insufficient amount to finance the type of school system needed.

Therefore, we, adult citizens of Prince Edward County, do petition the Board of Supervisors of Prince Edward County to allocate additional funds to be used for the purpose of public education.

NAME	ADDRESS

The petition we circulated in Prince Edward County, Virginia, 1964.

generously funding the private white academy. Not until 1986 did Prince Edward Academy accept Black students, and ultimately public schools would remain almost as segregated as they had been before *Brown*. But the summer of 1964 began with optimism about the battles yet to be won.

We quickly recognized that securing adequate funding for the fall opening of the public schools was the most immediate concern of Black community leadership. We joined with the teenagers who were serving as our hosts to canvass Black households, explaining what the Board of Supervisors had done, and urging signatures on a petition demanding adequate funding for public schools. Many of those who opened their doors were nervous about our presence, and our meetings with leaders on both sides of the conflict made clear to us why.

J. Barrye Wall, editor of *The Farmville Herald*, received us in his second-floor office with evident skepticism, declaring almost at once to our mixed-race group that he was unwaveringly opposed to integration and that *Brown* had been decided in error. "Prince Edward, Stand Steady" was his exhortation to his community, and he repeated it at the close of every editorial. Although he certainly planned to stand steady with us, he did not stand very tall. He was scarcely five feet, and I towered over him as he greeted us. I recall he did not offer to shake hands—no doubt to avoid doing so with the Black members of our group. With his shock of white hair and pronounced Southside Virginia accent, he seemed like something from another era—or even from a movie or a play—as he performed the part of a crusty and implacable segregationist. Whites pay more taxes, he explained, and therefore had the right to better schools. He hoped the new civil rights law, which he condemned, would not result in more test cases in Prince Edward; the community was already being used by outside agitators against the true desires of its residents—Black and white. At one point, I gingerly asked a question about miscegenation, which I knew was a loaded word. Just at that second, deafening alarms detonated, seemingly beneath our feet. I gradually realized it was from the hook and ladder in the fire station on the ground floor. But I was startled into silence, thinking that the very word had set off some sort of Race Alarm. Wall was unfazed, confirming that the ultimate source of his opposition to school integration was that it would inevitably lead to intermarriage and racial amalgamation, which he regarded as abhorrent. In this, he had the law on his side: in 1964, interracial unions were illegal in nineteen states, including Virginia and all others in the South.[9] There was no common ground that either he or we wanted to establish, and the alarms brought our meeting to an end. We knew we were not doing a very good job of either understanding or persuading those with whom we disagreed.

It is now hard to believe how openly and intensely the fear of racial mixing figured within the segregationist opposition to *Brown v. Board* and to civil rights more generally. Through today's eyes, the rhetoric seems almost bizarrely sexually obsessed; the historian Jane Dailey has characterized it as a kind of "sexual panic." Invocations of the cherished purity of the white race, warnings of "widespread racial amalgamation and debasement of society as a whole" and "mixed marriages, miscegenation, and the mongrelization of the human race" flowed from the pens of southern editors and the mouths of southern politicians. A Mississippi circuit judge insisted in an essay in *Life* that "segregation can be defended because it is the only reasonable and practical means to prevent racial intermarriage"; the Pulitzer Prize–winning Richmond journalist Virginius Dabney threatened that integration "will lead to ultimate racial amalgamation and make ours a nation of mulattoes." J. Edgar Hoover introduced Eisenhower to the term "mongrelization," which the president in turn used to explain white resistance to desegregation.[10] The proximity of Black and white youth—in schools or in groups like ours—seemed incendiary to the J. Barrye Walls of the South, and our very presence represented a provocation. Black and white teenagers—male and female together socializing, interacting as friends and equals—posed the greatest possible danger to the racial conventions of southern life.

But anxieties surrounding interracial sex, marriage, and dating extended well beyond the segregationist white South, as the reach of laws against mixed-race marriages suggests. In the mid-1960s, fewer than 20 percent of Americans nationwide approved of interracial unions.[11] Mixed-race relationships were rare and subject to public scrutiny and denunciation in the North as well as the South. When in 1965 the popular young singer Janis Ian released "Society's Child," a ballad she had written about an interracial romance, radio stations from across the country refused to play it, protesters disrupted her concerts, and she received threats against her life.

Yet, predictably, as our group lived and worked together, attractions across racial lines emerged. We were compelled to assess how deeply we had been branded by racial assumptions at odds with our own chosen integrationist commitments and beliefs. We talked openly about "the marrying a Negro thing," as I later put it in a letter to Linda Martin. One white southerner in our group, deeply committed to the civil rights struggle, confessed nonetheless that, as I wrote at the time, "she just never could marry a Negro because of those emotional things bred deep in her by her whole environment, things that reason just doesn't overcome successfully." But my friend Linda found herself falling in love with John, a Black member of our group, and wondering about the larger meaning and implications of the relationship. My major summer romance was with someone white, but I also grew closer and closer to George Crowell. It was a "beeyoutiful friendship," I wrote, but not more than that, I explained to Linda: "No lovers, no sweat." It was not till years later that I learned George was gay. I did not have to confront the dilemmas that were challenging Linda. But I offered her my advice: "If you fall in love with a Negro, you are falling in love with a man who just happens to be a Negro . . . The only thing you can do is just take it as it comes. If you fall in love with a Negro, I know you would have the courage to do what would be right for both of you."[12]

After our difficult meeting with J. Barrye Wall, we were relieved to find ourselves in friendlier company with Reverend Griffin. But his message was not an entirely easy one. His optimism had been tempered by a realism derived from years of efforts to mobilize Prince Edward County's Black community. "Docility had its premiere in this county," he told us. After a decade in the forefront of the civil rights struggle, he had few remaining illusions and understood the reluctance of many Black citizens to get involved. Segregationists had used economic pressure to quash dissent, threatening activists with mortgage foreclosures and loss of employment. Young people felt less "financial fear" than their parents and had thus become the heart of the movement. County leaders were committed to retaining cheap labor and keeping industry and accompanying opportunity out of Prince Edward, Griffin explained. A low-cost and poorly educated labor force perfectly suited their needs. Issues of race, justice, and morality could not be separated from economic and power realities.[13]

We saw such inequities on full display when we arrived in Orangeburg, South Carolina. One Black resident described the town to us as a "dislocated Mississippi community," and the historian I. A. Newby proclaimed it to be "the most racially troubled place in the state."[14] The presence of two Black institutions of higher education—Claflin College and South Carolina State—elevated racial tensions. Numbers of students were active in pressing for social change, and the very existence of a sizable community of middle-class, well-educated African Americans also heightened racial resentments among the many white residents who could not match their prosperity or professional attainments. From the time of Reconstruction onward, educated Black people had served as a particular target of white anger and violence. Their aspirations and achievements represented an inherent threat to both structures and ideologies of white supremacy. As the president of Claflin explained to us, Orangeburg's Black colleges made many whites feel they had more to resent and more to fear. Yet in spite of the positive impact of the two institutions on Black lives and prospects, median income overall for whites remained twice that of Black residents.[15]

Like Prince Edward County, Orangeburg had, since the early 1950s, been a site of civil rights struggle. In 1960, students launched their own sit-in campaign after protests first erupted at lunch counters in Greensboro, just a few hours' drive away. The summer of 1963 saw the escalation of direct-action protests in Orangeburg as in so many other locations across the South. When the city council refused to consider the Orangeburg Movement's demands for desegregation and expanded job opportunities, demonstrators were arrested by the hundreds day after day—with many simply rejoining the picket line and getting re-arrested as soon as they were released. Four days in late September saw more than a thousand arrests. In October, the movement leader Gloria Blackwell Rackley was dismissed from her teaching job—accused of "inciting youths to break laws" by encouraging their protests. Demonstrations further intensified, and Black schools were compelled to close in the face of a student boycott.[16] Young people were the heart of the Orangeburg Movement, and our group included some of those who had been most active. Eddie Sharperson, age sixteen, believed that the Orangeburg Movement fundamentally depended on teenagers like him, and he observed to us that Gloria Rackley, who served as a state NAACP vice president, was a rare exception in her willingness to risk her job. For the most part, it was people like Eddie, not adults, who were energizing the protests. The ten-year-old son of the family hosting me wore his multiple arrests like badges of honor. A fifteen-year-old girl we met shocked us with her story of being sentenced to a term in reform school for picketing.[17]

It was difficult for us to approach Orangeburg's white leaders with anything like an open mind, and what they chose to say to us did not make us any more sympathetic. Mayor S. Clyde Fair was reputed to be a tool of the Klan, and the views he expressed to our racially mixed group were uncompromising. We had scarcely entered his office when he declared himself "bitterly opposed" to integration. "Animal life is supposed to be separated," he insisted, although we weren't sure which animals, other than Black and white humans, he thought needed to be separated from which. He approvingly cited the Germans as closest to the ideal of race purity. Outsiders like the NAACP, the Congress of Racial Equality, and Dr. Martin Luther King, Jr., he insisted, had done nothing but harm.[18]

The Reverend W. W. Lancaster, pastor of the 2,100-member all-white First Baptist Church, regarded himself as a moderate and seemed eager to win our respect, if not our agreement. He was intent on demonstrating that he had taken considerable risk to be open and fair in the face of civil rights challenges. "There are many people," he told us, "who would be unhappy to know that George"—who was, of course, Black—"is sitting in my office right now . . . And that is no fault of George's," he hastened to reassure us. But like the mayor, Lancaster thought that "outside coercive means" had set the cause of racial harmony back by decades, and he repeatedly emphasized the importance of patience and time, especially in the face of what he saw as Black people's backwardness. "People have to be able to stand before they can run the hundred-yard dash."[19]

We evidently had tested his own patience, as well as his desire to appear reasonable and conciliatory. A few days after our meeting, Lancaster addressed the local Rotary Club with an account of our visit. "Their Attitude Caused Ire," the headline read in *The Times and Democrat*. Reverend Lancaster described himself as "infuriated" by us. We were "arrogant and unable to communicate," and it was clear we were not there to learn, "but to help us solve our problems immediately." He "took particular exception" to statements made by members of the group who had criticized the Constitution and Americanism as "myths." *The Times and Democrat* explained: "Following the interview, Mr. Lancaster became angry and, on searching for the roots of his anger, found it was not directed at the group, but the society and the homes that produced children such as they."[20]

I was the one who had talked about myths; I was the one to whom he was taking "particular exception." I was upset by how he had distorted my remarks and how he had characterized me—and all of us: "children such as they." We were not who or what he had accused us of being, and we certainly did not want to be dismissed as children. It seemed unfair that Lancaster hadn't made his objections directly to us, but instead decided to use them as the basis for a public address. I responded with a lengthy letter that, in retrospect, I see represented a kind of credo for me—what I believed in midsummer 1964, a little more than a month after the signing of the Civil Rights Act and four months before a presidential election that would pit the law's champion, Lyndon B. Johnson, against one of its most vocal opponents, Barry Goldwater. Insisting that Reverend Lancaster could not blame my views on my parents, I claimed the right to my own beliefs, and I articulated a perspective on America's racial dilemmas consistent with the concerns I had expressed from the time I was a young child.

My distress at the gap between the Christian and democratic principles I had been taught and the realities of race in America had only been reinforced in the weeks since I had embarked on this southern journey. "I cannot stand to see hypocrisy," I wrote, "without criticizing it in a desire to change and better things"—essentially the same point I had tried to make to President Eisenhower seven years before. But by now I had come to see the principles of Christian love established by Martin Luther King, Jr., as the most powerful weapon of the civil rights movement, and I tried to make use of that weapon the way he did: to call a professed white believer to task—to recognition of the implications of his own creed. Or, if it failed to enlighten or persuade him, I could reap the satisfaction of hoisting him on his own petard. I was no sophisticated student of the Bible, but I closed my letter by quoting to this Baptist minister a verse from 2 Corinthians that I had stared at almost daily for four years carved on the wall behind the altar in the Concord Academy chapel. I signed my letter "Faithfully." I was on God's side. I was on America's side. Which side, to borrow the words of the civil rights song, was *he* on?

Here is the heart of the letter:

> When I spoke of the "American dream" as a myth, I did not
> intend to sound Communistic, for I am not. I have visited
> East Germany, Czechoslovakia, and Yugoslavia, and the
> type of government that is in existence there does not appeal
> to me. Still, I find many, many inequalities and injustices that
> exist in the United States today, and I feel that only by rec-
> ognizing these injustices can we, as citizens, deal with them
> and improve the situation. Since the time I was very little, I
> heard from my parents, who are quite conservative and pres-
> ently support Goldwater, from the teachers in the Virginia
> schools I attended, and from the books I read, that America
> was a land of promise where every man had equal right and
> equal opportunity to succeed. But as I grew older, I began
> to see tremendous discrepancies in these ideals and in what
> actually was in practice. I saw Negroes in my community,
> all poor, all unable to procure employment as anything but
> maids or handy men; I saw the tenant farmer on my father's
> farm working extremely hard and succeeding at nothing but
> eking out a bare minimum for existence; I saw people with
> barely enough to eat and heard at the same time of the mas-
> sive grain surplus that the government threw into the ocean.
>   I see the inequality of opportunity very clearly in your
> state of South Carolina where poverty is so great that in one
> county the average income for a Negro family is less than a
> thousand dollars. One day, driving out from Orangeburg,
> we went to the house of a woman with thirteen children.
> Her husband had a very few acres of land and carried on
> subsistence farming. She worked in the fields of a nearby
> landowner for two dollars for a twelve-hour day. The only
> furniture in their house was a bed and two chairs. What op-
> portunity do her children have? Because the state does not

supply textbooks and she cannot afford to buy them, her children will never go to school. There is no law making education compulsory and so no one will protest this. Should their father produce a bad crop some year, the children would probably not have enough to eat, for South Carolina is one of three states that have no program of distributing to needy families the surpluses resting for a million dollars a day in grain elevators in the Midwest. This would not bother me so much if we were a little more honest about the problems, admitted them to children in school, in fact, made a point of teaching them to students so they could perhaps change things. Instead we set ourselves up as an example to other nations and say, "Give me your tired, your poor . . ."

I am not un-American, but I see a land of hypocrisy in what we as a nation say we are and what we as a nation are actually doing, Perhaps this has to be, but because I am sixteen, I am endowed with the honesty and the love of honesty that is so imbedded in the young, and I cannot stand to see hypocrisy without criticizing it in a desire to change and better things. Maybe I am very naïve; maybe no nation can do what it sets out to do, but I certainly want it to keep trying. The great value in the American system, I feel, is that it encourages criticism from within to help it evolve, correct itself, advance. I am criticizing. Only when individuals are aware enough to agree or disagree with the government's actions, and with all actions within the nation, can the system work . . . Granted, I did not set out with a completely open mind, for my moral beliefs dictate to me that segregation is wrong and that love greater than the patronizing affection of a white man of his maid must exist between the races. As far as methods of achieving this goal were concerned, however, I feel I was fairly objective, and therefore I think this trip has been of immense value.

So please do not think me un-American, and do not blame my parents, for they tried to bring me up in the most conservative tradition. If anyone is responsible for the way I think, it is I. And, please, do not feel sorry for me, for I have found something deep and meaningful in the civil rights movement, an idea with which I think even you would agree. The love of which Christ spoke is really the only answer; only by loving each man for himself, only by loving those that curse you, can one be a truly worthy person . . . As Paul said, "Though I speak with the tongues of men and of angels and have not love, I am as a sounding brass or a tinkling cymbal."[21]

I never received a response.

Reverend Lancaster was not the only person we succeeded in angering in Orangeburg. Whenever we appeared together as a biracial group, we challenged the existing racial order. Often we did this intentionally—to test compliance with the new Civil Rights Act by standing in line for a ticket at a movie theater or trying to order a meal at the Holiday Inn in accordance with the stated objective of the South Carolina NAACP to pursue "the task of implementing the civil rights act in an attitude which reflects a posture of firmness with restraint."[22] Sometimes we were served, grudgingly and with hostile looks and muttered threats. At other times we were ignored or turned away. But it seemed we provoked the most severe responses on occasions when we did not intend to be mounting a direct protest to segregation at all. Our simple presence together set off the alarm bell of "race mixing."

One hot afternoon, several of our group decided to go to a swimming area in a nearby river with young people from the Black families that were their hosts. White teenagers with knives appeared and began shouting and taunting the swimmers until several local Black youths managed to talk them down and maneuver everyone to safety.

We had all been instructed that if we encountered any trouble, we should try as quickly as possible to retreat into the sanctuary of the Black residential district. No one would dare chase us there. I found myself following this advice one afternoon when I was walking along a road with George Crowell. As a car drove by us, a bottle flew out the window and just missed our heads. Another car pulled up filled with angry, shouting white teenagers. George had the presence of mind to head away from the road toward a nearby cluster of Black homes, pulling me behind him, and the cars drove off. Incidents like these illuminated for me what I should already have known: no one, white or Black, was free to violate the taboos that governed racial interaction in the South. Segregation circumscribed the freedom of both whites and Blacks—a reality I had not fully understood. Racial hatred and white supremacy were upheld by a great deal more than simply a set of laws that either courts or Congress could change.

I had written my letter to Reverend Lancaster from Frogmore, South Carolina, where we had joined an NAACP Youth Conference at the historic Penn Center on Saint Helena Island in the heart of the Carolina Lowcountry. In this area about fifty nautical miles south of Charleston, white South Carolinians had in the years before the Civil War accumulated vast fortunes from the labor of enslaved Africans, cultivating first indigo, and then Sea Island cotton. The population had been overwhelmingly Black from the mid-1700s onward. African cultural forms—music, food, folklore, religion, the Gullah language—not only survived but also thrived in this environment. In late 1861, it became one of the earliest locations in the South to fall into Union hands. The fifty-five plantations on Saint Helena Island were abandoned by their white owners, leaving the Black residents in possession of the land. Expectations of permanent ownership were tragically dashed by the federal government at the end of the war, but Saint Helena nevertheless emerged as an important site in what evolved into the long struggle for freedom and justice.

The Penn Center was originally established by northern abolitionists, many of whom were Quakers, who arrived in the wake of Union troops to educate newly liberated residents who had been forbidden under slavery to learn to read or write. After World War II, the school evolved into a community center that trained midwives, provided a health clinic, and offered a space where civil rights groups could safely retreat for meetings and conferences like the one we were attending. It was one of very few locations in the South where interracial groups could stay in integrated facilities, a possibility that arose in no small part from its isolation. The National Association for the Advancement of Colored People (NAACP), the Congress of Racial Equality (CORE), the Student Nonviolent Coordinating Committee (SNCC), and the Southern Christian Leadership Conference (SCLC) all sponsored meetings there. Dr. Martin Luther King, Jr., and his lieutenants had gathered for a retreat and strategy discussions just a few months before our arrival. The Saint Helena we encountered was remote, poor, undeveloped, agricultural, and almost entirely Black. I have not returned since the region has become a booming resort area of golf courses, condominiums, and gated communities where descendants of many of the island's original Black families now provide a substantial portion of the labor in hotels and restaurants. But the Penn Center today continues its work in support of Black rights and the preservation of Gullah culture.[23]

Frogmore seemed an exotic landscape to me. The marshes punctuated with tidal pools and streams, the unrelenting heat and humidity, and the looming live oaks supporting curtains of Spanish moss exuded an aura of mystery and strangeness quite unlike any place I had ever been. And I knew this was hallowed ground, a site where freedom and slavery had battled for centuries in a combat I now wanted to join. Together with the forty-five or so other young people participating in the conference, I was to consider "NAACP history, Youth Council organization and administration, the Civil Rights Bill, voter registration and education."[24] In blue ink, in a notebook with lined, five-holed paper, I recorded my impressions. I had just finished reading two books recently published by Martin Luther King, Jr.—*Strength to Love* and *Why We Can't Wait*—that outlined his philosophy and strategy of nonviolence. I had been taken by his message and its powerful Christian framework, but my attraction derived not so much from any deep spirituality or from my own committed Christian belief. Virgin birth, resurrection, a Holy Ghost, loaves into fishes: all seemed fantastical in the context of the rationality I cherished. I was attracted, rather, to the logic of Christian ethics, to the fundamental fairness of the Golden Rule. This had been the basis for the little sermon I sent President Eisenhower when I was nine and the essence of the case I made to Reverend Lancaster at age sixteen. Theology was not important to me, but I became a true believer in Dr. King's vision of a Beloved Community on earth.

In lunch and dinner discussions, in conversations in the dormitories at night, I was impressed by the bravery and commitment of the young civil rights activists attending the conference, and there could be nothing more moving than to join them in the songs that had instilled them with courage. But during our days together, I came to recognize that they did not entirely share my idealism about nonviolence or fully embrace Dr. King's philosophy. In my mind, the principles of nonviolence had implications beyond the civil rights movement for issues of world peace, like those I'd explored behind the Iron Curtain the preceding summer. This seemed of little interest to my fellow conference attendees. "They had never thought about non-violence as anything but an expedient weapon to achieve their ends," I wrote in my notebook. I had encountered similar views in Orangeburg, where I remembered one boy said he was "non-violent most of the time," but did not reject physical confrontation when it seemed necessary. "The Negro movement is not perfect," I continued. "It too believes unidealistically that the ends often justify the means . . . The most important thing for the movement now as I see it is that all those involved realize that they are not fighting just to be able to go to a restaurant or a school or to get a better job, but to

A page from my notebook, summer 1964.

build a better society." Integration, I concluded, was just "the means." But my commitment to nonviolence seemed unrealistic, if not entirely misguided, to the young NAACP members.[25]

What I was seeing, but did not understand, was not just that the movement was imperfect, but that it was neither united nor monolithic, that cracks were already appearing that would soon marginalize King and his message. The ideology of Black Power and the increasing preeminence of SNCC, soon to be purged of white participation and leadership, would by 1966 take the freedom movement in a different direction. Integration would become neither an end nor a means, and nonviolence would be seen by many to represent weakness and submission instead of strength.

On August 4, the bodies of James Chaney, Andrew Goodman, and Michael Schwerner were discovered buried in an earthen dam not far from where they had disappeared. All three had been shot, and fragments of clay in Goodman's lungs suggested he had been buried alive. Chaney, who was Black and a local Mississippian— unlike the white New Yorkers Goodman and Schwerner—had been beaten and castrated. I had assumed the men were dead almost from the time they went missing, but the confirmation of their gruesome end still shocked, reminding us that the South was a dangerous place for anyone who challenged the racial status quo. And this evidence of raw brutality would come to sow further doubt in the movement about how nonviolence and peaceful persuasion could combat such unflinching cruelty.

These were hardly the first deaths of the civil rights movement. Medgar Evers, an NAACP field secretary, had been assassinated outside his home in Jackson a little more than a year earlier; a church bombing in Birmingham had killed four young girls attending Sunday school the preceding September; the local activists Herbert Lee and Louis Allen had been gunned down in Mississippi with no national attention or outrage.[26] But those were Black deaths. Goodman and Schwerner were white northerners, and their murders attracted a sense of connection and compassion from white Americans that earlier deaths had not. This was part of the strategy of the Mississippi program in which the three dead men had been participating. Freedom Summer was intended to bring northern college students to register voters and teach Freedom Schools. But its organizers also hoped to attract the public attention and sympathy that they knew would be accorded to young white students whose lives seemed at risk. White lives mattered to the press and to policymakers—and to white America—in a way Black lives did not. King had launched the Birmingham Children's Crusade of young protesters in spring 1963 in a similar effort to penetrate racial blindness and arouse broad sympathy for the movement. It was difficult to dismiss boys and girls as dangerous agitators and hard to condone the unrestrained violence of dogs and fire hoses used against them.

Birmingham, Alabama, summer 1964.

The Sixteenth Street Baptist Church bombing in September—which in addition to killing four girls left at least twenty other people wounded—lent a new urgency to civil rights demands, as at least some whites who had considered themselves moderates and had opposed Black activism found it difficult to reject King's designation of the killings as "one of the most vicious and tragic crimes ever perpetrated against humanity."

We arrived in Birmingham nearly a year after the bombing, but we found ourselves still caught up in the aftermath. The recent, long-fought battle for the Civil Rights Act had been aided and accelerated by the sympathy and horror the murders had aroused. But what we saw firsthand was the persisting grief of the Black community in Birmingham as it welcomed us. Our host families were the very ones that had been most affected by the previous year's violence and included the parents of one of the murdered girls. The houses where we stayed were all in the area of the city that had come to be known as "Dynamite Hill" because Klan members bombed and threatened its residents with such frequency. The community was a haven for the Black middle class, whose success had made them a target of white resentment and retaliation ever since families had begun to purchase homes from whites in the neighborhood in the 1950s. Now that so many of these families were active supporters of the movement, the danger had only intensified. This was the heart of the city that had come to be known as "Bombingham."

Cookie, the thirteen-year-old daughter of the family who welcomed me, had been a close friend of one of the murdered girls. "There was a kind of peaceful acceptance" in the way she described the loss of her friend, I wrote in my notebook. For Cookie, "living on what is known as 'Dynamite Hill' was just a part of her; the Movement, because of her parents' involvement in it was a part of her too." Her father, a physician, explained to me that the previous summer, during the height of the protests, "when houses all around his were being bombed, he had spent long nights lying on his living room floor," with a rifle, "staring out the picture window waiting for the car to come by with the bomb for his house." Although he was deeply committed to the movement, nonviolence had become a secondary concern in the face of this threat.[27]

When we accompanied our host families to Sunday services at the Sixteenth Street Baptist Church, we could see the lingering evidence of the destruction from the September explosion, just as we could hear the persisting sense of loss expressed to us by members of the congregation as they greeted us at the social hour after worship. A mass meeting of the Alabama Christian Movement for Human Rights that we attended the following day mourned the deaths as well, with the reading of a poignant poem written by a thirteen-year-old girl to honor "Six Little Friends," not just the four girls but also

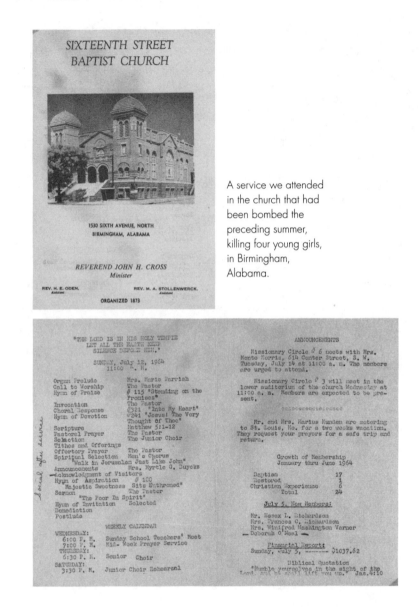

A service we attended in the church that had been bombed the preceding summer, killing four young girls, in Birmingham, Alabama.

two Black teenage boys who had been shot by white people later that same September day—one as a lark by two Eagle Scouts who were tried but never punished, the other by a policeman who saw the youth throwing rocks at a car painted with racist slogans. "The story does not end," the poem lamented.[28]

The ACMHR had been founded by the Reverend Fred Shuttlesworth in 1956 when the NAACP was outlawed in Alabama, and it had endured many instances of violent reprisal as it sponsored demonstrations, sit-ins, and boycotts. Shuttlesworth had been beaten; his house and his church had been bombed—the latter multiple times. More militant and less conciliatory than King, Shuttlesworth nevertheless had invited him to Birmingham in 1963 to bring broader visibility and intensified pressure from the ongoing demonstrations. Shuttlesworth saw his political action and his ministerial role as inseparable, and the ACMHR rally we attended was all but indistinguishable from a religious service.

We entered a church filled to overflowing. With the accompaniment of an organist, a choir of dozens of men and women dressed in black and white led the congregation in song and rhythmic clapping and shouting.[29] My repressed Episcopalian upbringing had not prepared me for such exuberance in a church, but I cautiously joined in with the words I knew. People turned to smile at us, and a woman passed me a paper fan advertising funeral insurance like the ones most of the congregation were waving to cool themselves in the hot and crowded room. Shuttlesworth's vice president, Edward Gardner, rose to the pulpit. The crowd quieted, and Gardner began to exhort them about the selective buying campaign against several downtown stores. "We don't want to buy from people who won't employ us, do we?" he demanded. I had already joined the picketers in front of the targeted stores, so I readily echoed the rest of the congregation. Gardner and Shuttlesworth had greeted the passage of the Civil Rights Act just a week earlier by checking in to Birmingham's most exclusive hotel, which as of July 2 could no longer legally exclude them. "And I said to Fred," he reported, "come on let's hurry up and go to sleep. We've got too much invested downstairs to sit around gabbing all night." The audience erupted in laughter and cheers. The evening concluded with the congregation on its feet, all holding hands and singing "We Shall Overcome."[30]

As the song ended, "people began swarming around me," I recorded, shaking my hand, smiling, welcoming me enthusiastically. These were people who had suffered bombings, killings, police brutality, "general oppression from whites, and here they were not hating me because I was white," I wrote in my notebook. I thought of the teenagers I had met who had been arrested so many times; I thought of those not far from my age who had been sentenced to reform school or even the chain gang because they would not abandon picketing; I thought of the ten-year-old in Orangeburg who had spent a week in jail; I thought of another young boy "who, when asked how he was going to spend his summer answered 'Fighting for Freedom.'" Boys and girls who dared. What could *I* be doing? What *should* I be doing? "This apparent devotion to an ideal that was almost not conscious was something I had never seen in the white community. It was a sense of purpose I envied," my notes concluded.[31]

I had no idea of the bitter resentments escalating between Shuttlesworth and King over both leadership and strategy in Birmingham; I had no notion that President Johnson, hero of the Civil Rights Act, would just a month later sell out the Mississippi Freedom Democratic Party by opposing their bid for seats at the Democratic National Convention; I did not know that two years later John Lewis would be ousted from the leadership of SNCC because he was too aligned with King's nonviolent integrationist philosophy; and I never thought about how our very presence might be endangering our hosts, who had so warmly welcomed us into their homes and lives. The morality play in which I pictured myself was far more complex than I understood.

I still remember a beautiful summer evening in Birmingham at a barbecue in George Crowell's family's backyard. The members of our group were joined by George's neighbors and friends, many of whom were movement activists. I recall almost unimaginable amounts and varieties of food. The Temptations sang from the record player as George tried to teach me a dance called the popcorn. People laughed and sang along, and some joined in the line dance on the grass. We felt happy—to be together defying convention and expectation, sharing a commitment to change we were convinced we could help bring about.

In an essay I wrote at summer's end, I mused about what it had all meant:

> I heard the word "freedom" used a great deal this summer. I think it has a much greater meaning than the one the Negroes have given it in the civil rights struggle. A free individual's actions are not controlled by his fear of public disapproval or of foreclosure of his mortgage or of death, but he consciously weighs all things and acts as he truly wishes. This kind of freedom can come only from a commitment to that about which one really cares, for only then do the superficial things cease to matter. In this sense, I feel that the Negroes who have involved themselves in the civil rights struggle have found a much greater kind of freedom than that liberty which they are trying to obtain from the white man who is owned by his car and his split-level house and dares not act for fear of losing them . . . What is wrong with the United States, both North and South, that people by silence give approbation to killing and violence?[32]

Could I live a life that transcended "superficial things"? That abandoned the safety of silence? What would I do with my own freedom?

A few days after we left Birmingham, George's house was bombed. The structure wasn't seriously damaged, and no one was hurt. George would live on to perish in a different national crisis. He died of AIDS in 1995 at age forty-six.[33]

10

THE CLASS OF 1968

I never realized until lately that women
were supposed to be the inferior sex.

(1937)

—KATHARINE HEPBURN, BRYN MAWR '28[1]

I am not entirely sure why I chose Bryn Mawr. Neither my mother
nor my grandmothers had attended college, and neither they nor anyone else in my family particularly cared where I went. I was in many
ways relieved to feel this sense of free rein in my college choice, un-
constrained by the family traditions and expectations that had all but
required my older brother to follow his father, uncle, and great-uncle
to Princeton. But Princeton did not admit women. Yale, Dartmouth,
Brown, and Columbia similarly remained all male. I had seen enough
of Radcliffe on visits from Concord to Cambridge to know that its
arrangements with Harvard amounted to something closer to second-
class citizenship than true coeducation. Radcliffe women were not
even allowed in the undergraduate library. But I knew little about
higher education and, apart from my teachers, few women who had
pursued it. Over the preceding decade, the top nineteen destinations
for Concord Academy graduates had been women's colleges. All but
three of the top twenty choices were in the Northeast. This was the
world my Concord advisers understood as they urged me toward the
Seven Sisters, seen then as the female equivalent of the Ivy League,
which they regarded as the most prestigious of my options.[2]

Bryn Mawr had a reputation as the most serious and academically rigorous of the group—"the most self-consciously intellectual of all the Seven Sisters," in the words of a leading college guidebook.[3] Close to half its senior class regularly went straight to graduate school, and it even had a small graduate school of its own. It seemed to be at once a small liberal arts college and a university. In addition to courses across the spectrum of the arts and sciences, it required advanced knowledge of not one but two foreign languages for the bachelor's degree, as well as an exacting yearlong course in philosophy. A Bryn Mawr director of admissions described it in the 1960s as "strenuously academic and distinctly non-vocational . . . an intellectual community which is . . . outstandingly able, well-trained, ambitious, disciplined and book-ish."[4] I had been so happy in the intimate community at Concord that I regarded Bryn Mawr's small size—fewer than eight hundred undergraduates—as a plus, and I welcomed its commitment to intel-

The Library Cloisters,
Bryn Mawr College.

lectual women. I had aspired to be such a person almost since I had first learned to read.

When I visited the campus in the spring of my junior year of high school, my mind was made up. I remarked to my parents that the campus seemed a lot like Princeton, and the two institutions had several collegiate gothic structures designed by the same architect. Bryn Mawr, with its towers and turrets, its arches, buttresses, and gargoyles, was what I understood a college ought to look like, and it promised to nurture the kind of person I thought I wanted to be.[5]

The freshman class I arrived to join on my seventeenth birthday in September 1964 included 199 students from 33 states and 6 foreign countries. We represented 175 high schools—126 of them public. A third of the students were receiving financial aid. A majority were in the top 5 percent of their high school class. Six of my classmates were Black. At Bryn Mawr, as at a number of its peer institutions, Black students were all assigned single rooms, presumably to avoid any possible objections from white roommates.[6]

Before we arrived on campus, each of us was supplied with a copy of the *Freshman Handbook*, intended to prepare us for our new lives.[7] The president, Katharine McBride, who had led the college for more than two decades, opened the booklet with a message of welcome. Neither her greeting nor any other entry in the handbook used the word "women"—or even "girls," which is how we customarily referred to ourselves[8]— yet the contents illustrated the many ways that our lives were to be shaped by assumptions about appropriate female behavior. Expectations—which took the form of what were known as "parietal rules"—were clear and specific: men were not allowed in student rooms after early evening, and doors were to remain at least partially open when they were visiting. For our safety, we were to sign out with our whereabouts when we were off campus in the evening and to return by 2:00 a.m., a much more lenient curfew than permitted most college women. All-but-unquestioned assumptions of female vulnerability masked underlying anxieties about female morality and justified a set of regulations that would have been unimaginable at nearby all-male Haverford. One product of these fears was the Lantern Men—Bryn Mawr's version of nighttime security guards—who opened the locked doors of the residence halls for students returning late at night and also escorted any young women who arrived after dark from Philadelphia on the Paoli Local, a train that stopped a few blocks from the college. I found something rather charming about the notion of protectors lighting our steps along campus pathways, but the swinging lanterns dotting the lawns amid the gothic arches and towers—keeping damsels from distress—would eventually come to seem medieval in conception as well as appearance. It wasn't long before we began to ask why we couldn't all just have our own keys.

The handbook explained that we would be expected to wear skirts to class and to any off-campus destination, out of "respect" for our professors and for the "reputation" of the college. But at least the Self-Government Association—Bryn Mawr students had claimed responsibility for setting their own rules for nearly three-quarters of a century—had just repealed the requirement for skirts at dinner. One item of clothing we were advised to bring was a "basic wool dress" that could "stand in good stead for church, Miss McBride's Tea and the Princeton Mixer." I had no intention of attending church or the Princeton Mixer, but Miss McBride's freshman-week tea was legendary. Elegant dishes of coffee ice cream and raspberry sherbet. Stockings a necessity. We were to be ladies as well as scholars.

Bryn Mawr represented a very peculiar sort of feminism. In the mid-1960s, there was not yet a women's liberation movement. Our consciousness was just beginning to be aroused and could certainly not be considered raised. Many of my classmates were like me, uneasy with the hurdles and injustices we recognized in our own lives. But we were not yet equipped with the language and insight to mount a systematic challenge to the world we found ourselves in. We accepted many constraints that today would seem unthinkable. Slowly, however, we had begun to identify and resist others.

Bryn Mawr assured us we could compete with men because we were special—intellectually gifted, ambitious, as good as—or even better than—any man. We would be able to transcend obstacles that would limit other women. To even speak of women as a category was seen as a kind of special pleading, an acknowledgment not so much of difference as of deficiency. As one member of the class of 1966 put it, "I feel like the administration and faculty think that being a woman is something you are supposed to overcome."[9]

But we, as outstanding individuals, need not concern ourselves with the broader circumstances or structures of women's lives. Bryn Mawr women had no deficiencies. Our education was designed to empower us, but to do so without ever requiring or encouraging us to think about our social or cultural place as females. Tellingly, Bryn Mawr declined to join Phi Beta Kappa, insisting that all its students were worthy of the honor. In some ways, the college and my mother shared a common outlook: both acknowledged that it was a man's world. My mother's conclusion was that I should accept the subordinate place that was my destiny. But Bryn Mawr, in contrast, intended to equip me with the individual strength and capacity to prevail in an arena that men had created and defined.

Much of Bryn Mawr's educational philosophy derived from its second—and first female—president, M. Carey Thomas, who had led the college from 1894 to 1922. The barriers she herself faced in pursuing higher learning made her a passionate advocate for women's education, and she was a leader as well in the movement for female suffrage. During her term as president, she lived in two sequential lesbian relationships, and expressed uncompromising opinions on marriage. To her mother, she described it as a "loss of freedom, poverty, and a personal subjection for which I see absolutely no compensation."[10] Her views lived on in legend in a statement we heard often repeated, even if she never actually uttered the words: "Only our failures marry." She is more likely to have said "Our failures *only* marry," and that message came to be regarded as equivalent to an inscription on the college seal.

In *The Feminine Mystique*, published just a year before I arrived at Bryn Mawr, Betty Friedan described with dismay the emergence at women's colleges of what she called "sex-directed education," courses designed to promote female "adjustment within the world of home and children."[11] These classes were a response to the "life-adjustment" movement in education that emerged in the 1950s, essentially equating emotional and mental health with accepting one's given lot. Bryn Mawr countenanced no such curriculum. Its only nod to any version of sex education was to require us all to pass a "hygiene test" based on a series of lectures given every fall that outlined male and female anatomy and explained how women got pregnant. These presentations seemed intended for those who had spent their adolescence in a cave. We mocked the lectures and asked absurd and embarrassing questions to torture the lecturers, especially the delectably named college physician, Pearl S. Pitt, who had the misfortune to be in charge of the whole enterprise.[12]

Bryn Mawr's academic program included essentially nothing about women. There were no courses in women's studies, no classes in women's history or literature or politics, and almost no mention of women at all even in the context of classes focused on broader themes. This was still the era where the designation "man" was unthinkingly used to encompass all humans. But if women were absent as the focus of our studies, they were omnipresent as instructors and administrators. The president and all the college deans were women, as was about half the faculty. Had I gone to Radcliffe, I would have likely never encountered the single tenured female in the arts and sciences faculty in that era. Princeton had no tenured woman on the faculty until 1968.[13]

At Bryn Mawr, women professors were everywhere. Inclined toward tweeds, laced Oxfords, and a no-nonsense attitude about life and learning, they appeared to me as unfathomably erudite. The historian Caroline Robbins, who was in her sixties when I encountered her, was an internationally renowned scholar of eighteenth-century English political thought. I always thought she looked rather like the figurehead on the prow of a ship sailing through the college corridors, but I was nevertheless in awe of her intellectual accomplishments and scholarly stature. During my senior year, I took a course with Miss Robbins on the Enlightenment in which she read to us in a monotone from her notes for two hours every Tuesday afternoon. I am sure she was sharing unequaled gems of historical insight, but it was all I could do to stay alert. Teaching as a craft, as a skill or an art, was regarded as almost irrelevant at Bryn Mawr. What mattered was the substance of the scholarly information that was being passed on from instructor to student, not the way that transmission occurred. It was up to us to find the material interesting, not up to our professors to make it so. With most of the faculty, we were on our own.

There were, of course, exceptions, especially among the younger professors. Richard DuBoff was an economist with progressive views and unbounded enthusiasm for his subject. He challenged us to challenge him as he paced back and forth on the dais at the front of the classroom. One day he became so impassioned that he fell off the riser into a wastebasket. He was undamaged, but after that we hardly took our eyes off him, worrying that it might happen again. As a leader among a group of young, left-leaning faculty, he grew increasingly vocal in his opposition to the war in Vietnam and helped us organize the teach-ins and protests that proliferated as the conflict escalated. Although I never took more than his introductory course in economics, he readily agreed to advise my senior thesis on the origins of the Vietnam War.

Mary Maples Dunn, who taught U.S. and Latin American history, was similarly lively and equally generous with students. She regularly emitted a deep-throated chortle that distinguished her from her unremittingly dour—and we assumed humorless—colleagues. She, moreover, was a female faculty member known to have a husband and children, and she even invited students to her house for dinner, where we could encounter them firsthand; scholarship and ambition need not require renunciation of marriage and family, M. Carey Thomas notwithstanding.

Bryn Mawr's insistence upon our intellectual superiority was accompanied by another sort of elitism as well. M. Carey Thomas had come from a background of wealth and privilege, and her philosophy of female education was shaped by hierarchical assumptions about race and intelligence, even as she rejected any such rankings of gender, unless, perhaps, to place women on top. She had actively blocked African Americans and Jews from either attending or teaching at the college. And she believed that superior minds should be freed from the mundane demands of daily life. She would liberate her women scholars from the drudgery of domestic work by shifting that burden to those she presumed to be less intellectually able. Even in 1964, nearly a half century after her death, this poisonous legacy lived on. We were waited on at linen-covered tables by maids in uniform, who cleaned our rooms and performed other menial tasks that enhanced our well-being. Heavier work was undertaken by male porters. The maids lived on the top floor of the residential halls; the porters, in the basement. In sharp contrast to the faculty and most of the students, all of them were Black.

Students had objected to these arrangements well before our class arrived. The system would gradually change, with fewer workers resident on campus, along with improved salaries and working conditions, but it would not fully come to an end until the 1980s. Early in my college career, I insisted that Mr. DuBoff come to inspect the dark basement living quarters with me, hoping to enlist him in my outrage, and he was readily persuaded that this was yet another issue that faculty and students must strive to change.

The maids' and porters' living and working conditions became part of a growing list of concerns for an increasingly politically aware college community. During my junior year, my classmate Margaret Levi united with a popular political science professor to help organize a union vote by the workers. She was stunned when the measure failed. "Much as we believed unions were what the maids and porters needed," she wrote, they "let us know it was not what they wanted." The following year, my friend Kit Bakke, editor of *The College News*, wrote an essay demanding that attention must be paid to this offensive system; this was followed in the next issue by photographs that I, together with another student, took of employees' attic and basement rooms. These living and working conditions, Kit asserted, "promote a 'plantation' atmosphere which is patronizing, stifling and uncomfortable."[14] But during our four years at the college, we managed to do little to improve the workers' lives.[15]

As Bryn Mawr students, we felt empowered, though at the same time intimidated, by the college's confidence in our intellectual capacities. We feared being seen as Bryn Mawr "failures." Yet most of us sought boyfriends and hoped to find husbands, investing much of our self-worth in the attention we garnered from men, while our gay classmates remained deeply closeted. This led us often to defer to men in relationships, in student organizations, and even in academic settings. In joint Haverford–Bryn Mawr classes, the women did all the reading; the men did most of the talking.

We felt growing unease about the assumptions of social and class superiority—symbolized by teas and servants—that seemed fundamental to Bryn Mawr's culture and identity, but increasingly at odds with an emerging hostility to hierarchies and privilege that marked the 1960s. And we were bewildered by the contradictory messages we received about our roles and opportunities as women. As my classmate Liz Schneider wrote, looking back from the "real world" a few years after our graduation, "The education of women—no matter how rigorous or inspiring—cannot overcome the wholesale prejudice of a society entrenched in its belief that women are inferior and properly excluded from the positions a first-class education might prepare them for." But Bryn Mawr made it difficult to acknowledge that these contradictions did exist, and we left college ill-equipped to deal with the barriers that would confront us as women beyond the college walls. "Most Bryn Mawr women are trapped," she wrote, "in a fundamental ambivalence: do they want to be the doctor or the doctor's wife?"[16] I remained blithely unaware that I might have to choose.

The seriousness of Bryn Mawr's intellectual culture suited me well. At the very end of freshman orientation week, our class gathered in cavernous Goodhart Hall, with its stained-glass windows and flying buttresses, for an address delivered by the formidable Miss McBride, who stood, stiff of spine and firm of countenance, on the stage before us. Bryn Mawr's Anglophilia included a requirement that students wear black Oxbridge-style academic robes at various occasions during the year as a tribute to centuries-long traditions of higher learning. The culminating event of freshman week, the day before classes began, marked the first station on this intellectual journey. We were to dress accordingly.

I have not forgotten Miss McBride's speech that day and her frequent allusions to what she in an almost reverential way called "our work." I had not previously been aware that I had "work." It sounded like possessing an artist's or a writer's oeuvre—something greater than the sum of its parts. I had taken courses and tests and written essays, but now I would have "work"—with the implications of vocation and purposefulness it seemed to entail. Yet this work, like all learning, she emphasized, must begin with humility. To truly learn, she insisted, you must open yourself up to the notion that you have a lot to learn, that what you do not know is close to infinite. A sense of ignorance fuels the desire to overcome it. Humility is a prerequisite for being educated. I had a kind of deer-in-the-headlights approach as I faced my first days of college. If I was supposed to be humble, it wasn't going to be all that hard. But Miss McBride was evoking a more lasting humility, not just for the initial weeks of college but also as a permanent commitment and condition. Because knowledge is endless, we would always have more to know.

Miss McBride's words from that September day more than a half century ago have stayed with me. Take your work seriously but always remember it is never complete, can always be better. I remember almost nothing else she said to us in my years at Bryn Mawr. She was not like Mrs. Hall, delivering regular exhortations about everything from what she had dubbed the Ten Deadly Virtues to our clothing choices. Miss McBride and, it often seemed, all of Bryn Mawr were concerned singularly with our minds. Our hearts, our souls, even our values seemed to warrant attention only as derivatives or offshoots of our intellect. I remember that at first I found the contrast with Concord and its atmosphere of constant moral challenge disconcerting, but over time I came to appreciate the Bryn Mawr approach, which—for the most part, and rightly or wrongly—assumed we were adults and should be treated as such. It represented a kind of respect for our independence as well as for our ability to use our brains and reason to figure things out for ourselves.

Yet in September 1964, I was also deeply torn about my academic inclinations and commitments. Just a few weeks before, I had been in the South, in the company of people risking their lives for justice and equality, in a world far removed from the peaceful campus of Bryn Mawr College. The immediacy and urgency of the civil rights struggle contrasted sharply with the abstractions of ancient history or French or German literature. How did these two parts of my life relate? In letters to Linda Martin, my friend from the summer, I wondered if I ought to be in school at all when so much was at stake in the South. "Life is just a series of rising and receding depressions about the uselessness of education," I wrote. "I have been thinking a lot about maybe taking a year off."[17] College seemed to be all about me; my summer had been all about others. My academic work transported me to an ethereal realm of ideas; the civil rights movement was about action in the here and now. Studying often just seemed *irrelevant*.

The notion of relevance had not occurred to those who had constructed the Bryn Mawr curriculum. Or perhaps they had envisioned a kind of timeless relevance; they would argue that Plato and Aristotle would always be important (and thus they required all of us to study them). But there were not many courses one could choose that addressed issues that only came to seem more pressing as my college years wore on. Not just nothing about women, but no courses in Black studies, nothing that might illuminate our increasingly significant and—to me—increasingly troubling engagement in Vietnam.

Although I could not take a course on the Black experience, I managed to find one on Native Americans, taught in the Anthropology Department by Frederica de Laguna, a very distinguished ethnologist who would in 1975 be one of the first two women elected to the National Academy of Sciences. (The other was Margaret Mead.) The Sociology Department offered a class called American Social Structure that covered class and poverty; the History Department provided a course on Latin American revolutions and another on revolutionary Europe.

In spite of what I saw in the catalog as rather slim pickings, I managed to create a measure of the relevance I sought. Nearly every Bryn Mawr course required a significant research paper, and whenever I could, I chose a subject that in some way related to my political concerns. For sociology, I wrote about race and the white church in the South; for U.S. history, I chose to explore federal Indian policy in the early twentieth century; for a class on Tudor–Stuart England, I wrote about a seventeenth-century radical democratic reform movement called the Levellers; for the senior thesis in my history major, I studied the origins of the U.S. involvement in Vietnam. And I wrote repeatedly about Albert Camus—for the big paper required at the end of freshman English and again in a philosophy course my sophomore year. Finally, as a kind of bookend to my freshman essay, I submitted a paper for European history in my senior year on the ethics of the French Resistance, a movement in which Camus had been a hero.

I had first encountered Camus in high school when I was assigned *L'Étranger* (*The Stranger*) in French class, but it was the exquisite moral intensity of *The Plague* and the powerful leanness of parable in *The Myth of Sisyphus* that captivated me. For my yearbook page both at Concord and four years later at Bryn Mawr, I chose the same quote from Camus: "For the plague stricken . . . peace of mind is more important than a human life . . . I have realized that we all have plague and I have lost my peace. And today I am still trying to find it . . . to understand all those others and not be the mortal enemy of anyone. I only know that one must do what one can to cease being plague-stricken."[18] In the proposal I submitted for my Bryn Mawr freshman paper, I explained, "Ever since I read *The Plague* I have liked Camus without really knowing why. I find much of what I think verbalized in what I have read of his work, and, therefore, I wish to know more about his thoughts and his method of creation."[19]

Camus's message to me was that we must combat evil, beginning with its presence within us. Life itself represented a moral emergency. One must recognize this and choose—to be victim or executioner—and act. This in itself created life's purpose and meaning. To deny that one was plague stricken was to accept the kinds of hypocrisies and blindnesses that had tormented me from the time I was a small child. "Once man has recognized plague, or absurdity," I wrote, "he must fight against it, for he cannot escape from himself." Camus's ideas seemed to me not only demanding in their emphasis on moral necessity but also empowering, for they endowed the individual with the capacity to create meaning. "To revolt, to say no," I wrote, "is to imply that somewhere there is a yes."[20]

Having discovered Camus because of a high school French assignment, I was unaware of his importance to many of those, just a few years older, who were assuming leadership roles in the emerging student movement. The civil rights leader Robert Moses invoked Camus in his address to the Mississippi Freedom Summer volunteers at their orientation in June 1964. "Race hatred" was an American epidemic, he declared. "There is an analogy to *The Plague*, by Camus. The country isn't willing yet to admit it has the plague, but it pervades the whole society."[21]

Tom Hayden, Todd Gitlin, and Carl Oglesby, who served as presidents of Students for a Democratic Society, have all written of being inspired by Camus. He would even appear in speeches at Vietnam teach-ins. To borrow the traditional Quaker parlance, he spoke to our condition, to young people growing up in the aftermath of a war that had represented an ethical catastrophe and had left the world confronting the possibility of atomic disaster. Like many others in college and young adulthood, I embraced his sense of moral and political urgency, its promise of agency, and its ethics of responsibility. As Todd Gitlin wrote me not long before he died in the winter of 2022, Camus taught us "that one finds freedom in the jaws of resistance to evil." The notion of freedom arising from commitment that transcended the self

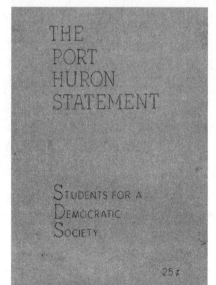

My copy of the SDS founding document.

appeared entirely consistent with the lives of the civil rights activists I had encountered during my summer in the South. It seemed, to me at least, a philosophy of salvation—ideally of others and perhaps even the world but, more certainly, of oneself.[22]

But throughout my college years, I would find the relevance I was seeking mainly outside the classroom. Soon after I arrived on campus in the fall of 1964, I attended a meeting of Students for a Democratic Society, then a fledgling organization, where I paid twenty-five cents for a fifty-two-page mimeographed document titled "The Port Huron Statement," SDS's defining "manifesto of values and beliefs," which offered an "Agenda for a Generation." I found its overarching principles inspiring and resonant with many of my own convictions. The statement began with the invocation of American ideals—of a "government of, by, and for the people," and a society of justice and equality. But it charted a growing generational "disillusion" as young people began to see "disturbing paradoxes" in American life. Instead of peace, a Cold War mentality had brought humankind to the brink of nuclear destruction. The "declaration 'all men are created equal . . .' rang hollow before the facts of Negro life in the South and the big cities of the North." America, it lamented, "is still white." But the statement was not simply a critique; it proposed a solution. The means to realizing America's ideals was the establishment of "participatory democracy," the engagement of all citizens in the decisions that shaped their lives. SDS called for a new society and new politics.

The final section of "The Port Huron Statement" was titled "The University and Social Change." Students, it declared, were poised to lead this national transformation not only because we had recognized America's failure to live up to its own values. We also happened to be located in an institution ideally suited to function as a force for change. The "university could serve as a significant source of social criticism and as an initiator of new modes and molders of attitudes." The document's final words merged a call to action and a cri de coeur: "If we appear to seek the unattainable . . . then let it be known that we do so to avoid the unimaginable."[23] Perhaps being a student didn't need to be so irrelevant after all.

Bryn Mawr's SDS members had joined an initiative launched by the national organization the previous year. The Economic Research and Action Project sought to build "an interracial movement of the poor." During the summer of 1964, SDS had begun work in ten northern cities, including Philadelphia, just a dozen miles from the college. Living in the neighborhood they were trying to organize, a group of students and recent graduates of area colleges stayed on into the fall, forming a core around which volunteers like me could gather. Once or twice a week, with a carful of students from Bryn Mawr and Haverford, I drove the half hour into the city. I was assigned a multiblock area in South Philadelphia and charged with helping to create a community organization intended to empower residents to pursue better lives through active engagement in the democratic process.

South Philadelphia was not the most destitute area of the city—that was North Philly, where, just weeks before, a riot sparked by charges of police brutality had led to more than seven hundred arrests. But South Philly did encompass sections of genuine poverty, both Black and white. Our instructions, from the three or four permanent ERAP staff members, were to knock on the doors of the brick row houses that lined every block and talk with residents about the issues that mattered most to them. We had no idea what we were doing. But we would, assured one SDS leader, learn "from the ghetto residents who really know what they need."[24]

Many doors slammed in our faces. The inhabitants who did open them usually had little to say. I did not find it easy to initiate conversation, to create a connection with people whose lives seemed so different from my own. I had never lived in a city. Just walking around the neighborhood with its empty lots, abandoned cars, and dilapidated buildings was a revelation to me. And the painstaking particularities of this work were distant from the grandiose abstractions that had motivated me to undertake it. Gradually, as the fall wore on, our little team managed to build trust with a few residents who agreed to open their homes for community meetings to discuss goals and strategies. I don't think we ever had more than a handful of attendees, but the consensus emerged that our organizing issue should be rat control. Now at least we had something tangible to talk about when we stood on stoops and knocked on doors. We would build a united front to demand the city take action against a growing and dangerous population of rodents.

The community residents probably anticipated how it would all turn out from the start. SDS national headquarters decided that ERAP initiatives needed to be consolidated. Before the winter of 1965 was over, the Philly operation had folded, and most of its few full-time staff had moved to join the project in Chicago. We ended our trips into the city. I don't remember that we ever explained to the South Philly community what had happened to our ambitions or our promises. I don't think we even said goodbye. It must have seemed that we just disappeared. Before long, SDS had abandoned ERAP altogether.[25]

By the beginning of a new year and a new semester, I was no longer trying to organize South Philadelphia, but I soon found myself drawn into a more dramatic expression of my concerns about racial justice and civil rights. As I look back, I think of a story that Bryan Stevenson, lawyer for the condemned and dispossessed and founder of the Equal Justice Initiative, tells about his life, a story that has helped me understand how I ended up in Selma, Alabama, in March 1965 when I was supposed to be back in Bryn Mawr, Pennsylvania, taking midterm exams and completing my first year of college. Bryan is a spellbinding speaker—maybe the best I have ever heard—who transports you into his world of experience and compassion. There is one personal memory he shares often. It is about his grandmother, who always held him so tight it hurt and offered words that he has never forgotten: "'You can't understand most of the important things from a distance, Bryan. You have to get close." Proximity, Stevenson came to recognize—to the condemned, to the oppressed, to the suffering—gave him a purpose and a foundation for action that the abstractions of newspaper articles or law school textbooks could never provide.[26]

My summer experience in the South had given me proximity. I had gotten close, and I could not see stories of racial injustice and white violence in the same way again. The incidents being reported from the voting rights drive that Martin Luther King, Jr., had joined in Alabama were not remote. Even if the particular individuals I had come to know—Eddie and Willie from Orangeburg, George from Birmingham, or the families of the four young girls who had been murdered in the bombing of the Sixteenth Street Baptist Church— were not the specific individuals now being beaten or killed, it was people like them, people who were confronting the same injustices and sharing the same dreams. I had become invested in them and in their struggle in a way I could not have been before they gave it tangible reality in my mind—and heart. I had to get close again. The moment of truth for me was Bloody Sunday, March 7, 1965, when I watched on television as unarmed protesters, including John Lewis and the formidable sixty-three-year-old civil rights crusader Amelia Boynton, were clubbed to unconsciousness by state troopers determined to prevent them from crossing the Edmund Pettus Bridge.

In 1963, Alabama's Dallas County Voters League, together with the Student Nonviolent Coordinating Committee, had begun a voting rights drive in Selma. But it had been stymied by violence, intimidation, arrests, and court injunctions. Selma was a city of about thirty thousand people, 57 percent of whom were Black. Fewer than 1 percent of the city's eligible African American population was registered to vote, and Selma was notorious for the violence of its response to any Black assertiveness or demands for change. Sheriff Jim Clark—close to a caricature but all too real in his beefy menace—led a posse of law enforcement officers who used nightsticks, whips, and cattle prods to impose what they called "public safety," by dispersing civil rights

meetings, beating Black leaders, and pummeling picketers and protesters. When these tactics seemed only to strengthen the burgeoning
Selma movement, national civil rights leaders recognized an opportunity for a battle over access to the vote that could draw widespread
attention and support. Selma's activists formally invited Martin Luther King, Jr., and the Southern Christian Leadership Conference to
join their campaign. They were correct in their assessment: as soon as
King joined their efforts, Selma began to appear on the front pages
across the country nearly every day. I and many thousands like me
were caught up by the drama.

King arrived on January 2, 1965, to address a crowd seven hundred strong gathered at Brown Chapel African Methodist Episcopal Church to celebrate the 102nd anniversary of the Emancipation
Proclamation. "Today marks the beginning," King declared, "of a determined, organized, mobilized campaign to get the right to vote everywhere in Alabama."[27] In the weeks that followed, several thousand
African Americans seeking to register were arrested, including King
himself. After law enforcement officers violently broke up a march
in mid-February, a young Black protester, Jimmie Lee Jackson, was
killed by a state trooper, who also brutally beat his eighty-year-old
grandfather.

The time had come, James Bevel of the SCLC proclaimed, "to do
something dramatic."[28] King would lead a fifty-four-mile march from
Selma to the state capitol at Montgomery. Alabama's bombastic segregationist governor, George Wallace, vowed he would never permit
it to happen. Bloody Sunday was the result, and it received all the national attention the march's organizers could have hoped for. As the
protesters, led by John Lewis of SNCC and Hosea Williams of the
SCLC, advanced peacefully over Selma's Edmund Pettus Bridge on
the afternoon of March 7, they encountered a wall of uniformed men,
armed with rifles, pistols, clubs, and whips, as well as hoses wrapped
in barbed wire. Many of the troopers were mounted on horses, and
many wore helmets bearing Confederate symbols. When the dem-

onstrators did not immediately obey an order to turn around, the police advanced into the crowd, swinging their weapons at anyone and everyone in their path. The marchers tried to flee, stumbling over those who had been beaten and wounded. But police continued to pursue them, donning masks to cover their faces as clouds of tear gas enveloped the scene. They had come prepared not just to stop the marchers but to punish them.

Photographers rushed films of the chaotic and bloody scene to their networks. In those days, news film for television had first to be developed, then placed in canisters to be flown to network headquarters in New York. CBS and ABC showed short clips on the 6:00 p.m. news, but by 9:00 p.m., ABC was ready to broadcast an entire fifteen-minute segment. It had no narration, which had the effect of inserting the viewer directly into the unmediated chaos. The unforgettable images of Alabama state troopers, mounted on horses, wielding billy clubs against helpless demonstrators have since become iconic. But as I watched on television, it was all too shocking and all too real.

From that moment, I knew I had to do something. If I did not stand up, if I did not act after witnessing this, I would be ashamed forever. What more clear-cut confrontation of good and evil could one imagine? What more urgent obligation of American citizenship and basic morality than not just to speak but to *act* against what had happened on that bridge? All Americans, King declared, "are involved in the sorrow that rises from Selma to contaminate every crevice of our national life."[29] I knew it didn't matter to the world at large what I did; I had no illusions that whatever action I took or did not take would have a significant impact on the fate of the Voting Rights Bill. This was an issue between me and my conscience about what was necessary for me to live my life.

Two days after Bloody Sunday, James Reeb, a Unitarian minister from Boston who had come to join the protests, was attacked and beaten by the Klan. On March 11, he died of his injuries, provoking further outrage across the nation—a level of indignation on behalf of a white victim, many Black activists noted, that had not been expressed over the earlier death of Jimmie Lee Jackson. SNCC, CORE, and other groups organized protests in more than eighty cities, including a noisy and disruptive demonstration outside the White House. Though President Johnson declared that he would not be forced into action, pressure to deliver a Voting Rights Bill and to protect demonstrators was mounting. And, as I closely followed the news from Selma and across the nation, I felt increasing urgency about what I should and would do.

On March 17, a Wednesday, an order issued by the federal district judge Frank Johnson paved the way for another attempt by protesters to make the journey from Selma to Montgomery. The march was scheduled for the following Sunday. King put out a call for "all of our friends of goodwill across the nation to join with us in this gigantic witness to the fulfillment of democracy."[30] I knew I was going to go, and I needed to quickly figure out how.

I enlisted my boyfriend, Adam,[31] to come with me; together, we persuaded his roommate to lend us his car, a blue Ford Falcon station wagon with room for one of us to sleep while the other drove. I entreated my best Bryn Mawr friend to type up the extremely rough—handwritten in those days—draft of my English term paper—the freshman capstone project—and submit it for me on the due date. I was also going to need to skip a sociology midterm exam, so I set off to tell my professor why, in the hope he might let me take a makeup.

Professor Eugene Schneider, like many on the Bryn Mawr faculty, had an office in the bowels of the college's faux-medieval library. Tucked behind the cloisters, just off a gray stone hallway, Mr. Schneider sat at his desk almost hidden behind piles of books and papers and the gloom of the pipe smoke that filled the room—a sweet-smelling cloud a world away from the fog of tear gas on the Edmund Pettus Bridge. His first question to me after I told him my plans was to ask if my parents knew I was doing this. My answer was an emphatic no.

I shared nothing of my political views or activities with them. They would disown me, I answered. He raised his eyebrows and puffed a few times on his pipe and then replied that since he believed I would be in danger, he wanted me to call him every twenty-four hours while I was south of the Mason-Dixon Line. If he didn't hear from me, he would take action. What action? Call out the cavalry, he said. We never specified what that meant. I suspect he had no idea and assumed he would figure something out in the moment if it became necessary. But he left me highly motivated to prevent the summoning of any cavalry. I readily agreed to call.

The trip to Selma from Philadelphia is about a thousand miles. Adam and I decided we would switch off driving every hundred miles so we could stay alert. We wanted to be scrupulously law-abiding, especially as we got farther south. I was well aware of many instances of police harassing those suspected of being "outsiders" or civil rights activists, and we would be heading into Dixie with Ohio license plates. That also meant that we didn't want to stay at motels or otherwise draw attention to ourselves, as I was only seventeen years old, and Adam could be subjected to various kinds of legal unpleasantness for traveling with a female minor across state lines.[32]

We stopped and regularly changed drivers as we had planned; we played the radio, ate the snacks we had brought along, talked about what might lie ahead, and unspooled our anxieties about whether this march would result in violence like the first. We were about halfway there when the radio announcer reported that President Johnson had decided to federalize the Alabama National Guard to protect the marchers. This made us believe we might survive our adventure.

By the time we got to Atlanta, about a twelve-hour drive from Philadelphia, we knew we had to find a way to get some sleep. It was well after midnight, and we were confident we would be able to complete the remaining leg to Selma in time for the start of the march later that day. Where could we stay? I had an idea. From the time I had spent in Atlanta in between stints in Birmingham and Orangeburg the preceding summer, I had a vague notion of how to get around the city. I suggested we go to Morehouse College—a historically Black institution and in my mind a safe haven—and find a parking lot where we could sleep in the car. I remembered the correct exit from the freeway, and we located an empty lot where we parked and quickly fell asleep. But before long, there came an insistent knock on the car window. There stood a Morehouse security guard, displeasure evident on his face. We were on our way to march at Selma, I explained, and needed to get some rest before we went any farther. "Bless you." He smiled and walked away.

We proceeded early the next morning, refreshed, and arrived in Selma as protesters were gathering at Brown Chapel, the SCLC headquarters and the starting point for the march. We were worried about where to park our borrowed car and about what might be done to it while it sat on the street during our absence. Jim Clark's posse had frequently targeted the cars of civil rights activists, smashing their windows and tires, then arresting drivers for possessing vehicles in violation of safety regulations. And at many sites of civil rights activity across the South, bombs had been placed in vehicles, as in houses and churches. Aside from choosing a fairly exposed parking spot, there was not much we could do except hope for the best—and trust in the effectiveness of the newly federalized troops charged with keeping peace and order in the town.

As we hurried along the sidewalk toward Brown Chapel, we encountered a pair of guardsmen headed in the opposite direction. I felt a sense of great relief as I saw them and may even have smiled in appreciation of the responsibilities they had assumed for our safety. But as they came alongside us and we passed on the sidewalk, the guardsman nearest me reached over and punched me in the breast. I lost my breath—from surprise and shock as much as from the blow itself. They proceeded down the sidewalk as if nothing had happened;

I turned and stood gaping at their backs as they moved away. I wasn't badly hurt; I just had the wind knocked out of me. But I had received a message: even the president of the United States cannot truly federalize the Alabama National Guard. I was reminded that "Alabama" precedes both "National" and "Guard" in their title. And white Alabama remained unwaveringly committed to the racial status quo. As Governor Wallace had put it in his 1963 inaugural address, "Segregation now, segregation tomorrow, segregation forever."[33]

We squeezed into Brown Chapel and found ourselves in the midst of a mass meeting very like the one I had attended in Birmingham the summer before. But the excitement of this crowd was electric as it swayed in time to the familiar anthems of the movement, although many of the words were specific to the place and occasion:

> Ain't gonna let nobody turn me 'round
> Turn me 'round, turn me 'round.
> Ain't gonna let no tear gas turn me 'round . . .
> Ain't gonna let no horses turn me 'round . . .
> Ain't gonna let George Wallace turn me 'round . . .
> Gonna keep on a-walking, keep on a-talking
> Marchin' up to freedom land.[34]

It seemed a bit like a pep rally in its joyous exuberance, but at the same time, there was apprehension about what might lie ahead. We were troops—albeit nonviolent ones—readying for battle, a band of brothers (and sisters), a happy few, exhorted by our own King to marshal our courage for the fight.[35]

The marchers poured out of Brown Chapel and snaked through Selma's streets toward the Edmund Pettus Bridge. I could see its arches above the heads of the crowd, and soon I was walking up its steep incline. I reached the highest point on the bridge and looked down. Instead of the menacing wall of uniformed troopers I had seen on television two weeks before, determined to halt the marchers at the bridge's end, National Guard members lined the road on either side, ensuring that the crush of onlookers did not block our way. Thirty-six hundred strong, we were a-walkin' and a-talkin' on our way to Montgomery and freedom land.[36]

We marched seven miles that day. Clots of people lined the road. Many were well-wishers—Black residents of Dallas County shouting encouragement and appreciation. I recall numbers of them as either quite elderly or very young. Perhaps they were unable to march but glad to cheer. There were white detractors, too, who shouted hostile epithets and carried signs supporting segregation and urging outside agitators to return from whence we came. I worried that there might be snipers on the tops of the buildings we passed, but the heavy law enforcement presence had accomplished its purpose. Johnson had not just federalized the Alabama National Guard but also sent one hundred FBI agents and U.S. marshals, one thousand military policemen, and two thousand U.S. Army troops, as well as an assistant attorney general to accompany us.[37] I had no notion of the number and variety of our protectors, but there were enough of them in evidence to give me confidence as we walked.

Adam and I were in the middle of the procession, able to see neither its beginning, where the dignitaries and civil rights leaders marched, nor its end. The people walking beside us were a combination of local Black citizens and visitors, like us, who had come south to join the effort. Ministers, teachers, ordinary people who had stories much like ours, they had watched the violence on TV and decided they had to come—for conscience, for America, for justice, and, often, for God. We marveled that we were there; we marveled that this was happening; we marveled at both the support and the opposition we witnessed along the way.

When Judge Johnson had ruled that the march could proceed, he had included a safety provision that had direct relevance for us. After the first day, Route 80 narrowed from a four-lane to a two-lane high-way. At that time, and until the road opened up to four lanes again as it entered Montgomery County more than twenty miles later, only three hundred marchers were permitted. These would, of course, be the individuals at the heart of the Selma movement, as well as the national leaders who had come to participate. It would not be until Wednesday afternoon that others would be able to rejoin the march for the triumphant entrance into Alabama's capital city.

The continuing marchers would spend the night in a field close to the designated route. Two local Black farm owners, David and Rosa Bell Hall, had overcome considerable fear of retribution to offer the use of their land as a campground. When we arrived, volunteers were spreading out blankets, singing as they worked. With the fading light of an Alabama early spring day, it seemed to me a pastoral setting—far removed from the fears and threats of violence that had surrounded us. We were directed to an area where other volunteers were assigning protesters to buses and cars for the return to Selma. There were also families offering to take marchers into their homes for the night. Suddenly I remembered I had not called Mr. Schneider for more than twenty-four hours. I had no phone or access to one. Not knowing what to do, I turned to a local woman I had been walking near during the day and asked if she would be willing to make a collect call on my behalf when she got home. She readily agreed, and Mr. Schneider received a mysterious call later that evening assuring him of my well-being. I was grateful he accepted the charges.

The couple who took us into their small and tidy house were elderly—at least to my seventeen-year-old eyes—and had long memories of the constraints and oppressions with which Black Alabamians had lived. They showed us to a well-appointed room—I suspect it was their own—where we collapsed from the exhaustion of a day that had begun in Atlanta so many hours before. When we had learned we would not be able to march again until at least Wednesday, we had decided to return north, as we had no idea where we could stay or how we would occupy ourselves for three days without becoming a burden to others like our generous hosts. In the morning, we were offered a ride back to downtown Selma and, we hoped, our car. The blue Falcon was where we left it, seemingly untouched, though we had a moment of fear about a possible explosion as we turned on the engine. But soon we were under way, feeling safer than we probably should have. Just four days later, at the end of the march, Klan members shot and killed Viola Liuzzo, a thirty-nine-year-old white woman who had come from Michigan to participate, as she drove away from Montgomery.

I remember nothing of the trip home. Soon I was back at Bryn Mawr, which had not changed a bit during the four momentous days I had been gone. Its quiet seemed surreal after the intensity of what I had experienced. But I soon received reminders that I had been gone as I confronted the havoc caused by my academic derelictions. My English paper—which my friend had indeed typed and submitted, but which I had never even seen—was returned to me covered with scribbled corrections and outraged comments. My professor, Robert Patten, minced no words about one outcome of my trip:

> While sympathizing as a person with your decision to in-volve yourself in Selma rather than staying at Bryn Mawr to proof-read your paper, as a teacher I cannot help deploring the effect on the paper that decision all too evidently had. The final version is characterized throughout by a degree of sloppiness and laxity that has never before been prominent in your work. This is all the more to be regretted, since you have the insight to have made this a really first-rate study of Camus' fiction. To begin with, the writing is consistently flaccid. You employ far too many imprecise formulations; there is too much bad jargon and shorthand . . . A certain imprecision in structure has led to two other flaws: para-

graphs are not crisply determined, and ideas and phrases are repeated far too often.[38]

On and on for several typed single-spaced pages.

Since kindergarten, I had strived to be a perfect student, but I received this chastisement with a certain satisfaction. I knew Mr. Patten was right. The paper was a mess. But I secretly wondered what Albert Camus, its subject, might have thought of the whole episode. I had originally chosen my topic and envisioned my paper as a sort of homage to him, but going to Selma was a far better one. We must live our lives, Camus had urged, so as not to be on the side of the executioners. That was the side I had been born on, the one I was struggling to escape.[39]

I thought of the many remarkable people I had encountered in Selma and the risks they took every day in pursuit of freedom and equality. The couple who permitted marchers to camp on their farm; the husband and wife who had welcomed us into their house; the thousands of marchers who had been in the fight for months, years, and even decades, their lives perpetually in danger. The sacrifice of my freshman English paper was the very least I could do. I knew I had not made much of a contribution to the civil rights cause, but I had done something important for myself. For me, going to Selma was an affirmation that some things matter more than others in life. And some things are bigger than any one of us. I had gone to Selma, as Dr. King had requested, to bear witness.

I had idealized the civil rights movement even before my trip, and my reverence was only strengthened by my days in Selma. It was a thrill when the Voting Rights Act we had marched for became law the following August. But the movement was coming apart, even as I walked down Highway 80. SNCC had refused to endorse the Selma march, resenting what it saw as King's high-handedness and hunger for celebrity. And challenges from Black activists to the philosophy of nonviolence were mounting. The assassination of Malcolm X in

February had fueled a rise in militancy and a growing commitment to Black Power as an alternative to the integrationist mode of earlier protests. After the passage of the Voting Rights Act, King himself began to redirect and expand his attention—to the North and to poverty and economic justice, issues that proved even more complex and divisive than his earlier efforts to end de jure segregation.

By the spring of 1966, SNCC had split with the mainstream civil rights movement, changing its official name from the Student Nonviolent Coordinating Committee to the Student *National* Coordinating Committee. The raised fist of Black Power was replacing the bended knee of nonviolence as both the emblem and the essence of the Black freedom movement. Selma was in many ways the end of a chapter. What the progressive social critic Marcus Raskin once called "the We Shall Overcome period of American life"[40] seemed to be over. Even though opening the rolls to Black voters would ultimately transform American politics, activists like Stokely Carmichael did not believe conventional measures could produce the deeper change they sought. The script for my morality play was being abandoned, and it was no longer clear where a white person could fit in with the movement's changing directions. There was no inspiring demonstration for me to attend, no organization to join, no specific piece of legislation to champion.

It may be that moral clarity inevitably becomes more elusive as one ages. Perhaps my generation understood this when we warned that you should never trust anyone over thirty. But even for Dr. King himself, the path forward became more difficult and less obvious. And the emerging tragedy of Vietnam would only make it more so. The first American combat troops arrived in Vietnam on March 8, 1965, the day after Bloody Sunday.

11

INSTEAD OF HAPPY CHILDHOODS

It is especially appropriate that we American students, fighting
for the right to determine our own future, support the right
of self determination throughout the world and call for
international opposition to the war in Vietnam.
—*THE COLLEGE NEWS*, BRYN MAWR COLLEGE, MARCH 17, 1967

On April 17, 1965, I attended my first antiwar rally in Washington,
D.C. I have lost track of how many Vietnam protests I participated
in during the next half decade. Usually I drove down with a carful of
friends from Haverford and Bryn Mawr. Sometimes I would leave
them after a Saturday rally and head to our Virginia farm two hours
away to spend Sunday with my family—especially, after my mother's
death in 1966, to see my ten-year-old brother. I never spoke of where
I had been, and no one ever asked.

The war would come to consume SDS—and many of us. Vietnam,
as the journalist Michael Herr once remarked, "was what we had instead of happy childhoods."[1] But the April 1965 rally still had an air
of novelty and a hopeful optimism that would be replaced as the years
wore on by a growing anger and a sense of futility. Both the war and
the size of the protests would steadily expand. From the time of the
Gulf of Tonkin Resolution in the summer of 1964, when Congress
gave President Johnson essentially blanket authority to wage war in
Asia, I had felt growing disquiet about the American presence in
Vietnam. I had supported Johnson's election as the "peace" candidate,
yet here he was betraying the very principles he had run on. By the

early winter of 1965, a number of us at Bryn Mawr and Haverford had begun to delve into the details of the conflict. We investigated the circumstances surrounding what seemed the highly dubious claim of an attack on American ships that had served as Johnson's justification for the Tonkin resolution, and we chronicled the impact of American air strikes and atrocities against Vietnamese civilians.[2]

Although most of my friends had approved of my trip to Selma, many had reservations about my growing preoccupation with foreign policy. I remember a heated argument with a roommate who refused to believe that our government was misleading us. She insisted that if we did not stop communism in Vietnam, the rest of the countries in Asia would fall like dominoes. What I had seen on my trip to Eastern Europe nearly two years before had led me to reject the pervasive and monolithic anti-communism that was propelling the nation into an ever-widening war. It was clear that we who opposed mounting conflict had a great deal of work to do, even within our own small college community.

After the University of Michigan invented the teach-in in March 1965, we called on the expertise of faculty from the wider Philadelphia area—including Temple, Penn, and Swarthmore as well as Haverford and Bryn Mawr—to sponsor marathon sessions of lectures and panels that often stretched well into the night. Together with thousands of other students and professors on campuses across the country, we explored Vietnamese history and the evolution of American foreign policy, as well as more recent political developments, reaching well beyond what was available in our regular curricula. As one Michigan student observed, "This teach-in shows me what a university has to be."[3] We were mobilizing our intellectual resources in support of our politics.

By April, some twenty thousand people—the D.C. police said fifteen thousand; we were sure it was at least twenty-five thousand—had been convinced to gather from around the nation to officially present our concerns in a petition to Congress. On a sunny spring day, we listened live to folksingers I had heard only on the records I played in my dorm room. Like many in the crowd, I knew almost all the words and sang along as Phil Ochs insisted "I ain't marching anymore" and Joan Baez assailed the "masters of war," in a rendition of Bob Dylan's angry anthem. It did not escape my notice that these songs—like many others embraced by the antiwar movement—reminded us that in war it was always the young who died. Vietnam was strengthening the already-growing awareness that we were a generation entirely apart from our parents in our values, our aspirations, our music, our sex lives, and—now with the threat of war and the draft—our basic self-interest.

A parade of speakers took the podium to charge that the United States had abandoned its democratic ideals by waging war in support of the dictatorship we had installed and supported in Vietnam. The conflict, SDS's Paul Potter proclaimed, "has provided the razor, the terrifying sharp cutting edge that has finally severed the last vestige of illusion that morality and democracy are the guiding principles of American foreign policy."[4] The betrayal of American ideals that had galvanized my engagement with civil rights also lay at the heart of my distress about our involvement in Vietnam. My concerns about racial injustice and about the Cold War were inextricably intertwined. The preceding summer, the civil rights icon Fannie Lou Hamer had traveled from Mississippi to the Democratic National Convention in Atlantic City, New Jersey, to demand that her vote be counted. She uttered three unforgettable words as she was turned away: "Is this America?" I now found myself asking that same question about the president's determination to escalate what I regarded as a cruel and illegitimate war in Vietnam.

In the early 1960s, fewer than ten thousand men were drafted into military service each month. By the end of 1965, that number approached fifty thousand. Escalation in Vietnam brought the war home to American campuses through its direct and growing impact on our own lives. Mounting numbers of troops were accompanied by

growing numbers of American casualties. We were increasingly concerned not just with the war's morality but also with its mortality, with
a burgeoning fear that boys we knew—perhaps at some point even
our own boyfriends—might be injured or die. Even though I had not
known him well, I was stunned and horrified when in the summer of
1967, one of my brother's former Princeton roommates was killed—in
"hostile action . . . small arms fire . . . Quang Tin province."[5]

Deferments that had provided a variety of ways to avoid the draft
were gradually disappearing. Being married no longer got you out;
graduate school, except for medicine and the ministry, no longer
provided exemption; undergraduates were informed that they would
need to be in the top half of their class or perform well on a "Vietnam
Test," given by the federal government to assess students' aptitude for
higher education, in order to receive a 2-S classification. A man was
eligible to be drafted until he was twenty-six, so a plan to avoid service in Vietnam had to involve a strategy that would be viable for a
number of years. The draft and what to do about it became a preoccupation for nearly every boy at Haverford and for every Bryn Mawr
girl who cared about him. As we came closer and closer to graduation—and the boys to full eligibility—the discussions became more
and more anguished.

The draft was administered by four thousand local boards, and
each had its particular approach to Selective Service and its own attitudes about approving deferments. In the South, some boards were
outright punitive, drafting civil rights protesters in retribution for their
activism, and in North and South alike, young Black men were more
likely to be enlisted and sent into combat. The burning or turning-
in of draft cards, which gained momentum after late 1965, also put
students at risk of being inducted. For many of the boys I knew, it was
their draft board's attitude toward conscientious objection that was
critical. Haverford and Bryn Mawr had both been founded by Quakers,
but Haverford had retained a direct and explicit connection to the
Society of Friends, nurturing a strong pacifist spirit in its students

and faculty. A man could receive exemption from the military draft if he could convince his draft board of his opposition to violence. A Supreme Court case in 1965 determined that this need not involve membership in a pacifist religious group such as Quakers or Mennonites, but many draft boards disregarded this ruling.

The real sticking point, however, was that a potential draftee had to be opposed to all violence—not just the Vietnam War—to be granted CO status. I remember endless inconclusive conversations about whether one would have fought Hitler. In addition, conscientious objector applicants had to be ready to answer the question that almost inevitably would be posed in their required interview with their draft board: If someone were attacking your girlfriend, would you use force to protect her? Many of my late nights during college were devoted not to parties but to gatherings of friends earnestly seeking answers to what might prove to be life-or-death questions.

Haverford's Quaker ties connected the college with a growing network of "draft counselors," individuals with expertise in how to mount a case for CO status, as well as in many other means of avoiding the draft. The challenge to conscience involved not just the purity of one's pacifist beliefs but other ethical questions as well. How much could one shade the truth? How far would one go toward outright deception in seeking a medical deferment—starving oneself to be below the required weight level, pretending to be insane, or addicted to drugs, or homosexual? Was the solution to try to join a branch of the service that would keep you out of ground combat—a choice that grew increasingly difficult as the National Guard filled to overflowing? Was the most virtuous decision to go to jail in dedication to your beliefs? How ethical was it to try to avoid the draft in the first place when that meant that many less well-connected and less privileged individuals, without draft counselors or student deferments, would have to serve instead? If it was immoral to go and immoral not to go, should you therefore just serve? Or should you flee to Canada or Sweden to escape the draft, but likely never be able to come home?

I knew men who made each of these choices and whose lives were shaped by them forever. It was an agony for them, and it was in many ways an agony for the women as well, for our lives were closely bound up with theirs: they were our friends, our lovers, our fiancés, in some cases even our husbands. Our futures were indivisible. But our futures and our agony were also different. I wasn't going to die in a jungle or a rice paddy. I didn't have to decide how deep my pacifist commitments really were. In my opposition to the draft, as with my concerns about civil rights, I was in a position of privilege; I was not a direct victim of the injustice I sought to oppose. The Vietnam generation—those of draft-eligible age during the war—included 53.1 million young Americans; 26.3 million of us were exempt because we were female. I had received as a birthright the best and most absolute and permanent draft deferment. "There but for fortune go you and I," Joan Baez sang in her 1964 hit. That sense of fortune, of unwarranted luck, haunted me. War had defined my parents' and my grandparents' generations. Now, in a very different way, it was defining mine. I began to wonder if that was what a generation is: not a biological measure so much as the maximum length of time human beings can forgo mobilizing to destroy one another.

The escalation of the draft radicalized the antiwar movement, pushing it, in its own description, from protest to resistance to rebellion. But our rising anger about the war was not just a matter of opposing conscription and its threats to our control over our own lives. The escalation of the war made us increasingly concerned about the suffering of the Vietnamese people. Johnson steadily intensified the bombing until ultimately the United States would drop more tons of explosives than it had in all of World War II. The government developed "pacification" policies for the South Vietnamese countryside that would require, in the words of one military officer, the destruction of villages in order to save them. Soldiers committed atrocities like the murder of some five hundred civilians at My Lai. But the personal horror of the draft, of having to participate in such a conflict, of forcing men to be soldiers in what seemed an immoral—and increasingly unwinnable—war: this changed the stakes. It brought the war home.

In "The Port Huron Statement," SDS had in 1962 proclaimed its "abhorrence" of violence in its pursuit of social change. The Vietnam War first eroded and then eliminated those compunctions. In Washington in October 1967, a protest of more than 100,000 people divided into two as a sizable portion of the demonstrators left the Lincoln Memorial to cross the Potomac and march on the Pentagon. The part of the protest I participated in was not very different from the many marches that had preceded it, though the crowds had grown bigger. Phil Ochs and Peter, Paul, and Mary sang; various notables spoke. But on the Virginia side, the demonstrators, who had signaled their intention to commit civil disobedience, were met by the 82nd Airborne, armed with rifles, bayonets, and tear gas. Militant law enforcement clashed with aggressive demonstrators and resulted in 683 arrests—as well as Norman Mailer's classic account of the confrontation, *The Armies of the Night*.[6] Several Bryn Mawr students were arrested. The *College News* editor Kit Bakke wrote of the impact of her experience at the Pentagon: "Everyone seems to recognize that this is a turning point in the movement, away from peaceful mass rallies . . . and toward more local and more militant action. We have been marching for over two years now and it does not seem to have done much good."[7]

Both literally and figuratively, I remained on the peaceful side of the river, uneasy about this new and violent turn within student activism. I had a kind of temperamental aversion to intimidation and force, one that had been nurtured by my exposure to Quaker precepts. I was much more comfortable with a politics grounded in debate and persuasion, and with power exerted through democratic expression, than with the new performative and coercive style coming to characterize young militants. I was drifting away from SDS as it abandoned its commitment to participatory democracy in deference to what it called its "action faction."

But I was finding other means of acting against the war. In the same month as the march on the Pentagon, three badly injured young Vietnamese arrived for medical treatment in the United States under the sponsorship of the Committee of Responsibility to Save War-Burned and War-Injured Vietnamese Children (COR).[8] One hundred more would eventually follow, and others would be cared for in a COR facility in Saigon. I had become aware of COR the preceding January when *Ramparts* magazine published a lavishly illustrated and horrifying photo essay titled "The Children of Vietnam."[9] It might more appropriately have been called "What the United States Has Done to the Children of Vietnam." Shocking color photographs depicted boys and girls with skin shredded or burned to ash from napalm, with faces disfigured from bombs, with limbs missing from land mines— or from amputation, a procedure used regularly as a "surgical shortcut" in Vietnam's inadequate and overtaxed medical facilities. Martin Luther King, Jr., wept when he saw these photographs and not long after that delivered the legendary Riverside Church speech in which he, for the first time, explicitly condemned the war. The *Ramparts* article didn't make me cry; I was too angry.

I cut out the horrifying photographs to create a display on a bulletin board in Bryn Mawr's main classroom building. It created an uproar. A group of students demanded that the pictures be taken down, declaring them offensive and in bad taste. Several complained they could not sleep at night after seeing them. Others argued that a consideration of the war should be based on facts and figures, not on a condescending appeal to emotions. Within a day, sheets of plain white paper had appeared to cover all the photographs. Declaring this response something "I could neither believe nor understand," I dispatched a letter to *The College News* in a steely rage:

> One of the more convenient aspects of modern warfare is that it can be waged by a people unaware of what it is doing . . . I do not believe . . . that anyone can develop a valid

opinion about this war without realizing to some extent the significance of the means being used to win it. War is not in good taste. The thousands of Vietnamese children with eyelids burned away by napalm cannot sleep easily either. Somehow facts and figures of millions wounded or thousands dead do not mean nearly as much as the picture of a single Vietnamese child with the skin peeling off his back from a war burn.

Suffering is not measured in millions or thousands but in many individual cases. It is only when we see the meaning of an individual's suffering that we can begin to multiply it into statistics. Each wounded child does not understand or even know how many children are wounded. He understands the war in Vietnam in terms of his own suffering. It certainly cannot hurt us to be exposed to his point of view . . . One cannot begin truly to solve a problem until one has admitted that it exists. Covering the pictures will not heal the children's wounds. If you are outraged by the pictures, you should be equally outraged by the existence of the untreated wounds . . . The war in Vietnam is at least partly our war; the wounded are at least partly our responsibility.[10]

I closed with my favorite quote from Camus: "I only know that one must do what one can to cease being plague stricken." At heart, I knew that my letter to *The College News* was both right and self-righteous, both absolutely true and highly disingenuous. I wanted to help the children. But I also wanted America to see what its war was doing. I envisioned political as well as humanitarian goals. To transport these children to the United States was a way for me to help to bring the war home.

Encouraged by the *Ramparts* article, I had discovered that COR had a very active presence in Philadelphia, based among a group of physicians at Temple University. The chair of the organization's national board, Dr. Herbert Needleman, lived only a few miles from the Bryn Mawr campus, and his wife was an alumna. He invited me to join COR's national committee. I worked to mobilize fellow students to raise money to bring children to the United States for medical care unavailable to them in Vietnam, distributing a flyer headed: "AN OPPORTUNITY FOR YOU TO DO SOMETHING ABOUT THE SUFFERING CHILDREN OF VIETNAM." It announced, "Committees have been set up to contact local churches, businessmen and other schools; to recruit doctors from the Main Line; to handle publicity and general fundraising; and to provide general manpower."[11] I began to speak at local high schools, spreading the word and seeking donations. The opposition I had encountered at Bryn Mawr was replicated on a broader level. Both the U.S. and South Vietnamese governments were uneasy about the effect badly injured children would have on American public opinion, and they posed every imaginable bureaucratic obstacle to bringing the children for care in the United States. It would require dogged persistence for COR to pursue its purposes.

The war continued, and so did we. We fasted, we protested, we held Vietnam Weeks filled with speakers and seminars, and we tried to spread antiwar sentiment with the community-organizing drive of 1967's Vietnam Summer. But the escalation and our sense of futility continued to rise. I could understand why many activists were becoming more militant.

Some of us in the student movement, frustrated at our inability to change foreign policy, began to look for victories closer to home. "The Port Huron Statement" had as early as 1962 pointed to the role universities might play in social change. Although SDS's leadership had come increasingly to regard higher education as reinforcing rather than challenging the status quo, students began to seize opportunities in their own backyards. Many grew directly out of the war and its demands—for reports of class rank to determine draft eligibility, for example. This became an obvious target for student pressure and protests. In Philadelphia, a consortium of research institutions that included Bryn Mawr was accepting government funds for studies of biological and chemical warfare, so we insisted that Miss McBride oppose these policies or withdraw the college from the organization. When we confronted her with our request—it was delivered in a manner too civilized to be considered a demand—she seemed bewildered, unaware of the nature of the research and surprised by our focus on it. It was a sign that students were getting well ahead of what educational administrators had even begun to imagine. But she took us seriously and entered our concerns into a debate that ultimately led to the establishment of constraints on classified research by the consortium.[12]

I had been involved in various positions of student leadership since my arrival at Bryn Mawr—as a class vice president, then president, and ultimately in my senior year as head of the college's Self-Government Association. Many of the duties associated with those roles were trivial, and even then some struck me as ridiculous. Bryn Mawr celebrated—and revered—a number of what it called "traditions," the most notable of which was May Day, another example of the college's Anglophilia. May Day's early and more extravagant versions at the beginning of the twentieth century aspired to emulate Elizabethan fairs, complete with farm animals, elaborate costumes, and the arrival of the college president on a horse. By the 1960s, it was somewhat toned down but still involved students dancing around maypoles in white dresses, with a pole for each college class, a hoop race to see who would be the first to marry, Morris dancers and pipers, and an anthem said to have been written by Henry VIII. In my four years of college, I never once attended, much less danced, but as sophomore class president it was my job to oversee May Day's organization and, most important, to make sure Haverford did not succeed in its annual effort to steal the maypoles.[13] The Bryn Mawr student body had not yet developed the sense of irony about this celebration that might have reconciled me to it. A feminist playfulness has enabled it to survive—beloved, as I understand it—into the twenty-first century. In addition to their homage to the traditional beribboned shafts, students now dance around a May Hole while chanting, "Hey hey, ho ho, the patriarchy has got to go." In my day, we had occasion to chant to the same tune, only it was at antiwar protests rather than celebrations of spring and it was Lyndon Johnson, not yet the patriarchy en masse, whom we sought to depose.

Introducing Professor Eugene Schneider at a Bryn Mawr symposium I helped organize about the urban crisis.

But my duties involved more than May Day. We inevitably confronted issues arising from a growing demand that students everywhere seize greater control over their own lives, free from any lingering bonds of in loco parentis. These were battles I had been fighting in some form since I was a toddler refusing to wear fancy pants. At a women's college, these imperatives derived both from a nascent feminism—why shouldn't we have the same freedoms men did?—and from another social upheaval that was taking place around us: the Sexual Revolution. Committed to freedom struggles in our own nation and abroad, we found ourselves fighting for new freedoms of our own. A *College News* article from March 1967, citing antiwar organizers, outlined the connection: "'It is especially appropriate that we American students, fighting for the right to determine our own future, support the right of self determination throughout the world and call for international opposition to the war in Vietnam.'"[14] And vice versa.

Young women of my college generation had been told all our lives that "nice girls don't." And we had been warned—even threatened—with tales of the dire consequences of "going too far." Once a man had made his conquest, he wouldn't respect us. We would get a "reputation." And worst of all, as the Bryn Mawr Hygiene Lectures reinforced, we could get pregnant—with the terrifying prospect of a dangerous illegal abortion or a "shotgun marriage," a squalling baby demanding our attention, and the demise of any hopes for further education or career. We all had acquaintances who had experienced these fates. I had seen friends return to campus bleeding from botched abortions, yet too frightened to seek medical help. I knew pregnant classmates who resigned themselves to marry boys they did not love. One girl disappeared from my biology lab and from the college in the middle of a semester to reemerge the next academic year as a wife and mother.

But the dark cloud of moral opprobrium that had surrounded premarital sex was lifting. Sex, my generation came to insist, was natural, a matter for joy, not shame. As the economists Claudia Goldin and Lawrence F. Katz have documented, the median age at first intercourse declined steadily from the 1960s onward. In 1960, it was twenty; by 1970, eighteen and a half; by 1980, seventeen and a half; by 1990, sixteen and a half. Yet for women of my college era, the fear of pregnancy remained real and realistic. We could rebel against our parents, but not against biology. Until Enovid. The Pill.[15]

Enovid was a combination of estrogen and progesterone first approved in 1957 for treatment of menstrual disorders and then, three years later, as a highly reliable form of contraception. It was easy to use and much more effective in preventing pregnancy than anything else available. But until the late sixties, it was illegal to prescribe an oral contraceptive to an unmarried minor without parental consent. I don't think there was anyone at Bryn Mawr in the 1960s who would have made such a request of her parents. A chasm was emerging between the generations on the acceptability of premarital sex. At Bryn Mawr, growing numbers of nice girls did. They just didn't tell their parents.

But the safety offered by the Pill was hard to come by. I got it without asking before I even thought I wanted it. Because I had irregular and painful menses, the college infirmary sent me to a local gynecologist for a consultation. She prescribed the Pill and renewed it regularly throughout my college years. I never had to worry about getting pregnant.

During my four years of college, I had a succession of three long-term boyfriends. I met Adam, who later would accompany me to Selma, when we were assigned to the same team in the SDS organizing project in South Philly. He had graduated from Haverford the year before and was living in a nearby house with two former classmates while he worked in a college biology lab. He shared my intensity and earnestness about changing the world, and he considered himself to be in constant moral combat with injustice and inauthenticity. During evenings at their house, he and his roommates would invent giant casseroles they called "gorp," designed to make a little meat go a long way while we all discussed the men's draft status and life plans. One roommate was a philosophy graduate student, so we often slipped into highly abstract considerations of the ethical choices that the rapidly escalating draft calls represented.

But it was not just the draft that presented a challenge. Nearly every life choice was fraught. Intensity seemed to prescribe a purity of action and commitment that verged on the exhausting. I remember I once secured a pair of front-section tickets to the Philadelphia Orchestra that had been passed on to the college by an alumna who could not use them. Adam was excited to come with me but insisted he would not dress up for the occasion. He would wear his customary blue jeans so as to remain true to who he believed he was. This was not yet an era in which one wore jeans to the Philadelphia Orchestra. Coats and ties were de rigueur, especially in the row of seats we were to occupy. Jeans would indeed be a statement—though of what I wasn't exactly sure. Épater le bourgeois, I supposed. But I was embarrassed by the notion of using the generosity of an alumna to make a political point I was sure she would have deplored. I was overruled when I suggested that perhaps the more honorable path would be not to go at all. I slunk down the aisle at the Academy of Music, keeping a considerable distance from Adam and hoping that the surrounding Philadelphia worthies would not report this transgression to our benefactor. Or at least not associate me with it. One of my greatest challenges as an activist was probably that I was too polite for the revolution.

If Adam was in constant struggle with himself and the world, his successor was the opposite. He, too, was a recent Haverford alumnus, a genuinely countercultural figure, at peace with being exactly himself and entirely different from everyone else. His parents had named him Terron, in hopes he would always have his feet on the ground. He was gentle and kind and had no reservations or doubts about being a conscientious objector. He, too, worked in a lab, though his was at Penn, and he lived in an apartment a few miles from Bryn Mawr. Raised in the Pacific Northwest, he had roamed woods and fields and had developed an array of practical skills absent in almost everyone else I knew. He slept on a mattress on the floor but made all his other furniture himself, baked his own bread, and was devoted to his pressure cooker, which I found rather unnerving, as I always feared it would explode. Educated as a scientist, he was also something of a mystic, captivated by Eastern philosophies and Native American religions. He was a follower of the teachings of Edgar Cayce, a clairvoyant who had died in the 1940s but still received the almost worshipful loyalty of a band of disciples who have been seen as important originators of what became the New Age movement.

Terry embraced many of Cayce's ideas about spiritual and physical health. I remember his regular applications to his stomach of poultices drenched in a forbidding dark substance. I regarded this as nothing more than an endearing weirdness, something far less frightening than the experiments with LSD and other mind-altering drugs with which numbers of my classmates were becoming involved. Terry never tried to push his beliefs on me, and I spent many evenings and weekends hanging around his apartment, studying and writing papers while he undertook his many projects. When we were apart, he wrote me lengthy letters, their pages filled with tiny, penciled words that now require a magnifying glass for me to read. My parents regarded him as an even more inappropriate boyfriend than Adam. Perhaps that is why I ended up treating him so badly after my mother's death. My father was dealing with so much that I felt reluctant to be the cause of additional worry and heartache. I found myself forgetting to return Terry's calls, discovering I had less time to spend at his apartment, drifting away without ever explaining what was happening either to him or to myself.

By the summer of 1967, six months after my mother's death, I had acquired a new, more acceptable boyfriend, Steve, a Haverford student I had met through my new role as president of the Self-Government Association. He was on the Haverford student council, a tall, handsome premed, involved, as I was, in the effort to expand students' power and responsibility. Together, we became caught up in the challenge to what seemed increasingly outdated restrictions on our freedom to make our own choices. An honor system of academic and community government could not survive if students didn't respect its claims on them. "We cannot base an honor system on a series of rules which students do not wish to uphold," I declared to the college newspaper. Soon after I took office in the spring of 1967, near the end of my junior year, Haverford made a decision that gave the issue a new urgency. Haverford's board declared that there would be no more restrictions on when women would be allowed in Haverford dormitories. As far as Haverford was now concerned, women could move in with their boyfriends. Bryn Mawr's Self-Gov was already undergoing a regular periodic review of its constitution—the rules and expectations it set for women students. How would we respond? How would the administration permit us to respond? How would we deal with "the problem of cohabitation posed by the absence of hours at Haverford?"[16]

In retrospect, the issues seem antiquated and insignificant. At the time, they appeared earthshaking, involving student freedom, the future of in loco parentis, the rights of women, and the legitimacy of student self-rule. "The Self-Government system cannot and should not act as a mother to the student body," I proclaimed.[17] In what *The College News* described as an "effort for collegiate grass-roots democracy," I called for an open meeting to consider whether Bryn Mawr women should be permitted to spend the night at Haverford.[18] Six hundred students would attend what was expected to be a tense and contentious gathering.

My involvement in civil rights and student activism had exposed me to assumptions about leadership and social change that I was now going to find myself putting into practice. The ideals of "participatory democracy" rejected hierarchy as well as the power or legitimacy of any single individual. I saw myself as the convener of a gathering of college citizens, a facilitator of their debate and decision making, a conductor rather than a commander. I approached the meeting as if I were leading a very large seminar. It seemed important to present all sides of the question, so I invited Miss McBride to offer her views. Even though I anticipated that the gathering would not be persuaded by her position, I hoped she would not be shouted down.

Miss McBride had been president of the college since before we were born. Most students found her distant and intimidating; to many she just seemed archaic. As she walked down the long aisle of Goodhart Hall to join me on the stage and make her remarks, we could not help but speculate about how someone who had never married and who seemed so resolutely single could understand the issues before us. Seeing her in my mind as she made her way alone through the silent, cavernous auditorium, twelve hundred skeptical eyes fixed upon her, I am certain this could not have been her favorite presidential moment. But given these circumstances, she spoke effectively, explaining that rules were established not to exert control over us but to ensure student well-being. Pointedly invoking the wisdom derived from her long experience, she noted that students sometimes found themselves in situations they were not equipped to handle or resolve, and she wished to protect us from such occurrences. Casting the question as one of student welfare and interests rather than rights and power, she defused at least some of the mistrust in her audience. She came off as calm and thoughtful, respectful of us—even if we believed her to be wrong and somewhat patronizing. Her words re-

Goodhart Hall, Bryn Mawr.

inforced the tone of civil interchange that I had hoped for and made it easier for me to lead a reasoned discussion after she departed. Many students participated, expressing varied perspectives and opinions not just about the particular Haverford question, but about larger issues of student rights and privileges and the role the college should play in managing our lives. After considerable debate, the meeting concluded with an affirmation that students should be able to sign out for overnights anywhere, including Haverford. One classmate remembers that the civility of the gathering was constructively at odds with "sixties style" confrontations. "We were arguing," she noted, "that we were capable of handling these freedoms, so did not need to look sassy and petulant."[19] The grass roots had shown up, and they had spoken.

Over the months that followed, Bryn Mawr would abolish its system of parietals and eliminate curfews. It didn't happen as a revolution or an uprising, but as a series of further consultations and negotiations that reflected the halting shifts in values of the moment in which they occurred. Students themselves were divided about many of the provisions they were asked to consider in the constitutional revision ballot. Faculty weighed in on all sides, but the views of the popular political science professor Peter Bachrach were widely greeted with approval. Deploring a pernicious "double standard"—even as he referred to us as "girls" and Haverford students as "men"—Mr. Bachrach stated definitively, "If Bryn Mawr girls are expected to be the intellectual equals of men, then there should be social equality as well: if men had no curfew, neither should women."[20] This was the fundamental issue of fairness—of boys' freedoms versus girls' rules—that had challenged me since I had been a small child.

Small-scale meetings scheduled in all the residential halls generated debate not only about curfews and sign-outs but about a range of other issues as well. It was no longer a question of itchy organdy, but girls' freedom of choice in clothing still mattered. Students voted to repeal the requirement that skirts must be worn when one left campus. "The voting reflects a change in the mores of society . . .

The wearing of slacks in public places is no longer considered out of the ordinary," Self-Gov explained in an election summary. But the mandate for skirts in class—framed by its supporters as a gesture of respect for the faculty—was retained by a 66 percent majority.[21]

The most controversial provision, permitting overnights at Haverford, won decisively. The students had spoken. But in what was usually a formality, the board of directors—Bryn Mawr's name for trustees—had final sign-off on Self-Gov decisions. How would they respond? Miss McBride had made it clear that she was uncomfortable with the measure. Would she urge the directors to overrule the student vote? The justifications students advanced publicly to support this desired change tended not to be as straightforward as the position taken by Mr. Bachrach. Likely anticipating what they expected the views of the directors to be, most advocates avoided the subject of sex altogether and even argued only glancingly about personal freedom. A great deal of attention was devoted to the activities that women might wish to pursue in the middle of the night at Haverford apart from sexual intercourse. Curfews should not interrupt intense and extended discussions of Kierkegaard. This was the essence of Bryn Mawr: we believed we made our strongest argument by grounding it in intellectual opportunity.

It was the responsibility of Self-Gov officers to make the case to the directors. We did so in the most peculiar and unforgettable of circumstances. I cannot remember what conflicts made the only possible meeting date and place late August in Atlantic City. I do know that the board chair, a distinguished judge, had to be there then for a Bar Association conference, but he could make time for the session with us if we would travel to him. We scrambled to arrange rides as we rehearsed our arguments. When we arrived, we soon realized that the Bar Association wasn't the only convention in Atlantic City. The city was also hosting, as it did annually, the Miss America Pageant. Bryn Mawr and Miss America might well be regarded as the polar opposites of 1960s American womanhood. Our competitiveness revolved around brains, not beauty. Few Bryn Mawr girls even wore makeup.[22] The following summer, women's liberationists would stage one of their best-publicized early demonstrations at Atlantic City, a protest against the "degrading Mindless-Boob-Girlie Symbol" celebrated by the Miss America Pageant.[23] In 1967, however, I was not yet that politically enlightened or mobilized, and was instead quite fascinated by glimpses of glamorous young women darting from one event to another. I felt like an ethnographer deposited in a strange land.

Around a large green felt-covered table in a dark windowless hotel conference room, we met with a half dozen directors. We students talked as little as possible about sex and as much as possible about trust, rights of self-determination, and the educational value of the freedom to choose. We left the directors to deliberate. They agreed to the removal of curfews for a trial period; by the end of the academic year, they were gone altogether. The little Bryn Mawr laboratory experiment in participatory democracy had worked.

A number of years ago, I was explaining to my then-college-age daughter what my own college experience had been like. I proudly—and rather self-importantly—proclaimed, "*I* eliminated parietals at Bryn Mawr!" My daughter looked at me blankly and asked, "What are parietals?" I will choose to consider her question a tribute to our success.

12

THIS IS THE END

The ceremony of innocence is drowned.

—WILLIAM BUTLER YEATS[1]

I thought the last day of March 1968 might change everything. For one brief shining moment, it appeared we had won. But then the world seemed to unravel right in front of our eyes—just as we stepped forth to join it. It was a Sunday night. Spring break was over, and only six weeks of college remained before graduation. Celebrations were already beginning to dot the calendar. The weather was warming, and national politics were heating up as well. In January, the Tet Offensive, penetrating the actual and symbolic heart of American power in Vietnam, had seemed to expose President Johnson's assurances of imminent victory as entirely meretricious. His promises of light at the end of the tunnel appeared to be no more than delusions—or outright lies. We in the antiwar movement already distrusted nearly every word he said, and we embraced this new and compelling evidence of military and intelligence failures as proof we were right to do so. Not only was the war morally wrong; we were losing it. The peace movement was gaining new traction, and now it could claim a foothold in electoral politics: Eugene McCarthy had announced his candidacy for the White House on a platform of ending the war. In early March, a campaign staffed by hundreds of student volunteers brought him close to defeating Johnson in the New Hampshire primary, an almost unimaginable blow to an incumbent president.

And now Johnson was announcing he would deliver a speech to

the nation about the war. My boyfriend, Steve, lived in a Haverford dorm in a four-man suite that boasted a comfortable sofa and a television. We decided we would watch Johnson there.

By 1968, the United States had nearly 500,000 troops in Vietnam, and draft calls were rising, an increasingly relevant issue for college seniors like those at Haverford whose 2-S deferments would soon expire. Although I found the growing militance—and even violence—in the antiwar movement distressing, I was angry, too. Angry at Johnson for lying, angry at how his lies betrayed what I believed America ought to be, angry at how his distortions seemed to be not just prolonging the war but tearing the nation apart and fracturing and radicalizing a student movement in which I had so fervently believed. "Credibility gap" became the term of art for the chasm between what the president and his administration were saying and what growing numbers of the American people regarded as fact or truth. Would Johnson be announcing yet another escalation? Or might Tet and McCarthy have convinced him of the need for at least a slight change of course? Would we even be able to believe or trust anything he said?

Johnson delivered a very long speech. Steve's suitemates hooted at the TV screen when he said something particularly deceptive or misleading. But so much of what he was saying seemed like what we had heard before. It was numbing. As the speech wore on, Steve began to nod off. He knew he would be getting a medical school deferment from the draft, so Johnson's words weren't immediately relevant to him. But suddenly his suitemate Jack Rakove was shoving him awake. We could not believe what we had just heard, and we turned to one another for confirmation. "I shall not seek, and I will not accept, the nomination of my party for another term as your president," Johnson had declared.[2]

"Did he say that?" "Did you hear that?" "Could it be an eve-of-April-Fool's joke?" We leapt from our chairs in delight and disbelief. Johnson was quitting. We could hear shouts from rooms down the hall and across the campus. This was a clear victory for the antiwar movement that had detested him. "Hey hey, LBJ, how many kids did you kill today?" Surely this meant that whoever succeeded him would have to be committed to ending the war. Even in my cynicism and distrust, I could not have imagined that American troops would remain in Vietnam for seven more years. Between 1968 and the 1975 evacuation of Saigon, 38,156 more Americans would die. Nearly two-thirds of the eventual American losses were still to come. But I did not know that. In this moment, it seemed the nearly unimaginable had happened. We were rid of Johnson. Peace was certainly at hand. And we in the antiwar movement took satisfaction that it was at least partly our own doing.

Jack had spent a junior year abroad in Edinburgh and remembers that when he returned to Haverford in the fall of 1967, it had seemed different. The first thing he noticed was that drugs were everywhere—mostly marijuana, but LSD and other hallucinogens as well. As senior year unfolded, Jack recalls, conversations overwhelmingly focused on two topics: first, the draft and what each of his classmates was going to do about it, and second, *Sgt. Pepper's Lonely Hearts Club Band*, the Beatles album released late the preceding spring. Who *was* Mr. Kite? Was "Lucy in the Sky with Diamonds" just a code for LSD? Did Harry the Horse represent a drug dealer? Did the song title "Fixing a Hole" refer to shooting up heroin? What message were the Beatles sending? What did it all mean?

The album was itself a kind of drug trip—from its psychedelic cover mixing the dead and the living, the real and the invented, to the songs and lyrics themselves, involving a fantastical world of "tangerine trees and marmalade skies." Meaning was upended as the Beatles invited us into a realm of higher consciousness. "I'd love to turn you on." No one doubted that the Fab Four were themselves tripping as they recorded the album, but theirs were upbeat hallucinations expressed in the cheerful rhythms and oompah-pahs of an English music hall band. Together with the single "All You Need Is Love," released in

July, *Sgt. Pepper* had served as the background music for 1967's Summer of Love, anthems for the emerging counterculture of freedom and self-expression. We all returned to college in the fall knowing every word and singing every melody.

But the academic year ahead would not sustain this optimism. The good trip that was *Sgt. Pepper* would become the bad trip of assassinations, political turmoil, and social upheaval that was 1968. Psychedelic skies darkened, and it would be not the Beatles but Jim Morrison and the Doors who would come to represent an increasingly embittered and alienated youth culture. "This is the end," Morrison warned us. Many of those who remained committed to social change turned in frustration toward violence; others abandoned their search for relevance and engagement in favor of drug-fueled oblivion— a retreat from the world into the workings of their inner psyche. Jim Morrison was high on LSD when he recorded "The End," and its ominous invocations of death, murder, and pain made listening to it feel something like living through a nightmare. When Morrison sang, "All the children are insane," we came close to believing that he meant us and that it was all too true. We embraced "The End" because it was as scary as the world unfolding around us, which made it seem indispensable.[3]

Although I smoked marijuana a few times, I was not an active participant in the drug scene. I was writing a senior thesis, and Steve and I were deeply engaged with our academic work, including a class in European history taught at Haverford that we were both taking. Serious studying didn't fit very well with getting high. But drugs affected my life nonetheless, as an issue for student government. In a meeting with Miss McBride soon after I was elected Self-Gov president in the spring of 1967, I raised drugs as an issue I thought the campus would be confronting in the coming year. Miss McBride expressed surprise and communicated her certainty that Bryn Mawr students were too intelligent to be lured into such distractions, which were both illegal and a possible threat to health. Her comment seemed revelatory to me. Her confounding of intelligence and judgment struck me as misguided—even naïve, yet somehow a wonderfully traditional Bryn Mawr point of view. I also realized how out of touch she was. The Self-Gov board estimated that at least half the student body had been experimenting with drugs. Reality would ambush her soon enough. By midsummer, she felt compelled to release a letter to the community declaring that a student ought "not to plan to return to Bryn Mawr unless she is convinced that she will not be using drugs."[4]

Now it was my turn to be surprised. The college's president had issued this statement about student conduct without consulting the students. The realm of behavior and discipline belonged by custom to the students themselves, through the mechanism of their Self-Government Association. I was concerned more about college governance and student power than I was about drug policy. Already caught up in the long struggle for freedom from my own parents' constraints, I was determined that the college should abandon, not expand, any parental role.

I posed a series of questions to the Self-Gov Board, once again reflecting my sense of myself as convener not commander. I presided over the Self-Gov Association as if it were a kind of class discussion. "Do you think she should have said it? Does she have a right to tell students what to do in this way? Beyond question of whether she has this right, should she invade students' private lives?" I asked the Self-Gov Board. If we asserted our responsibility for dealing with drug use, would Miss McBride be willing to back away from the stark position she had articulated?

Our elaborate deliberations involved matters of law, morality, medical risk, individual freedom. I wrote to the board:

> It seems to me we do not know enough about effects of drugs, esp. marij. to be sure we do not want anyone to try it ever. Nor do I feel that it is my job to forbid someone to break a law—I think that law-breaking is one's own decision

if one is aware of and ready to take legal consequences of an
action. We do not want to set up a double jeopardy . . . We
want to maintain an atmosphere of decision as free as is possible about this—as w/ any other personal decision among
the student body.

We concluded that Self-Gov would intervene only if a student was
engaging in behavior that posed a legal threat to the larger community. Not that we—or the larger student body—knew what that might
mean. In the months that followed, we handled only a few incidents
under what could hardly be characterized as a "policy," and we admitted in our end-of-the-year report to the student body that that we had
"no definitive answer to the 'drug problem'" at Bryn Mawr. Yet Miss
McBride had seemed almost relieved to yield the front line on this
vexing issue to us, and we were happy to have made our point about
student authority and responsibility.

Despite our lofty rhetoric, we had little influence over the escalation in drug use in 1968 and beyond. Our idealistic notions about
choice and freedom collided with the terrible outcomes that drugs
yielded for some students: their disappearance into a nether world of
hallucinogens and alternative realities. "One pill makes you larger /
One pill makes you small," often with the consequence, as Jefferson
Airplane sang, that "logic and proportion" disappeared.[5]

You didn't have to be taking drugs to find that logic and proportion were in short supply in the spring of 1968. On April 4, four evenings after Johnson made his announcement, I was eating ice cream
at a party for graduating history majors at the house of the department chair when someone rushed in to say that the Reverend Martin
Luther King, Jr., had been shot and killed in Memphis, Tennessee.
Johnson's message on Sunday had been shocking, but this news was
unthinkable: intolerable, not to be borne, received with the force
of a bullet. The news physically hurt, made it almost impossible to
breathe, left me doubled over. But the cries of "Oh, no!" or efforts to

deny—"This can't be true!"—could not rewind reality, could not keep Dr. King from walking out on the Lorraine Motel balcony, could not prevent him from going to Memphis to support the striking workers, could not bring him back. King's campaign for nonviolence, already under political threat from all sides, had now been terminated with the murder of this man of peace. I felt it not just as the death of a man, but of a moment and a possibility. The end of a movement I had so strongly identified with, and of the life of a man I had regarded as a hero. For me, like so many other Americans, it seemed a personal as well as a public tragedy. I thought back to hearing him speak at Groton five years earlier about the "appalling silence of good people." King's eloquent words and courageous actions had helped me imagine so much of what I wanted to be and do.

Miss McBride convened a Quaker meeting—a ritual that at least as far as I was aware had never before occurred at the college. We gathered once again in Goodhart Hall, the largest indoor space on campus, where I had served as an usher when King had spoken not

Dr. Martin Luther King, Jr., and President Katharine McBride at King's baccalaureate address at Bryn Mawr College, 1966. I was an usher.

quite two years earlier at the baccalaureate service for the class of 1966. Invited to sit on a traditional Friends' Facing Bench at the front of the room, I looked out on the silent assembly and tried to imagine—to borrow the title of the book King had completed the previous year—*Where Do We Go from Here?* Would it be, as King had asked, *Chaos or Community?*[6]

The immediate answer was chaos. For thousands of Americans, there would be no quiet mourning. In more than a hundred cities across the nation, violence erupted as rioters set fires and threw rocks and bottles at the police. Army troops were ordered to Washington, Chicago, and Baltimore; National Guard troops were called out in Chicago, Detroit, Boston. In Chicago, nearly twelve thousand soldiers were deployed, and Mayor Richard J. Daly urged an antilooting policy of "shoot to kill." In Washington, "panic threatened" the city, the journalist Tom Wicker reported in *The New York Times*, as white-collar and government workers created traffic gridlock fleeing their desks in pursuit of safety in the Maryland or Virginia suburbs. President Johnson convened a joint session of Congress to address the crisis. Europe, the journalist Anthony Lewis reported, was reacting with "intense horror" and "fear for the stability of American society."[7] In New York, Black "militants," as the *Times* described them, worked to keep the peace, but not because of any respect for the beliefs of Dr. King. As a representative of CORE explained: "We hold no love for nonviolence—it is a philosophy that went bankrupt a long time ago. We simply don't believe in having black people slaughtered going up against armed police . . . Before we go to war we should know we are fighting from a position of strength, not weakness." The civil rights leader Floyd McKissick proclaimed that not just King but nonviolence was dead.[8]

I began to wonder if the revolution that had become the goal for so many radicalized student activists had arrived. There had been urban riots every summer of my college years—in New York in 1964, Watts in Los Angeles in 1965, Chicago in 1966, Newark and Detroit and dozens of other cities in 1967. But April 1968 seemed different. The *Times* editorialized four days after King's death, "Not since the Civil War has this country experienced an epidemic of domestic violence so widespread as it was this weekend."[9] The war, as threatened, was no longer confined to Vietnam; it had come to America.

I remember the rest of the spring at Bryn Mawr as subdued, muted. The celebration of our history degrees had ended so badly on April 4 that I didn't have much appetite for more festivity. Bryn Mawr, ever serious, expected us to continue our academic endeavors at full throttle until the very end—requiring papers and formidable comprehensive exams in our majors in the very last weeks of school. It was in many ways a relief to have so much work to do. Better to worry about the Congress of Vienna or the Monroe Doctrine than the tumult beyond the college walls. Yet as I made my way through the customary rituals and requirements of senior spring, it was hard not to notice that the world seemed to be coming unglued. The decorous student activism we had championed at Bryn Mawr was taking on a much more confrontational character elsewhere, as students at dozens of colleges and universities mounted their assault on the values and practices of American higher education, occupying buildings, holding deans captive, physically battling with the police. "Recognizing the failure of the liberal university to exist in accordance with its own philosophy," I wrote in a paper for a class on the history of education, "the protestors challenge liberalism itself." The university, like so many other institutions, was facing "a crisis of legitimacy."[10] The power of mind was yielding to the power of force. Nothing could be again as it once appeared. "All You Need Is Love" seemed like something from another planet.

On May 27, Bryn Mawr awarded 167 bachelor of arts degrees. Sixty percent of the class was headed straight to graduate or professional school. My friends and teachers had assumed I would go to law school, but I could not imagine devoting myself to the details of torts or civil procedure. If I decided to pursue further education, I knew it would be for graduate work in history. What had always captured me intellectually was the broad sweep of ideas and social forces. And having grown up in a changing and not-changing Virginia, I knew how those assumptions and circumstances exerted their power through time, often creating silences and blindnesses that undermined human possibility. From at least when I had written to Eisenhower as a nine-year-old, I had recognized the force and the burden of history; I understood the words of the white southern poet and novelist Robert Penn Warren: "History is what you can't / Resign from."[11] Coming to terms with the past would ultimately become an intellectual and professional commitment as well as a personal necessity. I grew up to be a historian.

CATHERINE DREW GILPIN

For the plague-stricken . . . peace of mind is more important than a human life . . . I have realized that we all have plague and I have lost my peace. And today I am still trying to find it . . . to understand all those others and not be the mortal enemy of anyone. I only know that one must do what one can to cease being plague-stricken.

— Albert Camus

My page in the Bryn Mawr college yearbook, 1968. On my right wrist I am wearing the bracelet my grandmother gave me the night my mother died.

But not yet. I had decided I needed to be in the real world for a while. I had loved school since I began kindergarten at the age of four, and at Bryn Mawr I had become caught up not just in learning itself but also in issues of higher education, its shape and future.[12] Could it provide sufficient relevance to the social and political questions that consumed me? I felt I couldn't know until I tried to live outside it. I accepted a job in the Philadelphia regional office of the Department of Housing and Urban Development, a cabinet-level federal agency established just three years before and charged with addressing urban poverty and unrest. I'd be dealing with policies and politics, well removed from the ivory tower.

I had told friends that I didn't even want to go to graduation—partly reflecting a 1960s-era disdain for pomp and circumstance, partly because I felt so disheartened about the world around me. But at Bryn Mawr you had to show up to collect your diploma, so I joined my classmates on an unusually cold spring morning to mark the end of my college experience. My father, no doubt even less excited about the event than I, dutifully came to attend the ceremony, driving up in a pickup truck so he could haul all my possessions home. I avoided having to go back to Virginia with him by planning to stay on in Pennsylvania with friends until my job began.

Bryn Mawr graduation, May 27, 1968.

Thirty-two members of the class that had entered with me in 1964 were no longer with us, a sizable 16 percent of our original cohort. Some had transferred; some had just dropped out. But in one way or another, many represented casualties of the sixties—and some of those who did graduate with me in 1968 and adjacent years would eventually join that category as well. The upheavals in values and possibilities, the new freedoms and accompanying dangers, the intensity and engagement of our college generation, the specter of Vietnam and the draft—all conspired in a way that made coming of age as a thinking and feeling person in those years like walking on the edge of a precipice. An accumulation of often casually made choices could lead to disaster; commitments to principled action could entail enormous risks or sacrifices; toxic relationships, bad drug trips, sexual experiments, and errors of human judgment could yield outcomes that distorted or damaged lives—sometimes irreparably. It felt like there was more at stake—more at risk—for my generation than for those that had preceded us. Mary Patterson McPherson—by that time dean of the college, later Bryn Mawr's sixth president—has described to me the atmosphere of almost constant crisis in which she had to operate: "I spent night after night in the Bryn Mawr Hospital hoping . . . somebody wouldn't die" from a drug overdose, or alcohol poisoning, or a suicide attempt. She regularly bailed out Haverford and Bryn Mawr students arrested at protests or political confrontations; she was constantly "worried about people doing themselves in, in one way or another." As I graduated, I looked back and thought how lucky I was to have skirted catastrophe. More than a half century later, I can imagine the myriad ways it might have been otherwise.[13]

I did not disappear, like my friend Kit, into a Chicago jail and then into the Weather Underground; I did not blow myself up building a bomb in a Greenwich Village townhouse, as one Bryn Mawr graduate a few years ahead of me did; I did not have to seek a back-alley abortion or drop out of school after the effects of a botched one, as one close friend did; unlike the girl in my biology class who disappeared in the middle of the semester, I did not get pregnant and have to marry (and later divorce) my boyfriend; I didn't have to go to Canada or prison to escape the draft, and I did not die in Vietnam—or have to endure its cruelties; I did not get beaten or killed in the South; I was not convicted of felony murder for my role in a Black Liberation Army robbery of a Brinks van, as was a member of the Bryn Mawr class of 1965; I did not descend into the fantastical universe of mind-altering drugs; and unlike Holly Maddux, who was a freshman at Bryn Mawr when I was a senior, I was not murdered, dismembered, and stashed in a trunk by a charismatic but crazy countercultural Penn boyfriend. I had managed not to become a victim, and I was still struggling not to be an executioner.

Yet even in the nightmare of 1968, even as the Black freedom and student movements embraced violence and veered in directions I could not follow, even as American politics all but destroyed what Kit had described as our "enduring, but inaccurate faith in America,"[14] I remained glad to have had a time when I had a reason to believe, ideals to strive for, a glimpse of a Beloved Community. In the long run, it would prove sustaining because I could always hope to find it again.

A week and a day after my graduation, Robert F. Kennedy was assassinated.

American troop levels in Vietnam would rise to 549,500 in the course of the year. By the end of December, 296,406 more men would be drafted; 16,899 more Americans would die.[15]

There would be no antiwar candidate in the 1968 presidential election.

EPILOGUE: FREE, WHITE, AND TWENTY-ONE

We must be free not because we claim freedom,
but because we practice it.

—WILLIAM FAULKNER[1]

It felt strange to be back in my childhood room, trying to go to sleep in the twin bed in which I had spent so many nights over so many years. Shivering and shaking with cold and shock the Christmas Eve my mother died. Sticking to the sheets on hot summer nights while the hassock fan whined uselessly in its effort to move the still and heavy Virginia air. Lying on my back with my arms rigidly at my side looking up for bombs Sputnik might drop on me as it flew by.

The 1960s were nearing their end, but the room remained a kind of Museum of Toys of the Fifties. On the bookcases sat Silly Putty eggs; wind-up chomping teeth; a collection of ceramic horses, several wounded and missing a leg or a tail; brightly colored antennae and proboscises left over from a game of Cootie; a Magic 8 Ball to tell me my future—"Signs Point to Yes"—or urge me to "Ask Again Later." A small dressing table held a set of pink combs and brushes painted with my initials. To sleep in that room was to be transported back into another self, one I had struggled for years to leave behind. Growing up had been about freeing myself from that time and place, and from all it thought I was destined to be. Now I would have to enact—to "realize," in the literal nineteenth-century usage of "make real"—my confidence in the person I had fashioned. The room would always be there in my mind, but I needed to make sure it lived on as a

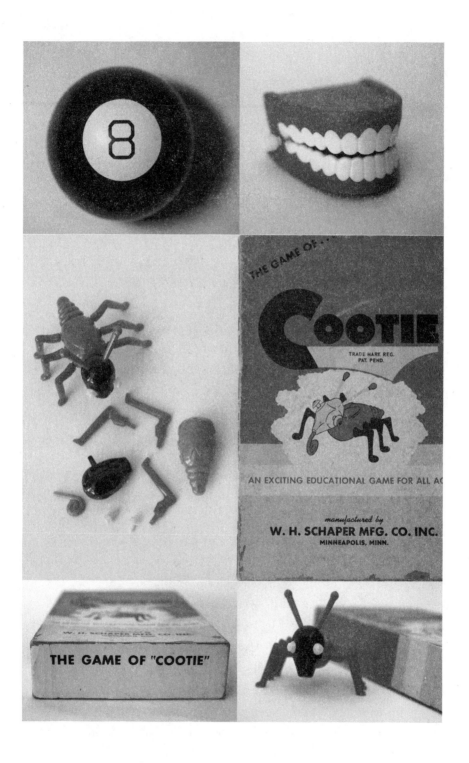

memory and not a trap. I was an adult now, a college graduate, someone supporting herself with a full-time job, but I still feared Virginia
would swallow me. Perhaps it was those chomping teeth.

I had come home to vote in the 1968 presidential election. I had
turned twenty-one in September, so I was at last going to be able, in
that pre–Twenty-Sixth Amendment era, to cast a ballot.[2] As the second anniversary of my mother's death approached, I was still not used
to the house without her. For years, I had not wanted to go home because she was there. Now I didn't want to go home because she wasn't.
After a year in which my father had formally marked his status as a
grieving widower with black neckties and a black ribbon on his coat
lapel, he had embarked on a new existence as a highly eligible bachelor, pursued alike by those seeking a date, a mate, or perhaps just a
single "extra man" for a dinner party. The center of his life was not
Lakeville, but the social whirl he was enjoying in the world beyond it.
The house seemed neglected, almost as if it, too, had died. But I had
come for a purpose. My father had said not a word to me about the
election when I arrived. Bumper stickers on his car made it clear he
was voting for Nixon, but I expressed nothing about my intentions—
or about what I regarded as his appalling politics.

"Free, white, and twenty-one." I had heard my mother say it a
thousand times. It appeared so often in the movies and popular culture of the 1930s and '40s that it has been called an "all-American
catchphrase": characters played by the likes of Ginger Rogers, Jean
Harlow, and Inger Stevens all used it. Henry Ford had been quoted
saying it in 1919 and FDR in 1933. In a 1959 film, *The World, the
Flesh, and the Devil,* Harry Belafonte declared it "an arrow in my
guts." Malcolm X referred to it derisively in the last public speech he
made before his assassination in 1965.[3]

It was my mother, not my father, who invoked it with such frequency. In popular culture, too, the words were overwhelmingly spoken by women. In Hollywood classics, actresses declare themselves
"free, white, and twenty-one" and then follow with "I am going to

do what I please" or "I am going to lead my own life" or "I've got a right to happiness like anyone else."[4] They were claiming their entitlement—of citizenship, race, and age. Asserting their privilege in the face of power challenged or denied. Embracing it at the expense of the rights of others. But privilege, I had learned, is a complicated heritage.

Freedom had been a pressing concern for me from the time I was a small child and first launched battles with my mother about clothes and hair and girls' rules. But freedom had become a great deal more than just not being treated differently from my brothers. There was my gradual discovery that others around me confronted far greater injustices, the growing awareness beginning at age eight or nine of being white, with all it entailed in a society of manifest inequality just beginning to move away from the legal foundations for segregation. And there was my emerging comprehension that freedom meant not just "freedom from" but "freedom to"—a distinction that I had first explicitly recognized on my travels in Eastern Europe but that applied as well to the hierarchies of class and privilege in my own life and nation. "Freedom to" had given me an outstanding education, a veritable bounty of advantages. I had been enabled—to do what? Now I was legally free of any parental constraint. Not that anyone had done much to try to constrain me since my mother's death. But I was at last officially an adult. I could—in the words of the Hollywood stars—"lead my own life" and "do what I please." And what about Camus's notion of freedom as commitment? I had encountered girls and women who dared. Would I dare, too?

That moment in 1968 was a difficult one in which to determine a course for one's life. It was also a difficult moment to contemplate casting a ballot for the first time. The violence that had characterized the spring had reached new heights at the Democratic National Convention in August when Chicago police had assaulted antiwar demonstrators. At the same time, a fractious Democratic Party bowed to Johnson's continuing control and nominated his vice president, Hubert Humphrey, a candidate who had not mustered the courage to defy the president and speak out against the war. Humphrey seemed cowardly and out of touch. It was as if the antiwar movement and the successes of Eugene McCarthy's campaign had never happened. I found the direct attacks on the student movement by his Republican opponent, Richard Nixon, and the overtly racist third-party candidacy of George Wallace of Alabama entirely abhorrent, but I transferred my long-standing anger with Johnson to his vice president.

I began to wonder, too, if Johnson had planned his withdrawal as a way to avoid an election he feared he would lose yet at the same time retain control—and continue the war—by means of a toady. My reaction to the presidential race closely paralleled that of many other young people. *The New York Times* reported that "4 of 8 Ivy League Papers Back Humphrey Reluctantly." The other four supported write-ins. Columbia endorsed Eldridge Cleaver, a Black Panther recently released on parole from San Quentin, while *The Daily Pennsylvanian*, *The Harvard Crimson*, and *The Dartmouth* urged votes for the comedian and Black civil rights activist Dick Gregory. The Rutgers paper reflected my sentiments, encouraging students to "opt out of the system by voting for Dick Gregory, who is running a symbolic campaign against the very power structure that ignores us." The being ignored part rang true for me, as it did for the many student activists who in their frustration were propelled leftward by the recognition that no one was listening. What would it take to seize American attention? To make our truths and our passions felt and heard? To stop the slaughter in Vietnam? The violence of the Weather Underground that emerged at the end of the decade represented one answer to that question. Voting for Dick Gregory was a less dramatic gesture that arose from the same impulse.[5]

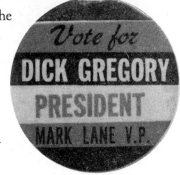

Declaring himself the candidate of the Freedom and Peace Party, Dick Gregory published a campaign biography that combined elements of absurdist humor with pro–civil rights, antiwar statements and positions. His first act as president, he announced, would be to paint the White House black; he would replace the annual Easter egg roll with a watermelon roll; he would bring the troops home from Vietnam and send LBJ instead. But he had a serious message as well. The "moral revolution" he called for in America, he insisted, was "not a fight of blacks against whites; it is a united struggle of right against wrong." He believed that Dr. Martin Luther King, Jr., had been "the greatest moral force on the face of the earth," and, he observed, "The supreme hypocrisy of America is that this nation is not disturbed by white violence. But it is scared to death of black violence." His would be, he declared, a campaign for the enforcement of the Constitution in "the cause of human decency."[6]

I knew Dick Gregory had no chance; I knew mine would be a vote of futile protest—a "waste" of a vote. I feared a Nixon presidency, but I just could not stomach Humphrey. I had spent four years—almost a fifth of my life—trying to call the administration and the Democratic Party to account over Vietnam, and Humphrey's candidacy was a denial that any of it had even happened. Not unlike my bereaved great-grandfather in his heartbroken maiden speech in the U.S. Senate more than four decades earlier, all I was saying was give peace a chance.

The polls for the precinct in which I was registered were located about ten minutes' drive from our house in a settlement of a dozen or so structures called White Post. My weekly 4-H club meetings had taken place in the parish hall of the White Post Methodist Church, so this was familiar territory. My write-in vote for Dick Gregory was one of 1,680 votes he received in Virginia. It was one of 2 votes he received in Clarke County, where Nixon's total was 1,127, Humphrey's 768, and Wallace's 742.[7] Oddly, given that my ballot was in some sense a waste, I could actually see it represented in the official statewide tally. I have often thought about the identity of Gregory's

Dick Gregory's
half-serious,
half-comic campaign
manifesto, published
January 1, 1968.
I wrote him in.

other Clarke County supporter; I wonder if it might have been Raphael.

My trip home proved to be something of an archaeological excursion into the memories and remnants of my childhood, and the vote tallies revealed a great deal about the community I had left. The sizable showing for George Wallace represented the white backlash against the nation's changing racial landscape. The totals reflected the dramatic movement away from the old Solid South of the Democratic Party, an outcome Johnson himself had predicted when he signed the 1964 Civil Rights Bill. The majority of citizens of Clarke County had embraced the Republican candidate, Richard Nixon, whose calls for "law and order" promised a return to the denials and injustices of 1950s complacency. My own lonely ballot symbolized my estrangement from this childhood world. And yet my vote, "wasted" though it might have been, represented something more as well. It was a vote cast for a Black candidate in a Clarke County election, something unimaginable just a few years before. And I had cast it. Someone who, fewer than fifty years earlier, would herself have been denied the franchise.

When my grandfather, Kenneth Gilpin, returned from Europe at the end of World War I, he was elected to the Virginia House of Delegates, representing the district in which I was now a constituent. His work as a legislator involved many very local questions like road development and farm policies. But as a candidate for House Speaker, he took on a national issue. He opposed the ratification of the Nineteenth Amendment and the extension of suffrage to women.[8] Yet here I was. Educated, employed, and enfranchised. I was free. The embodiment of one dimension of progress, intent on helping to overturn other forms of injustice and inequality. I think of how Martin Luther King, Jr., had closed his speech at Groton—with words he told us he'd heard from an old Black preacher: "Lord we ain't what we want to be; we ain't what we ought to be; we ain't what we gonna be. But thank God, we ain't what we was."[9]

Forty years and ten White House races later, Virginia would cast its electoral ballots for the first Black president.

A Note on the Title

In the course of the last decade of John Lewis's life, I was the privileged and grateful recipient of a number of his acts of kindness and generosity. He opened the event at the Kennedy Center where I delivered the National Endowment for the Humanities' 2011 Jefferson Lecture; he invited me to speak about my participation in the 1965 march to members of Congress sharing a bus from Montgomery to celebrate Selma's fiftieth anniversary; he offered moving remarks at the dedication of a plaque to commemorate the stolen lives of four enslaved persons who had worked in the house of Harvard presidents in the eighteenth century; he delivered the address at my final commencement as Harvard's president.[1] In March 2020, just months before he died, I called him to describe this book project and tell him why I hoped to title it with his words. He responded with customary grace: he would be honored.

Since his death, John Lewis has been elevated to an iconic place in American culture and history. He is invoked by those dedicated to his legacy and by those who wish to use the power of his name as they work to destroy what he stood for. I have worried that titling this book with his words might seem either an act of unwarranted appropriation or a cliché. But remembering our last conversation, I believe that my using his words has his blessing. I do so as a gesture of respect and tribute to a man who inspired me from the era of the Freedom Rides to the confrontations of Lafayette Square and the emergence of Black Lives Matter. So much of our ability to continue to struggle and to hold on to the dream of a Beloved Community of justice and peace is, to borrow the words of President Barack Obama, "because of you, John."

Acknowledgments

I have been assisted and uplifted by remarkable acts of generosity as I have worked on this book. My brothers, Tyson, Donald, and Lawrence Gilpin, responded to my queries, shared memories and photographs, and trusted me with my story. My aunt Bettie Gilpin Petith, who blazed a trail, helped this time via Zoom from her apartment in Rome. Teachers and classmates from Concord, Bryn Mawr, and Haverford joined me on Zoom, and the more than one hundred–strong Google Group of Bryn Mawr's Class of 1968 weighed in on matters ranging from the prevalence of makeup during college to the impact of Sputnik. My deepest gratitude to Kitty Fisk Ames, Kit Bakke, Marcia Young Cantarella, Annie Morgenthau Grand, Liz Thacher Hawn, Terry Hirshorn, Deborah Jackson Weiss, Beverly Lange, Margaret Levi, Mary Patterson McPherson, Susan Sherer Osnos, Jack Rakove, Elizabeth Schneider, Melvin Scult, and Kate Douglas Torrey for Zoom conversations. The late Suzy Kagey, my father's longtime secretary, shared her memories of him not long before her untimely death.

Friends and traveling companions from my summers in Eastern Europe and the American South helped me sharpen my memories of those experiences. Thank you to Chuck Lawrence, Beverly Mikuriya, Madelyn Nix, Mary Noland, Harry Nussdorf, and Linda Martin for joining me on Zoom. It was a pleasure to reconnect with you after so many years.

From the time of the first phone call about the book proposal, Jonathan Galassi's engagement, responsiveness, and wisdom have been fundamental, as he encouraged and pushed me in ways that transformed the original project. I feel I have been enrolled in a master class in writing and editing. My only regret about finishing the book is that the interchanges that have been both so enlightening and so much fun will come to an end.

My thanks to Andrew Wylie for taking me on, for helping me craft a proposal, and for connecting me with FSG and Jonathan. The unsurpassed speed with which he responds to emails is a sign of the careful attention he directs to every issue or question.

Cullen Murphy of *The Atlantic* edited an article that has now evolved into a section of the book, and he has supported me and this project from the start. He gave me excellent advice about the book proposal and has continued out of the goodness of his heart to read and react throughout my writing process. It is a much better book because of his extraordinary editorial eye, his suggestions, and his confidence in what the book could be.

A number of friends and colleagues carefully read the whole manuscript and offered wise suggestions and a few warnings. I am deeply grateful to Liz Cohen, Christine Heenan, Stephanie McCurry, Tamara Rogers, Tony Rogers, Amy Rollins, Jessica Rosenberg, Barbara Savage, and Jonathan Walton.

Gene Atkinson, Donald Davis, Beverley Driver Eddy, David Frey, Julia Heaton, Beth LaDow, Sharon Miles, Hayes Mizell, Jeannie Norris, Alice Roebuck, Allen Stokes, and June Manning Thomas all helped me find important research material. Dr. Herbert Schaar, who followed us around Europe in 1963, generously shared photos of that summer from his retirement home in the Canary Islands. The work of my student and research assistant Emmy Cho was invaluable and included not just expert sleuthing in libraries and on the web, but also an astute reading of the entire manuscript. The Southern Historical Collection at the Wilson Library of the University of North Carolina, Chapel Hill, digitized many manuscripts and scanned key photographs to enable my work. The Special Collections Department of the Bryn Mawr College Libraries was unfailingly helpful, as was the Schlesinger Library at the Radcliffe Institute for Advanced Study at Harvard. Trevor Plante at the National Archives once again aided my research with his unparalleled understanding of those rich collections. Rich Burns, Tom Lingner, and Robert Zinck of the Imaging Department of Harvard's Widener Library created high-resolution scans of dozens of snapshots, portraits, and documents to enable the bulk of the book's illustrations. Stephanie Mitchell took key additional photographs. Clark Schuler of Harvard IT saved me from my technological incompetence more times than I can count.

Portions of chapter 4 previously appeared, in slightly different form, in *The Atlantic* ("Carry Me Back") and *Harvard Magazine* ("Living History"). Many thanks to those publications.

I am grateful to Stephen Faust for his efforts to supply me with photographs and for permission to use his wonderful portraits of Virginia, many taken with a large format view camera that so powerfully captures the landscape.

Katie Liptak at FSG has smoothed the production process with her supreme competence and good cheer.

Katie Tiger, as usual for more than a decade, has done everything imaginable to make my life and work possible. She helped at every stage of this project, but her heroic efforts on photo permissions deserve special appreciation.

Charles Rosenberg has heard me tell many of these stories for nearly half a century. He is a discerning reader and a very fine editor, not to mention a distinguished historian. But for this book he has been even more valuable as a participant observer and as interpreter of so many of the experiences the book details. My own life was transformed by the fact that from so early on in our time together, he understood.

This book is, of course, dedicated to Jessica. This is her legacy, too, one that she cannot, as Robert Penn Warren puts it, "resign from." But at least she has never had to worry about parietals.

Notes

PROLOGUE

1. James Baldwin, "Introduction to *Notes of a Native Son*," in *Baldwin: Collected Essays* (New York: Library of America, 1998), 7. Citations for quotes on epigraph page: Harper Lee, *To Kill a Mockingbird* (1960; repr., New York: Harper Perennial, 2002), 90; John Lewis to Drew Gilpin Faust, in Harvard Commencement Speech, Harvard University, May 24, 2018, www.youtube.com/watch?v=XRjAzepG-bA.

1. A DEATH IN THE FAMILY

1. James Agee, *A Death in the Family* (New York: McDowell, Obolensky, 1957), 304.
2. Isabella Tyson Gilpin, "Short History of a Long Life," Gilpin Family Papers, Southern Historical Collection, University of North Carolina at Chapel Hill.
3. Elizabeth Bocock to Isabella Gilpin, December 26, 1966, manuscript letter in possession of author. All manuscript materials are in possession of the author unless otherwise noted.
4. Mira Hall to My dear Catharine [Mellick], January 21, 1932, Miss Hall's School (MHS) Archives, Pittsfield, Mass.
5. James H. S. Fair to Miss [Mira] Hall, June 23, 1932, MHS Archives; James H. S. Fair, "Teacher's Statement, Catherine M. [*sic*] Mellick," MHS Archives.
6. Mira Hall to Mr. F. E. Shnyder, February 10, 1939; Mary L. Stoughton to Miss Margaret Hall, October 8, 1937, MHS Archives.
7. Catharine Ginna Mellick to Daddie and Mummie, on board the SS *Washington*, United States Lines, n.d. [1936]. See also Edith May Papers, Schlesinger Library, Radcliffe Institute for Advanced Study, Harvard University.
8. Catharine Ginna Mellick to Dad and Mum, Letter #9, Sunday, n.d. [1936].
9. Catharine Mellick to Dad and Mum, Letter #9, Sunday, n.d. [1936]; Catharine Mellick to Mum, Letter #4, n.d. [1936]; Catharine Mellick to Dad and Mum, March 1, 1936.
10. Margot Garrett Zuberbuhler to Catharine Ginna Mellick, July 19, 1940.
11. See Melanie Beals Goan, *Mary Breckinridge: The Frontier Nursing Service and Rural Health in Appalachia* (Chapel Hill: University of North Carolina Press, 2008), and Drew Gilpin Faust, "Mary Breckinridge," in *Notable American Women: The Modern Period* (Cambridge, Mass.: Harvard University Press, 1980), 125–26.
12. Catharine Ginna Mellick to Grandma, Sunday, n.d. [1940]; Catharine Ginna Mellick to Mum and Daddy, November 22, 1940.
13. "University Foibles," *Esquire*, September 1940, 103.
14. McGhee Tyson Gilpin, response to questionnaire for 50th Reunion Book, Class of 1942, in McGhee Tyson Gilpin, Princeton Alumni Files, Princeton University, Princeton, N.J.
15. "Baby Boomers," History, May 17, 2010 (updated June 7, 2019), www.history.com /topics/1960s/baby-boomers-1.
16. Betty Friedan, *The Feminine Mystique* (1963; repr., New York: W. W. Norton, 2013), 1, 373, 371.
17. Letter of recommendation to Bryn Mawr College from Harriet A. Olmsted, Concord

Academy, September 19, 1963, Catharine Drew Gilpin Student File, Bryn Mawr College Archives, Bryn Mawr, Pa.

18. Helene Deutsch, quoted in Friedan, *The Feminine Mystique*, 200. "Well-adjusted" was the ideal for child-raising in the 1950s; it was no accident that the Reverend Martin Luther King, Jr., made specific allusion to this mark of complacency in a 1957 speech: "God grant that we will be so maladjusted that we will be able to go out and change our world and our civilization." See King, "The Power of Non-violence," June 4, 1957, webs.wofford.edu/whisnantdm/Sixties/Civil-Rights/The%20Power_Non-violence.pdf.

19. Thomas Piketty and Emmauel Saez, "Income Inequality in the United States, 1913–1998," *Quarterly Journal of Economics* 118, no. 1 (February 2003): 12, 13, 31.

20. See Thomas D. Snyder, "Education Characteristics of the Population," chap. 1 in *120 Years of American Education: A Statistical Portrait*, ed. Thomas D. Snyder (Washington, D.C.: U.S. Department of Education, 1993), 8, nces.ed.gov/pubs93/93442 .pdf; and "Percentage of U.S. Population Who Have Completed 4 Years of College or More, 1940–2020, by Gender," Statista, www.statista.com/statistics/184272 /educational-attainment-of-college-diploma-or-higher-by-gender.

2. A GIRL ISN'T THE SAME

1. Lucy Rebecca Buck, *Sad Earth, Sweet Heaven: The Diary of Lucy Rebecca Buck*, ed. William Pettus Buck (Birmingham, Ala.: Cornerstone, 1973), 50.

2. Isabella Tyson Gilpin to Lawrence Davis Tyson, November 13, 1918, and November 19, 1918, Lawrence Davis Tyson Papers, Southern Historical Collection, University of North Carolina at Chapel Hill (hereafter LDTP); Lawrence Davis Tyson to Bettie McGhee Tyson, October 10, 1918, LDTP. Late in her life, Isabella would describe her brother's death as the result of fire from a submarine. Correspondence from 1918 between her father and McGhee's commanding officer makes clear this was not the case. Airplane malfunction and pilot error (McGhee was operating as gunner, not pilot, on that day) were the cause.

3. Lawrence Davis Tyson to Bettie McGhee Tyson, October 4, 1918, LDTP; Lawrence Davis Tyson to James Neely, October 18, 1918, LDTP.

4. See Samuel Hynes, *The Unsubstantial Air: American Fliers in the First World War* (New York: Farrar, Straus and Giroux, 2014).

5. Lawrence Davis Tyson to Bettie McGhee Tyson, October 22, 1918, Tyson Papers; Colonel T. J. Wyrick, General Tyson's chief of staff, is quoted in an unidentified newspaper clipping, LDTP; "Lieutenant McGhee Tyson While Flying for Freedom Is 'Probably Drowned,'" *Knoxville Sentinel*, October 15, 1918; Lawrence Davis Tyson to Bettie McGhee Tyson, October 22, 1918, LDTP.

6. Isabella Tyson Gilpin, "Short History of a Long Life," Gilpin Family Papers, Southern Historical Collection, University of North Carolina at Chapel Hill (hereafter GFP); Lawrence Davis Tyson to Bettie McGhee Tyson, September 20, 1885, LDTP.

7. Lawrence Davis Tyson to Bettie McGhee Tyson, October 22, 1918, October 28, 1918, and October 23, 1918, LDTP; Lawrence Davis Tyson to Bettie McGhee Tyson and Isabella Tyson Gilpin, November 9, 1918, and November 11, 1918, LDTP; Lawrence Davis Tyson to Bettie McGhee Tyson, November 11, 1918, and December 20, 1918, LDTP.

8. Alice Lombard to Bettie McGhee Tyson, December 10, 1917, LDTP.

9. Bettie McGhee Tyson to Lawrence Davis Tyson, October 19, 1918, LDTP; S. W. Duggan to Lawrence Davis Tyson, November 13, 1918, LDTP.

10. Isabella Tyson Gilpin to Lawrence Davis Tyson, October 19, 1918, LDTP; Anna Staub to Bettie McGhee Tyson, n.d. [1918], LDTP.

11. Josephus Daniels to Mrs. L. D. Tyson, October 12, 1917, LDTP.

12. Isabella Tyson Gilpin to Lawrence Davis Tyson, October 19, 1918, LDTP; "Who Am I?," Isabella Tyson Gilpin, scrapbook in possession of the author.

13. Isabella at times later in life stated her birth year as 1895. However, on her birthday in 1918, she writes of turning twenty-four years old. I take this as definitive. Isabella Tyson Gilpin to Lawrence Davis Tyson, June 1, 1918, LDTP.

14. Miss Spence's School for Girls, brochure, 13, 4, 13, LDTP.

15. Isabella Tyson to Lawrence Davis Tyson and Bettie McGhee Tyson, October 10, 1909, and April 8, 1910, LDTP; Isabella Tyson Gilpin, "Short History of a Long Life," GFP.

16. Isabella Tyson Gilpin, "Short History of a Long Life," GFP; Thomas Gailor to Kenneth Newcomer Gilpin, February 25, 1918, GFP; James Neely to Lawrence Davis Tyson, April 27, 1918, LDTP; Unknown to Bettie McGhee Tyson, July 19, 1918, LDTP; Robert Williams to Kenneth Newcomer Gilpin, February 3, 1918, GFP; author's Zoom conversation with Bettie Gilpin Petith, June 4, 2020. *The Knoxville Sentinel* declared Isabella to be the "most beautiful girl in the South," clipping, March 23, 1918, LDTP.

17. Isabella Tyson Gilpin, "Short History of a Long Life," GFP; Isabella Tyson Gilpin to Kenneth Newcomer Gilpin, September 10, 1917, GFP.

18. Isabella Tyson to Kenneth Newcomer Gilpin, November 11, 1917, GFP.

19. Lawrence Davis Tyson to Bettie McGhee Tyson, November 29, 1918, copied by Bettie McGhee Tyson, LDTP; Lawrence Davis Tyson, draft of Senate speech, n.d., LDTP; "Anglo-Saxons Composed the Famous 'Fighting Thirtieth,'" *Knoxville Journal*, September 28, 1932, 5, clipping, LDTP. On the 30th Division, see Geoffrey Wawro, *Sons of Freedom: The Forgotten American Soldiers Who Defeated Germany in World War I* (New York: Basic Books, 2018); Elmer A. Murphy and Robert S. Thomas, *The Thirtieth Division in the World War* (Lepanto, Ark.: Old Hickory Publishing Company, 1936); *30th Division: Summary of Operations in the World War*, prepared by the American Battle Monuments Commission (Washington, D.C.: U.S. Government Printing Office, 1944).

20. Francis Russell, "When Gentlemen Prepared for War," *American Heritage* 15 (April 1964), www.americanheritage.com/when-gentlemen-prepared-war; J. Garry Clifford, *The Citizen Soldiers: The Plattsburg Training Camp Movement, 1913–20* (Lexington: University Press of Kentucky, 1972).

21. Isabella Tyson to Kenneth Newcomer Gilpin, November 17, 1917, December 25, 1917, January 23, 1918, and January 26, 1918, GFP.

22. Isabella Tyson to Kenneth Newcomer Gilpin, February 4, 1918; GFP; Kenneth Newcomer Gilpin to Isabella Tyson, March 14, 1918, GFP; [A cousin] to Kenneth Newcomer Gilpin, February 12, 1918, GFP; Kenneth Newcomer Gilpin to Isabella Tyson Gilpin, n.d. [1918], GFP.

23. Kenneth Newcomer Gilpin to Isabella Tyson Gilpin, October 8, 1918, GFP.

24. Kenneth Newcomer Gilpin to Isabella Tyson Gilpin, October 15, 1918, GFP.

25. Lawrence Davis Tyson to Bettie McGhee Tyson, December 8, 1918, LDTP; Lawrence Davis Tyson, speech on World Court, *Congressional Record* 2642, January 23, 1926.

26. Isabella Tyson Gilpin to Kenneth Newcomer Gilpin, n.d. [1941], GFP.

27. Author's Zoom conversation with Bettie Gilpin Petith, June 4, 2020.

3. SHOOTING THE DOG

1. Socrates, quoted on Goodreads, www.goodreads.com/quotes/139940-the-greatest-way-to-live-with-honour-in-this-world.

2. McGhee Tyson Gilpin, Jr., conversation with the author, May 26, 2013. Many thanks to Barbara Savage, who described to me traditions of hunting in the Black community where she grew up in southern Virginia.

3. George Fitzhugh, *Sociology for the South, or The Failure of Free Society* (Richmond, Va.: Morris, 1854), 214–17.

4. McGhee Tyson Gilpin to Jessica Rosenberg, January 5, 1995. In possession of the author.

5. McGhee Tyson Gilpin to Isabella Tyson Gilpin and Kenneth Newcomer Gilpin, April 14, 1942, and n.d., GFP.

6. Beverley Driver Eddy, *Ritchie Boy Secrets: How a Force of Immigrants and Refugees Helped Win World War II* (Guilford, Conn.: Stackpole Books, 2021), 347.

7. McGhee Tyson Gilpin to Isabella Tyson Gilpin and Kenneth Newcomer Gilpin, November 1, 1944, GFP.

8. McGhee Tyson Gilpin to Donald N. Gilpin and Madelaine Gilpin, December 23, 1944, and October 14, 1944, GFP.

9. McGhee Tyson Gilpin to Isabella Tyson Gilpin and Kenneth Newcomer Gilpin, December 4, 1944, and October 27, 1944, GFP.

10. Christopher R. Gabel, *The Lorraine Campaign: An Overview, September–December 1944* (Fort Leavenworth, KS: Combat Studies Institute, General Staff College, 1985), 3.

11. McGhee Tyson Gilpin to Isabella Tyson Gilpin and Kenneth Newcomer Gilpin, January 8, 1945, GFP.

12. Ibid.
13. McGhee Tyson Gilpin to Isabella Tyson Gilpin, January 3, 1945, GFP.
14. McGhee Tyson Gilpin to Isabella Tyson Gilpin and Kenneth Newcomer Gilpin, August 31, 1945, and September 26, 1945, GFP; McGhee Tyson Gilpin, response to questionnaire for 50th Reunion Book, Class of 1942, in McGhee Tyson Gilpin, Princeton Alumni Files, Princeton University, Princeton, N.J.
15. McGhee Tyson Gilpin to Isabella Tyson Gilpin and Kenneth Newcomer Gilpin, October 27, 1944, GFP; McGhee Tyson Gilpin to Isabella Tyson Gilpin, July 7, 1944, GFP.
16. Ernie Pyle, *Brave Men* (1944; repr., Lincoln: University of Nebraska Press, 2001), 491, 493. See also Rick Atkinson, *The Guns at Last Light: The War in Western Europe, 1944–1945* (New York: Henry Holt, 2013); George S. Patton, *War as I Knew It* (New York: Houghton Mifflin, 1947); Oscar W. Koch, *G-2: Intelligence for Patton* (Atglen, Pa.: Schiffer Military History, 1999); George F. Hofmann, *The Super Sixth: History of the 6th Armored Division in World War II* (1975; repr., Nashville: Battery Press, 2000); Charles B. Blackmar, ed., *The Princeton Class of 1942 During World War II* (Princeton, N.J.: Princeton University Press, 2000); United States Army, "Combat History of the 6th Armored Division" (1946), *World War II Regimental Histories* 41, digicom.bpl.lib .me.us/ww_reg_his/41.
17. McGhee Tyson Gilpin, responses to questionnaire for 50th Reunion Book, Princeton Alumni Files.
18. Handwritten note by unidentified Princeton official regarding McGhee Tyson Gilpin's admission to Princeton, in McGhee Tyson Gilpin File, Princeton Alumni Files, Princeton University, Princeton, N.J.
19. See "Horseman," for example, on my Bryn Mawr College application, Catharine Drew Gilpin Student File, Bryn Mawr, and entry for McGhee Tyson Gilpin in Princeton University, *Now We Are Forty-Two: The Class of 1942* (Princeton, N.J.: Class of 1942, 1962), 92; Suzi Kagey, quoting McGhee Tyson Gilpin in phone conversation with the author, August 12, 2020.
20. Kenneth Newcomer Gilpin to Isabella Tyson Gilpin, February 19, 1944, and [1943] GFP.
21. "The Lexington Suite in a Virginia Hunt Country Estate," *American Standard: Pure Luxury* (1986), 27.
22. Charles Dickens, *David Copperfield* (1850; repr., New York: Modern Library, 1934), 185.
23. William Shakespeare, *Hamlet*, Act 5, Scene 2.
24. W. C. Fields has been quoted as saying, "Horse sense is a good judgment that keeps horses from betting on people," www.quotetab.com/quote/by-w-c-fields/horse -sense-is-a-good-judgement-which-keeps-horses-from-betting-on-people.

4. MANY FEELINGS ABOUT SEGREGATION

1. James Baldwin, "The Negro Child—His Self-Image," *Saturday Review*, December 21, 1963, reprinted as "A Talk to Teachers," in James Baldwin, *The Price of the Ticket: Collected Nonfiction, 1948–1985* (New York: St. Martin's, 1985), 83–84.
2. Charlie McIntosh to author, email, January 6, 2021.
3. Michael Leeds and Hugh Rockoff, "Jim Crow in the Saddle: The Expulsion of African American Jockeys from American Racing," working paper 28167, National Bureau of Economic Research, Cambridge, Mass., December 2020; Katherine C. Moody, *Race Horse Men: How Slavery and Freedom Were Made at the Racetrack* (Cambridge, Mass.: Harvard University Press, 2014).
4. Vicky Moon, *Sylvia Rideout Bishop Had a Way with Horses* (Middleburg, Va.: Country Zest, 2020).
5. Douglas Southall Freeman quoted in Keith Dickson, *Sustaining Southern Identity: Douglas Southall Freeman and Memory in the Modern South* (Baton Rouge: Louisiana State University Press, 2011), 43, 202, 96; Douglas Southall Freeman, "Virginia: A Gentle Dominion," *The Nation* 199 (July 1924), 68–71; J. Douglas Smith, *Managing White Supremacy: Race, Politics, and Citizenship in Jim Crow Virginia* (Chapel Hill: University of North Carolina Press, 2002).
6. Drew Gilpin Faust, "Carry Me Back," *The Atlantic*, August 2019, 52–61.

7. See Fred Hobson, *But Now I See: The White Southern Racial Conversion Narrative* (Baton Rouge: Louisiana State University Press, 1999).

8. Sally Mann, *Hold Still: A Memoir with Photographs* (New York: Little, Brown, 2015), 263.

9. Drew Gilpin Faust, "Living History," *Harvard Magazine*, May–June 2003, 38–46, 82–83. Catharine Drew Gilpin to President Dwight D. Eisenhower, February 12, 1957, Eisenhower Presidential Library, Abilene, KS.

10. The Hymnal of the Protestant Episcopal Church in the United States of America (Greenwhich [*sic*], Conn.: The Seabury Press, 1943), n.p.

11. Martin Luther King, Jr., *Letter from Birmingham City Jail* (Philadelphia: American Friends Service Committee, 1963), 12.

5. LIFE IN THE FIFTIES

1. See Michael DiBari, Jr., *Advancing the Civil Rights Movement: Race and Geography of* Life *Magazine's Visual Representation, 1954–1965* (New York: Lexington Books, 2017), 8; Loudon Wainwright, *The Great American Magazine: An Inside History of* Life (New York: Alfred A. Knopf, 1986), 179; *Looking at* Life *Magazine*, ed. Erika Doss (Washington, D.C.: Smithsonian Press), 2001; Wendy Kozol, *Life's America* (Philadelphia: Temple University Press, 1994).

2. *Life*, back covers, February 14, 1955, and March 5, 1955; "The First Baby," *Life*, December 24, 1956, 61.

3. "Why We Have the Youngest Customers in the Business," *Life*, September 12, 1955, 100; "Southwest Barbecue," *Life*, July 11, 1955, 44; "Ways to Cut Down Kitchen Work," *Life*, January 3, 1955, 17.

4. "The 80-Hour Week," *Life*, August 15, 1955, 93.

5. "The All-American Girl at Her Beautiful Best," *Life*, December 24, 1956, 7; "An Introduction by Mrs. Peter Marshall," *Life*, December 24, 1956, 2; "Women, Love and God," editorial, *Life*, December 24, 1956, 36; "Tough Training Ground for Women's Minds: Bryn Mawr Sets High Goals for Its Girls," *Life*, December 24, 1956, 102.

6. J. Rosenberger, letter to the editor, *Life*, January 14, 1957, 21.

7. "Playtex Magic Controller," *Life*, February 14, 1955, 79; "New Greaseless Way to Keep Your Hair Neat All Day," *Life*, June 14, 1954, 1. Marge Piercy described the "litany of bras, garters, boning, girdles" as "rubber coffins," in Piercy, "Through the Cracks: Growing Up in the Fifties," in *Parti-Colored Blocks for a Quilt* (Ann Arbor: University of Michigan Press, 1982), 120–121, quoted in Wini Breines, *Young, White, and Miserable: Growing Up in the Fifties* (Chicago: University of Chicago Press, 1992), xiv.

8. "The Peak Year for Pink," *Life*, May 2, 1955, 76; "True Pink Anchorglass Dinnerware," *Life*, November 21, 1955, 99.

9. "The U.S. Purrs with Satisfaction," *Life*, July 4, 1955, 2.

10. William Faulkner, "A Letter to the North," *Life*, March 5, 1956, 52; DiBari, *Advancing the Civil Rights Movement*, 34, 38, 43.

11. "The Background of Segregation," *Life*, September 3, 1956, 43; "Freedom to Jim Crow," *Life*, September 10, 1956, 96; "Time of Power, Then Humiliation," *Life*, 101, 102; "Nobody Is Mad with Nobody," *Life*, July 4, 1955, 2.

12. Charlayne Hunter-Gault, "Fifty Years After the Birmingham Children's Crusade," *New Yorker*, May 2, 2013.

13. *Hungary's Fight for Freedom: A Special Report in Pictures* (New York: Time-Life, 1956), 5; "A Desperate Fight for Freedom," *Life*, November 5, 1956, 37; "To the Heroes of Hungary," *Life*, November 19, 1956, 55; "Elvis: A Different Kind of Idol," *Life*, August 27, 1956, 101; cover photo of Richard Nixon and Hungarian girls, *Life*, January 7, 1957; *Weekly Reader: 60 Years of News for Kids* (New York: World Almanac, 1988), 123; Marc Richards, "The Cold War According to My Weekly Reader," *Monthly Review* 50 (October 1998): 33–46.

14. Annie Dillard, "To Fashion a Text," in *Inventing the Truth: The Art and Craft of Memoir*, ed. William Zinsser (Boston: Houghton Mifflin, 1998), 148–49.

15. "Nuclear Wars Can Be Small," *Life*, July 25, 1955, 26; "A Scare Felt Around the World," *Life*, March 24, 1958, 48.

16. Paul Dickson, *Sputnik: The Shock of the Century* (Lincoln: University of Nebraska Press, 2001), 116; "The Feat That Shook the Earth," *Life*, October 21, 1957, 21.

17. Stephen King, *Danse Macabre* (New York: Everest House, 1981), 23–24.

18. On girls, girl groups, and rock and roll, see Susan J. Douglas, "Why the Shirelles Mattered," chap. 4 in *Where the Girls Are: Growing Up Female with the Mass Media* (New York: Times Books, 1994), 83–98.

19. "500 Greatest Songs of All Time: 10. Ray Charles, 'What'd I Say,'" *Rolling Stone*, December 11, 2003.

20. Harper Lee, *To Kill a Mockingbird* (New York: J. B. Lippincott, 1960), 155.

6. GIRLS WHO DARE: NANCY, ANNE, AND SCOUT

1. Jason Epstein quoted in Christopher Lehmann-Haupt, "Jason Epstein, Author, Editor and Publishing Innovator, Is Dead at 93," *New York Times*, February 5, 2022, B8.

2. Theodore Bradley, comments, Blue Ridge Country Day School, report card for Drew Gilpin, June 1954, in possession of the author.

3. The Nancy Drew Conference held for five hundred participants at the University of Iowa in 1993 concluded that most readers began with Nancy Drew books between first and third grades. *Rediscovering Nancy Drew*, ed. Carolyn Stewart Dyer and Nancy Romalov (Iowa City: University of Iowa Press, 1995), 120. A Google Group of more than one hundred members of my Bryn Mawr class of 1968 hailed Nancy Drew as a childhood favorite. Many spontaneously mentioned the blue roadster as one of their most enduring memories. A number of members of the group also brought up pony books as favorite childhood reading.

4. Gillian Brockell, "Nancy Drew: How a Teen Detective Inspired Girls Who Went On to Make History," *Washington Post*, March 15, 2019; Polly Shulman, "Spunky Nancy Drew Faces Her Hardest Case," *New York Times*, May 6, 2007.

5. Carolyn Keene, *The Bungalow Mystery* (New York: Grosset & Dunlap, 1930), 11.

6. Carolyn Keene, *The Clue of the Broken Locket* (New York: Grosset & Dunlap, 1934), 15, 53.

7. Carolyn G. Heilbrun quoted in Michael Cornelius and Melanie Gregg, eds., *Nancy Drew and Her Sister Sleuths: Essays on the Fiction of Girl Detectives* (Jefferson, N.C.: McFarland and Co., 2008), 78; Carolyn G. Heilbrun, "Nancy Drew: A Moment in Feminist History," in Dyer and Romalov, *Rediscovering Nancy Drew*, 11, 17. On quest and romance plots, see Carolyn G. Heilbrun, *Writing a Woman's Life* (New York: W. W. Norton, 1988).

8. Anne Frank, *The Diary of a Young Girl: An Extraordinary Document of Adolescence* (Garden City, N.Y.: Doubleday, 1952), 9.

9. Tony Kushner, "'I Want to Go On Living After My Death': The Memory of Anne Frank," in *War and Memory in the Twentieth Century*, ed. Martin Evans and Ken Lunn (Oxford: Berg, 1997), 197.

10. Judith Miller, *One, by One, by One: Facing the Holocaust* (New York: Simon & Schuster, 1990), 287.

11. John Berryman, "The Development of Anne Frank," in *Anne Frank: Reflections on her Life and Legacy*, ed. Hyman Aaron Enzer and Sandra Solotaroff-Enzer (Urbana: University of Illinois, 200), 78; Frank, *Diary of a Young Girl*, 57, 274.

12. Frank, *Diary of a Young Girl*, 192, 237, 55–56, 211.

13. Ibid., 56, 192.

14. Primrose Cumming, *Silver Snaffles* (London: Blackie and Son, 1937), 134. Maxine Kumin also loved this book. See Maxine Kumin, "Silver Snaffles," in *In Deep: Country Essays* (New York: Viking, 1987). The following title serves as an explanation in itself: Jane Badger, *Heroines on Horseback: The Pony Book in Children's Fiction* (Coleford, Somerset, England: Girls Gone By Publishers, 2013).

15. Alice L. O'Connell, *Pamela and the Blue Mare* (Boston: Little, Brown, 1952).

16. Powhatan School, mimeographed yearbook, June 1960, n.p., in possession of the author.

17. Harper Lee, *To Kill a Mockingbird* (1960; repr., New York, Harper Perennial, 1968), 143.

18. Ibid., 252, 258.

19. Dale Rusakoff, "The Atticus We Always Knew," *New Yorker*, July 17, 2015, www.newyorker.com/books/page-turner/the-atticus-we-always-knew; Harper Lee, *Go Set a Watchman* (New York: HarperCollins, 2015). See also Casey Cep, *Furious Hours: Murder, Fraud, and the Last Trial of Harper Lee* (New York: Knopf, 2019).

20. Lee, *To Kill a Mockingbird*, 242.

21. Ibid., 228–29.

7. FRIDAY FOR REVOLUTIONS, WEDNESDAY FOR LIFE

1. Elizabeth B. Hall, "Ladies, Be Ladies," *Through Crowded Ways* (Concord, Mass.: Concord Academy, 1959), 29.
2. Ibid., 6; Phillip McFarland, *A History of Concord Academy: The First Half-Century* (Concord, Mass.: Concord Academy, 1986), 127.
3. Author's Zoom conversation with Susan Osnos, May 26, 2020.
4. Elizabeth B. Hall, address, January 4, 1961, box 10, folder 2, series I, subseries B, Elizabeth Blodgett Hall Papers, Schlesinger Library, Radcliffe Institute for Advanced Study, Harvard University (hereafter Hall Papers).
5. See McFarland, *History of Concord Academy*.
6. Elizabeth B. Hall, journal (typed), May 7, 1963, box 8, folder 10, Hall Papers.
7. Unsigned note, n.d., box 11, Hall Papers. See also frontispiece to Elizabeth B. Hall, *Ladies: 1962 and Other Talks at Concord Academy* (Concord, Mass.: Concord Academy, 1962).
8. McFarland, *History of Concord Academy*, 119.
9. Hall, *Through Crowded Ways*, 39, 28.
10. Hall, "Ladies, Be Ladies," in *Through Crowded Ways*, 29; McFarland, *History of Concord Academy*, 119; Elizabeth B. Hall, "Grow Up and Be a Woman," baccalaureate address, June 9, 1960, box 10, folder 2, Hall Papers. Hall borrowed the great-grandmother phrase from a Concord commencement address by Archibald MacLeish. See Hall, *Ladies*, 1.
11. Hall, "Grow Up and Be a Woman."
12. Elizabeth B. Hall, "Vespers," September 18, 1960, Hall Papers.
13. The classic statement on "separate spheres" is Barbara Welter, "The Cult of True Womanhood, 1820–1860," *American Quarterly* 18, no. 2 (Summer 1966): 151–74, but see also a revision and an elaboration: Linda K. Kerber, "Separate Spheres, Female Worlds, Woman's Place: The Rhetoric of Women's History," *Journal of American History* 75, no. 1 (June 1988): 9–39; Hall, *Ladies*, 52.
14. Imani Perry, writer, Harvard professor and member of the Concord Class of 1990, reflects on the history and meaning of race in the town of Concord, "Remembering Thoreau and the Black Residents of Concord," *Atlantic*, August 19, 2022, newsletters .theatlantic.com/unsettled-territory/62ff794cebf53e0022ce23c2/emembering-thoreau -black-residents-concord/.
15. Author's Zoom conversation with Melvin Scult, January 12, 2021.
16. Statistics on Black students from "The Status of African Americans at the Nation's Most Prestigious Boarding Schools," *Journal of Blacks in Higher Education*, no. 14 (Winter 1996–97): 27.
17. Martin Luther King, Jr., speech at Groton School, February 4, 1963, www.groton.org /about/history.
18. Ibid.
19. Hall, *Ladies*, 53.
20. The flyer is quoted in "Across Frontiers, June 19–August 21, 1963: A Report of a Nine Week Trip through West Germany, East Germany, Czechoslovakia, and Yugoslavia in the Summer of 1963," ed. Fritz Kempner and Chuck Lawrence, typed mimeographed document in possession of the author, 1–2.

8. ACROSS FRONTIERS

1. Mark Twain, *The Innocents Abroad, or The New Pilgrim's Progress* (New York: Harper and Brothers, 1905), 440.
2. Author's Zoom conversation with Beverly Mikuriya, May 4, 2021. See also Jay Caspian Kang, "The Puzzle of Asian American Identity," *New York Times Magazine*, October 10, 2021, 30–35, 38, 49–50. In an email to Chuck Lawrence, August 11, 2020, Herbert Schaar describes falling in love with Beverly and with the music Chuck introduced him to: "You cannot know how much YOU had an influence on me and my whole life." Schaar was one of the young men who followed us to Dubrovnik. My thanks to him for sharing his photographs and memories with me; email to author, May 11, 2022.
3. Iain MacGregor, *Checkpoint Charlie: The Cold War, the Berlin Wall, and the Most Dangerous Place on Earth* (New York: Scribner, 2019). Crowd estimate on page 99.
4. Drew Gilpin to Mummy and Daddy, n.d. [July 1963].

5. "Across Frontiers, June 19–August 21, 1963: A Report of a Nine Week Trip Through West Germany, East Germany, Czechoslovakia, and Yugoslavia in the Summer of 1963," ed. Fritz Kempner and Chuck Lawrence, typed mimeographed document in possession of the author. See also Fritz Kempner, *Looking Back* (privately printed, 2006).

6. See Anna Funder, *Stasiland: Stories from Behind the Berlin Wall* (New York: Harper Perennial, 2003), 57.

7. Quoted in Tanya Crawford, "Living Legacies: A Historical Analysis of the Atlanta Nine Who Desegregated Atlanta Public Schools" (PhD diss., Georgia State University, 2019), 86, 96. See Barbara Harper, "The Desegregation of Atlanta Public Schools," These Halls Can Talk: The Booker T. Washington High School Oral History Project, thesehallscantalk.com; Rebecca H. Dartt, *Women Activists in the Fight for Georgia School Desegregation, 1958–1961* (Jefferson, N.C.: McFarland, 2008).

8. Robert Coles, *Children of Crisis*, vol. 1: *A Study of Courage and Fear* (Boston: Little, Brown, 1967).

9. *Time*, September 8, 1961, 52.

10. Madelyn Nix, quoted in Karen Carnabucci, "Madelyn Nix Is Still Learning After All These Years," *Intelligencer Journal* (Lancaster, PA), July 28, 1982; Nix, telephone conversation with the author, April 21, 2021; Dartt, *Women Activists*, p. 139.

11. Author's phone conversation with Chuck Lawrence, September 15, 2020. Chuck's sister, Sara Lawrence Lightfoot, has written a biography of her mother, *Balm in Gilead: A Journey of a Healer* (New York: Addison Wesley, 1988). See also "Margaret Lawrence, 105, Dies," *New York Times*, December 8, 2019, 10.

12. Chuck Lawrence, "The Race Question," in "Across Frontiers," 26; Madelyn Nix, "As I Look Back . . . ," in "Across Frontiers," 24; Madelyn Nix, telephone conversation with author, April 21, 2021.

13. MacGregor, *Checkpoint Charlie*, title page and back cover.

14. Drewdie Gilpin, quoted in "Across Frontiers," 9–10.

15. I of course had no idea that Isaiah Berlin had delivered a famous lecture titled "Two Concepts of Liberty" at Oxford in 1958, but when I did read it in college, I saw my enlightenment in 1963 as a much cruder and simplistic version of what he was writing about as a serious philosophical problem.

16. Lawrence, "Race Question," 26.

17. Roland, quoted by Drewdie Gilpin in "Across Frontiers," 10. I met and conversed with Roland in Berlin in October 2016.

18. Kempner, *Looking Back*, 141–42.

19. Fritz Kempner to Bev, Bill, Chuck, Dave, Drewdie, John, Mat, and Shirley, September 13, 1963; Kempner, *Looking Back*, 142.

20. Kevin McDermott, *Communist Czechoslovakia, 1945–1989: A Political and Social History* (New York: Palgrave, 2015), 91; Thomas K. Murphy, *Czechoslovakia Behind the Curtain: Life, Work and Culture in the Communist Era* (Jefferson, N.C.: McFarland, 2018).

21. Aleksandar Hemon, "My Mother and the Failed Experiment of Yugoslavia," *New Yorker*, June 15, 2019; Aleksandar Hemon, *My Parents: An Introduction* (New York: Farrar, Straus and Giroux, 2019).

22. "Across Frontiers," 25.

23. Nix, telephone conversation with author.

9. CATCHING UP WITH THE REVOLUTION

1. Martin Luther King, Jr., quoted in Gary May, *Bending Toward Justice: The Voting Rights Act and the Transformation of American Democracy* (New York: Basic Books, 2013), 93.

2. Quotes from mimeographed flyer from Dick Hiler: "United States Travel Seminar [1964] Sponsored by East-West Study Program," in possession of the author.

3. These contradictions between goals of building interracial understanding and supporting civil rights were a fundamental challenge within the numerous programs the American Friends Service Committee sponsored in the South, and our group's mixed agenda was no doubt reflective of that outlook. See an excellent description of how this played out in Prince Edward County, one site for our own program, in Jill Ogline Titus, *Brown's Battleground: Students, Segregationists & the Struggle for Justice in Prince Edward County, Virginia* (Chapel Hill: University of North Carolina Press, 2011), 41 and throughout.

See also Bob Smith, *They Closed Their Schools: Prince Edward County, Virginia, 1951–1964* (Chapel Hill: University of North Carolina Press, 1965).

4. Mary Noland, a member of the group, told me in a Zoom conversation on May 10, 2021, that it was her understanding that the American Friends Service Committee had originally intended to sponsor our trip but withdrew because they determined it was too dangerous. This left Dick to take full responsibility through the organization he had created for the Russian and Eastern European trips, the East-West Study Program.

5. Quote in John Egerton, "A Gentleman's Fight," *American Heritage* 30, no. 5 (August/September 1979): 56–65, www.americanheritage.com/gentlemens-fight.

6. Brian E. Lee and Brian J. Daugherity, "Program of Action: The Rev. L. Francis Griffin and the Struggle for Racial Equality in Farmville, 1963," *Virginia Magazine of History and Biography* 121, no. 3 (2013): 256.

7. Titus, *Brown's Battleground*, 128.

8. See William J. van den Heuvel, *Hope and History: A Memoir of Tumultuous Times* (Ithaca, N.Y.: Cornell University Press, 2019), chap. 3. Van den Heuvel presents a narrative of his assignment from Attorney General Robert Kennedy to establish Free Schools in Prince Edward County.

9. The Supreme Court ruled in *Loving v. Virginia* (1967) that prohibition of interracial marriage was unconstitutional. For a chart delineating when miscegenation laws were passed and when repealed, see "Anti-miscegenation Laws in the United States," *Wikipedia*, en.wikipedia.org/wiki/Anti-miscegenation_laws_in_the_United_States.

10. Jane Dailey, *White Fright: The Sexual Panic at the Heart of America's Racist History* (New York: Basic Books, 2020), title page; James Kilpatrick, quoted in John Kyle Day, *The Southern Manifesto: Massive Resistance and the Fight to Preserve Segregation* (Jackson: University Press of Mississippi, 2014), 19. Tom P. Brady, "Black Monday: Segregation or Amalgamation," *Life*, February 6, 1956, 24–25; Virginius Dabney, "Virginia's 'Peaceable, Honorable Stand,'" *Life*, September 22, 1958, 51. On Hoover, see Dailey, *White Fright*, 223, and Elizabeth Jacoway, *Turn Away Thy Son: Little Rock, the Crisis That Shocked the Nation* (New York: Free Press, 2007), 126.

11. Frank Newport, "In U.S., 87% Approve of Black-White Marriage, vs. 4% in 1958," Gallup, July 25, 2013, news.gallup.com/poll/163697/approve-marriage-blacks-whites .aspx. Fewer than 0.75 of 1 percent of marriages were of mixed race in the early 1960s. See Thomas P. Monahan, "An Overview of Statistics on Interracial Marriage in the United States, with Data on Its Extent from 1963–1970," *Journal of Marriage and the Family* 38, no. 2 (May 1976): 224.

12. Drew Gilpin to Linda Martin, September 15, 1964. I am deeply grateful to Linda Martin for saving my letters and returning them to me.

13. Drew Gilpin, notes on meetings in loose-leaf notebook, 1964.

14. I. A. Newby, *Black Carolinians: A History of Blacks in South Carolina from 1895 to 1968* (Columbia: University of South Carolina Press, 1973), 345–46.

15. Steven A. Davis, "National Register of Historic Places Multiple Property Documentation Form: Resources Associated with the Civil Rights Movement in Orangeburg, South Carolina," United States Department of the Interior National Park Service, April 7, 1995; H. V. Manning, Claflin president, remarks to our group, n.d. [1964], Drew Gilpin, notes on meetings. Manning's daughter June Manning Thomas kindly shared with me a draft of part of her book in press, now published as *Struggling to Learn: An Intimate History of School Desegregation in South Carolina* (Columbia: University of South Carolina Press, 2021).

16. See the following articles from *The New York Times*: "162 Negro Demonstrators Jailed at Orangeburg, S.C.," September 28, 1963, 77; "333 More Jailed by South Carolina City," September 29, 1963, 17; "189 More Seized in South Carolina City," October 1, 1963, 22; "1,000 Negroes Jailed," October 2, 1963, 26; "100 in Rally Seized," October 8, 1963, 37.

17. The photographer Cecil J. Williams documented the Orangeburg Movement and the civil rights struggle more generally in thousands of photographs, many of which have been collected in two books: *Freedom and Justice: Four Decades of the Civil Rights Struggle as Seen by a Black Photographer of the Deep South* (Macon, Ga.: Mercer University Press, 1995), and *Out-of-the-Box in Dixie: Cecil Williams' Photography of the South Carolina Events That Changed America*, 3rd ed. (Orangeburg, S.C.: Cecil B. Williams Publishing, 2010). The latter volume includes photographic reproduction of *The Torch*,

the underground newsletter of the Orangeburg Movement, distributed by mimeograph April 1963–February 1964. Each issue lists recent arrests, often separating adults from "juveniles." Eddie Sharperson and John A. Williams, of our group, are listed multiple times; see pages 218–40.

18. Drew Gilpin, "Mayor Fair," loose-leaf notebook, July 22, 1964.
19. Drew Gilpin, "Rev Lancaster," loose-leaf notebook, n.d.
20. "Their Attitude Caused Ire," *Times and Democrat* (Orangeburg, S.C.), July 29, 1964, 10.
21. Drewdie Gilpin to Rev. Lancaster, July 31, 1964.
22. I. DeQuincey Newman, *Annual Report*, South Carolina Conference of Branches, NAACP, 1964, University of South Carolina University Libraries, Digital Collections, digital.tcl.sc.edu/digital/collection/idn/id/1380.
23. Efforts have been made to preserve Saint Helena's traditional culture from these encroachments. Unlike nearby Fripp and other islands, Saint Helena itself does not permit condominiums or gated communities. See Orville Vernon Burton, Wilbur Cross, and Emory Campbell, *Penn Center: A History Preserved* (Athens: University of Georgia Press, 2014).
24. Newman, *Annual Report*.
25. David Dennis's powerful memoir offers a rich portrait of the limits of nonviolence in the movement at this juncture. See David J. Dennis, Jr., in collaboration with David J. Dennis, Sr., *The Movement Made Us: A Father, a Son, and the Legacy of a Freedom Ride* (New York: HarperCollins, 2022).
26. See also the names of those killed for civil rights activism during the 1950s who are memorialized at the Peace and Justice Memorial Center in Montgomery, Alabama: Hilliard Brooks, Harry and Harriette Moore, George Lee, Lamar Smith, and Thomas Brewer.
27. Drew Gilpin, loose-leaf notebook; Gilpin quoted in *York (Pa.) Gazette and Daily*, August 17, 1964, clipping in possession of the author.
28. "Six Shocking Deaths," mimeographed poem collected by Linda Martin at an Alabama Christian Movement for Human Rights rally, July 1964. In possession of the author.
29. This would have been the Alabama Christian Movement for Human Rights Choir, also known as the Birmingham Movement Choir. It had nearly seventy members and had been created by Fred Shuttlesworth in 1960 to perform at mass meetings. The Pulitzer Prize–winning author Diane McWhorter, who grew up in Birmingham, offers a clear-eyed view of the complexities of the Birmingham Movement and of how the choir and music more generally fit within its strategy in *Carry Me Home: Birmingham, Alabama: The Climactic Battle of the Civil Rights Revolution* (New York: Simon & Schuster, 2001), 327: "The Movement was going to have to give people courage and hope in order to give them nonviolence . . . The Movement choir, which the ACMHR had established in 1960, would have to lead endless wails of gospels, incantations of 'Free-e-e-dom,' 'Ain't gonna let nobody turn me 'round,' and 'We shall overcome'" in order to transform "the angry Negroes of Birmingham into nonviolent soldiers."
30. All quotes from Drew Gilpin, loose-leaf notebook, 1964.
31. Ibid.
32. Drew Gilpin, "Thoughts on the Silent Majority," typescript, 1963.
33. Obituary of George Crowell, *Washington Post*, August 25, 1995, C5.

10. THE CLASS OF 1968

1. "15 Katharine Hepburn Quotes Every Woman Should Live By," Bryn Mawr College Admissions Blog, brynmawrcollegeadmissions.tumblr.com/post/96279473817/15 -katharine-hepburn-quotes-every-woman-should-live-by.
2. Smith, Radcliffe, Vassar, and Wellesley—all Sisters—were the top four destinations. Bryn Mawr was ninth. The coed school highest on the list was Carleton, at twentieth. Mills, Hollins, and Carleton were the only schools in the top twenty outside the Northeast. See "The Graduate Record," Concord Academy, 1962–63, 11.
3. Peter Sandman, *Where the Girls Are: A Social Guide to Women's Colleges in the East* (New York: Dial Press, 1965), 169.
4. Ellen Silberblatt and Elizabeth Vermey, "Admissions," *Bryn Mawr College Alumnae Bulletin*, Spring 1969, 13.
5. Bryn Mawr boasts the first examples of American collegiate Gothic architecture, mod-

eled after Oxford and Cambridge, and designed by the Philadelphia firm Cope and Stewardson, which later built some of Princeton's most significant structures. On coeducation (or lack thereof) in this era, see Nancy Weiss Malkiel, *"Keep the Damned Women Out": The Struggle for Coeducation* (Princeton, N.J.: Princeton University Press, 2016).

6. BMC Faculty Minutes, 1964–65, meeting of September 30, 1964. Room assignments reported by Marcia Young Cantarella, Zoom conversation with the author, August 24, 2020.

7. *Bryn Mawr College Freshman Handbook, Class of 1968*, Bryn Mawr Archives.

8. See, for example, Kit Bakke, editorial, *College News*, October 6, 1967, 2, describing Bryn Mawr as a "school of 750 girls."

9. Quoted in Elizabeth Schneider, "Our Failures Only Marry: Bryn Mawr College and the Failure of Feminism," in *Woman in Sexist Society: Studies in Power and Powerlessness*, ed. Vivian Gornick and Barbara K. Moran (New York: Basic Books, 1971), 584.

10. M. Carey Thomas, quoted in Helen Lefkowitz Horowitz, *The Power and Passion of M. Carey Thomas* (New York: Knopf, 1994), 173.

11. Betty Friedan, *The Feminine Mystique* (1963; repr., New York: W. W. Norton, 2013), 181 and chap. 7 overall.

12. See the following articles from Bryn Mawr's *College News*: Emily McDermott, "'What ABOUT Calamity Jane?' Asks Hygiene Lecture Audience," September 30, 1966, 2; "Health Education and Farewell," September 30, 1966, 2; and "Acid Remarks Trip Up First Hygiene Lecturer," October 20, 1967, 7. On life adjustment, see American Education Reform: History, Policy, Practice, episode 7.1: Life Adjustment Education, University of Pennsylvania, posted on Coursera, www.coursera.org/lecture/edref/episode-7-1-life-adjustment-education-9wttA.

13. "Women," Princetoniana, princetoniana.princeton.edu/history/women.

14. [Kit Bakke], "Attention Must Be Paid," *College News*, November 3, 1967, 1; photos, November 17, 1967, 5.

15. Margaret Levi, "The Power of Beliefs," *Annual Review of Political Science* 25 (May 2022).

16. Schneider, "Our Failures Only Marry," 588, 589.

17. Drewdie Gilpin to Linda Martin, November 11, 1964.

18. Concord Academy yearbook, 1964, 40.

19. Drewdie Gilpin, proposal, box 36, Drew Gilpin Faust Papers, Harvard University Archives, Cambridge, Mass. (hereafter Faust Papers).

20. Drewdie Gilpin, "Artistic Creation in the Philosophies of Aristotle and Albert Camus," January 14, 1966, 4, 5, box 36, Faust Papers.

21. Robert Moses, quoted in Taylor Branch, *The King Years: Historic Moments in the Civil Rights Movement* (New York: Simon & Schuster, 2013), 83.

22. Todd Gitlin to author, email, November 7, 2021. Gitlin also emphasized in his message to me the importance of Camus's opposition to violence, which I would have found very important. The literary scholar Germaine Bree delivered a speech about Camus at the University of Wisconsin Teach-In of April 1, 1965. See *Teach-Ins: U.S.A.; Reports, Opinions, Documents*, ed. Louis Menashe and Ronald Radosh (New York: Frederick A. Praeger, 1967), 246. See Tony Judt, "The Reluctant Moralist: Albert Camus and the Discomforts of Ambivalence," chap. 2 in *The Burden of Responsibility: Blum, Camus, Aron, and the French Twentieth Century* (Chicago: University of Chicago Press, 1998), 87–136; see Todd Gitlin on Camus in *The Sixties: Years of Hope, Days of Rage* (New York: Bantam Books, 1987), 31, 34, 66, 76, 147, 148, 266, 381; Carl Oglesby, *Ravens in the Storm: A Personal History of the 1960s Antiwar Movement* (New York: Scribner, 2008); Robert Moses interview with Julian Bond, posted to YouTube, March 24, 2014, www.youtube.com/watch?v=lebuaHS3-DI; Richard Rothstein, "A Short History of ERAP," Online Archive of California, oac.cdlib.org/view?docId=kt4k4003k7. On devotion to Camus by another young woman of my era, see Elizabeth Hawes, *Camus: A Romance* (New York: Grove Press, 2009).

23. The quote "manifesto of values and beliefs" is from the endpaper of the mimeographed copy of "The Port Huron Statement" in possession of the author. Other quotes are from "The Port Huron Statement of the Students for a Democratic Society" (New York: SDS, 1962), 3, 4, 7, 8, 33, 61, 63.

24. Rothstein, "A Short History of ERAP."

25. On ERAP's rise and fall, see Kirkpatrick Sale, *SDS* (New York: Vintage, 1973), 130–50.

On Philadelphia, see Paul Lyons, *The People of This Generation: The Rise and Fall of the New Left in Philadelphia* (Philadelphia: University of Pennsylvania Press, 2003).

26. Bryan Stevenson, *Just Mercy: A Story of Justice and Redemption* (New York: Spiegel & Grau, 2014), xx.

27. Martin Luther King, Jr., quoted in Gary May, *Bending Toward Justice: The Voting Rights Act and the Transformation of American Democracy* (New York: Basic Books, 2013), 54. See *New York Times*, January 3, 1965.

28. James Bevel, quoted in May, *Bending Toward Justice*, 80.

29. Martin Luther King, Jr., quoted in May, *Bending Toward Justice*, 93.

30. Ibid., 130.

31. "Adam" is a pseudonym.

32. The great anxiety in this era was the Mann Act, passed in 1910, which prohibited transporting women and girls across state lines for immoral purposes. It was used most extensively to prosecute men for sexual relationships with underage girls.

33. George Wallace, "Segregation Now, Segregation Forever," inaugural speech, January 14, 1963, posted at BlackPast, www.blackpast.org/african-american-history/speeches -african-american-history/1963-george-wallace-segregation-now-segregation-forever/.

34. See "Freedom Songs: Selma, Alabama," documentary recording on CD made by Carl Benkert, Folkways 5594, 1965.

35. I have, of course, borrowed here from the St. Crispin's Day speech in Shakespeare's *Henry V.*

36. Estimates of the number of marchers on March 21 vary, but the figure 3,500–3,600 is widely used. See May, *Bending Toward Justice*, 131.

37. May, *Bending Toward Justice*, 130.

38. Robert Patten, comments on my paper, Bryn Mawr College, March 1965. In possession of the author.

39. See Albert Camus, "Neither Victims nor Executioners," adamgomez.files.wordpress .com/2011/01/camus-neither-victims-nor-executioners.pdf.

40. Marcus Raskin, quoted in Gitlin, *The Sixties*, 168.

11. INSTEAD OF HAPPY CHILDHOODS

1. Michael Herr, *Dispatches* (1977; repr., New York: Everyman's Library, Knopf, 2009), 244.

2. See "Vietnam," February 17, 1965, typed carbon in possession of the author.

3. See *Teach-Ins: U.S.A.: Reports, Opinions, Documents*, ed. Louis Menashe and Ronald Radosh (New York: Frederick A. Praeger, 1967), 16.

4. Paul Potter, quoted in Kirkpatrick Sale, *SDS* (New York: Vintage, 1973), 187.

5. "Straughan D. Kelsey, Jr.," Honor States, www.honorstates.org/index.php?id=281868.

6. "The March on the Pentagon: An Oral History," *New York Times*, October 20, 2017, www.nytimes.com/interactive/2017/10/20/opinion/sunday/march-on-the-pentagon -oral-history.html; Norman Mailer, *The Armies of the Night: History as a Novel, the Novel as History* (New York: New American Library, 1968).

7. *College News*, October 27, 1967, 4. A longtime pacifist and the march's organizer, David Dellinger declared October 17 the end of the peaceful phase of antiwar protest; see "The March on the Pentagon: An Oral History."

8. See "First Injured Vietnamese Children Arrive for Treatment," *College News*, October 20, 1967, 1.

9. William F. Pepper, "The Children of Vietnam," *Ramparts* (January 1967), 45–68.

10. Drewdie Gilpin, "Children and War," *College News*, February 10, 1967, 2. See Lyons, *People of This Generation*, 69.

11. Typed manuscript in "Students: Issue on Campus. Vietnam War," Bryn Mawr Archives.

12. Kit Bakke, Drewdie Gilpin, Margaret Levi, Sharon Metcalf, and Kathy Murphey, "Open Letter to the College Community," *College News*, April 14, 1967, 3.

13. See "Filched Maypoles Will Land Two Haverfordians in Court," *College News*, April 21, 1967, 4.

14. "Vietnam Week Set in April; Area Colleges Plan Teach-In," *College News*, March 17, 1967, 5.

15. Claudia Goldin and Lawrence F. Katz, "The Power of the Pill: Contraception and

Women's Career and Marriage Decisions," *Journal of Political Economy* 110, no 4 (August 2002): 730–70. Goldin and Katz note that a diaphragm was sixty times more risky and a condom thirty times more risky than the Pill in preventing pregnancy, 731.

16. Drewdie Gilpin, statement for Ad Hoc Student Affairs Committee of the Board of Directors, May 16, 1967, Self-Gov File, Bryn Mawr Archives.

17. Drewdie Gilpin, "Election Statement," *College News*, March 3, 1967, 4.

18. "Self-Gov Begins Grass Roots Drive with Hall Councils," *College News*, April 21, 1967, 3; Drewdie Gilpin, "Gilpin on the Questions of Honor," *College News*, May 1, 1967, 3.

19. Patty Monnington Bonner, to author and Bryn Mawr College Google Group, email, March 20, 2022.

20. "Faculty Members Offer Differing Responses to 'In Loco Parentis,'" *College News*, April 14, 1967, 10.

21. "Meeting with Ad Hoc Student Affairs Committee of the Board of Directors," 3, Self-Gov Files, Bryn Mawr Archives. See also Self-Government Constitutional Revision Ballot, FINAL, Self-Gov, Bryn Mawr Archives, with vote tallies inscribed in author's handwriting, Bryn Mawr Archives.

22. Statement on makeup is based on responses to a question the author posed to the Bryn Mawr Class of 1968 Google Group.

23. The 1969 demonstration at Atlantic City included a Freedom Trash Can where women could dispose of bras, girdles, and curlers. Roxane Gay, "Fifty Years Ago, Protestors Took On the Miss America Pageant and Electrified the Feminist Movement," *Smithsonian*, January 2018, www.smithsonianmag.com/history/fifty-years-ago-protestors-took-on-miss-america-pageant-electrified-feminist-movement-180967504/.

12. THIS IS THE END

1. William Butler Yeats, "The Second Coming," www.poetryfoundation.org/poems/43290/the-second-coming.

2. millercenter.org/the-presidency/presidential-speeches/march-31-1968-remarks-decision-not-seek-re-election.

3. The Beatles, *Sgt. Pepper's Lonely Hearts Club Band*, 1967; Jim Morrison and the Doors, "The End," 1967. On the Doors, see Joan Didion, *The White Album* (New York: Simon & Schuster, 1979).

4. "President Opposes Statement, Wants Emphasis on Students," *College News*, October 6, 1967, 4.

5. Drew Gilpin, small brown notebook, 1967–68, in possession of the author; Drewdie Gilpin, "Report on Self-Government's Handling of Drug Cases," 1968, Self-Gov File, Bryn Mawr Archives; Jefferson Airplane, "White Rabbit," 1967.

6. Martin Luther King, Jr., *Where Do We Go from Here: Chaos or Community?* (New York: Harper & Row, 1967).

7. Clay Risen, *A Nation on Fire: America in the Wake of the King Assassination* (New York: Wiley, 2009), 161; Tom Wicker, "Thousands Leave Washington as Bands of Negroes Loot Stores," *New York Times*, April 6, 1968, 23; Anthony Lewis, "Europe Dismayed by Slaying and Fearful over U.S. Stability," *New York Times*, April 6, 1968, 1; Thomas A. Johnson, "Negroes Strive to Ease Tensions," *New York Times*, April 6, 1968, 1, 26.

8. "McKissick Says Non-Violence Has Become Dead Philosophy," *New York Times*, April 5, 1968, 1, 26.

9. Editorial, *New York Times*, April 8, 1968, 46.

10. Drewdie Gilpin, "The Liberal University and the Student Revolution: The Crisis of Legitimacy," box 36, Faust Papers.

11. Robert Penn Warren, "Shoes in Rain Jungle," *New York Review of Books*, November 11, 1965, www.nybooks.com/issues/1965/11/11/.

12. I was the organizer of the conference "The Student and the University in Society" in March 1967. See *College News*, March 10, 1967, 3.

13. Author's Zoom conversation with Mary Patterson McPherson, May 13, 2020. For two revealing memoirs of those for whom it did become otherwise, see Mark Rudd, *Underground: My Life with SDS and the Weathermen* (New York: William Morrow, 2009), and Cathy Wilkerson, *Flying Close to the Sun: My Life and Times as a Weatherman* (New York: Seven Stories Press, 2007).

14. Author's Zoom conversation with Kit Bakke, May 20, 2020. Kit reemerged from underground after two years, pursued degrees in nursing and public health, and worked in pediatric nursing for fourteen years. She has since become a writer and published three books. See her "bio-memoir": Kit Bakke, *Miss Alcott's E-mail: Yours for Reforms of All Kinds* (Boston: David R. Godine, 2006).
15. "Vietnam War U.S. Military Fatal Casualty Statistics," National Archives, www.archives.gov/research/military/vietnam-war/casualty-statistics.

EPILOGUE: FREE, WHITE, AND TWENTY-ONE

1. William Faulkner, *William Faulkner: Essays, Speeches, and Public Letters*, ed. James B. Meriwether (1965; repr., New York: Modern Library, 2004), 151.
2. Three years later, in 1971, the Twenty-Sixth Amendment to the Constitution lowered the voting age to eighteen.
3. Andrew Heisel, "The Rise and Fall of an All-American Catchphrase: 'Free, White, and 21,'" *Jezebel*, September 10, 2015; Malcolm X, "Educate Our People in the Science of Politics," speech at Ford Auditorium in Detroit, February 14, 1965, in *Malcolm X: The Final Speeches, February 1965* (New York: Pathfinder, 1992), 103.
4. *Jezebel*, "Free, White and 21: The Buried Catchphrase of Classic Hollywood," www.youtube.com/watch?v=t23nvB4gcL8; Heisel, "Rise and Fall of an All-American Catchphrase."
5. E. James West, "Pushing Beyond the Two-Party System: Dick Gregory's 1968 Presidential Campaign," *Black Perspectives*, online publication of the African American Intellectual History Society (AAIHS), www.aaihs.org/dick-gregorys-1968-presidential-campaign/; "4 of 8 Ivy League Papers Back Humphrey Reluctantly," *New York Times*, November 3, 1968, 79; "Gregory Backed at Rutgers," *New York Times*, November 4, 1968, 16.
6. Dick Gregory, *Write Me In* (New York: Bantam Books, 1968), 18, 33, 58.
7. L. Stanley Hardaway, secretary of the State Board of Elections, Commonwealth of Virginia, *Statement of the Vote . . . General Election Tuesday, November 5, 1968* (Richmond: Commonwealth of Virginia Department of Purchase and Supply, 1968), 2.
8. John W. Carter, Jr., to Kenneth Newcomer Gilpin, November 12, 1919, GFP.
9. Martin Luther King, Jr., speech at Groton School, February 4, 1963, www.groton.org/about/history.

A NOTE ON THE TITLE

1. It was on that occasion that he said the words I have used as an epigraph at the beginning of this book. John Lewis to Drew Faust in Harvard Commencement Speech, Harvard University, May 24, 2018, www.youtube.com/watch?v=XRjAzepG-bA.

Index

Page numbers in *italics* refer to illustrations.

Illustration Credits

97   Cover painting by Robert Riggs. Cover treatment from the pages of *Life*. *Life* and the *Life* logo are registered trademarks of Meredith Operations Corporation. Used under license. Copyright © 1956 Meredith Operations Corporation. All rights reserved. Cover treatment reprinted/translated from *Life* and published with permission of Meredith Operations Corporation. Reproduction in any manner in any language in whole or in part without written permission is prohibited.

100 *Life* cover featuring Richard Nixon and Hungarian refugee children, published January 7, 1957, courtesy of Shutterstock.

113 In the author's personal collection.

115 *Nancy Drew 15: The Haunted Bridge*, by Carolyn Keene, copyright © 1972, 1965, 1937, by Simon & Schuster, Inc. NANCY DREW MYSTERIES® is a registered trademark of Simon & Schuster, Inc. Used by permission of Grosset & Dunlap, an imprint of Penguin Young Readers Group, a division of Penguin Random House LLC. All rights reserved.

116 *Anne Frank: The Diary of a Young Girl*, by Anne Frank, copyright © 1952. Used by permission of Penguin Random House LLC. All rights reserved.

123 In the author's personal collection.

123 In the author's personal collection.

130 Image courtesy of Concord Academy, from the Elizabeth Blodgett Hall Papers, 1617–2006; MC 603. Schlesinger Library, Radcliffe Institute for Advanced Study, Harvard University.

131 Schlesinger Library, Radcliffe Institute for Advanced Study, Harvard University.

147 In the author's personal collection.

148 In the author's personal collection.

149 In the author's personal collection.

153 In the author's personal collection.

158 In the author's personal collection.

165 Photograph courtesy of Dr. Herbert Schaar.

169 In the author's personal collection.

171 In the author's personal collection.

176 In the author's personal collection.

190 In the author's personal collection.

192 In the author's personal collection.

194 In the author's personal collection.

194 In the author's personal collection.

199 Bryn Mawr College Libraries Special Collections.

211 In the author's personal collection.

238 Bryn Mawr College Libraries Special Collections.

244 Bryn Mawr College Libraries Special Collections.

254 Bryn Mawr College Libraries Special Collections.

257 Bryn Mawr College Libraries Special Collections.

258 Photograph by Stephen Faust.

262 Photographs by Stephanie Mitchell.

265 Photograph by Stephanie Mitchell.

267 *Write Me In!*, by Dick Gregory, copyright © 1968. Used by permission of Penguin Random House LLC. All rights reserved. Cover photograph by Sam Falk / *The New York Times* / Redux.